MAX RIDE
ULTIMATE FLIGHT

JAMES PATTERSON

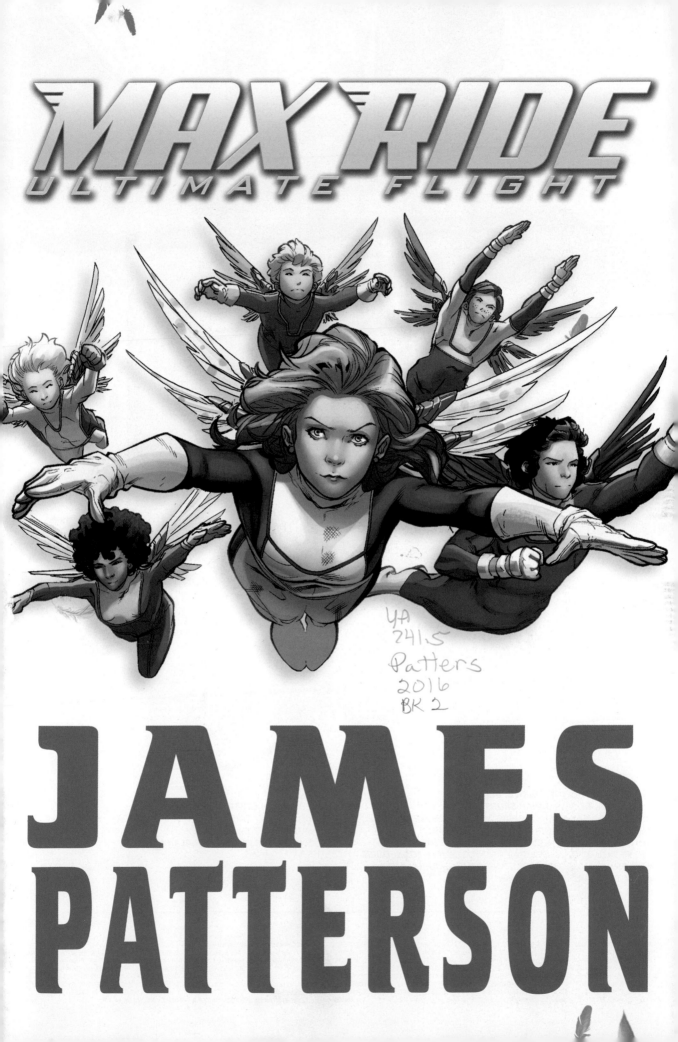

COLLECTION EDITOR *MARK D. BEAZLEY*
ASSOCIATE EDITOR *SARAH BRUNSTAD*
ASSOCIATE MANAGER, DIGITAL ASSETS *JOE HOCHSTEIN*
ASSOCIATE MANAGING EDITOR *ALEX STARBUCK*
EDITOR, SPECIAL PROJECTS *JENNIFER GRÜNWALD*
VP, PRODUCTION & SPECIAL PROJECTS *JEFF YOUNGQUIST*
SVP PRINT, SALES & MARKETING *DAVID GABRIEL*
BOOK DESIGNER *ADAM DEL RE*

EDITOR IN CHIEF *AXEL ALONSO*
CHIEF CREATIVE OFFICER *JOE QUESADA*
PUBLISHER *DAN BUCKLEY*
EXECUTIVE PRODUCER *ALAN FINE*

MAX RIDE: ULTIMATE FLIGHT. CONTAINS MATERIAL ORIGINALLY PUBLISHED IN MAGAZINE FORM AS MAX RIDE: ULTIMATE FLIGHT #1-5. FIRST PRINTING 2016. ISBN# 978-0-7851-9585-6. PUBLISHED BY MARVEL WORLDWIDE, INC., A SUBSIDIARY OF MARVEL ENTERTAINMENT, LLC. OFFICE OF PUBLICATION: 135 WEST 50TH STREET, NEW YORK, NY 10020. COPYRIGHT © 2015 BY JAMES PATTERSON. ALL RIGHTS RESERVED. ALL CHARACTERS FEATURED IN THIS ISSUE AND THE DISTINCTIVE NAMES AND LIKENESSES THEREOF, AND ALL RELATED INDICIA ARE TRADEMARKS OF JAMES PATTERSON. NO SIMILARITY BETWEEN ANY OF THE NAMES, CHARACTERS, PERSONS, AND/OR INSTITUTIONS IN THIS MAGAZINE WITH THOSE OF ANY LIVING OR DEAD PERSON OR INSTITUTION IS INTENDED, AND ANY SUCH SIMILARITY WHICH MAY EXIST IS PURELY COINCIDENTAL. MARVEL AND ITS LOGOS ARE TM MARVEL CHARACTERS, INC. **PRINTED IN THE U.S.A.** ALAN FINE, PRESIDENT, MARVEL ENTERTAINMENT; DAN BUCKLEY, PRESIDENT, TV, PUBLISHING & BRAND MANAGEMENT; JOE QUESADA, CHIEF CREATIVE OFFICER; TOM BREVOORT, SVP OF PUBLISHING; DAVID BOGART, SVP OF BUSINESS AFFAIRS & OPERATIONS, PUBLISHING & PARTNERSHIP; C.B. CEBULSKI, VP OF BRAND MANAGEMENT & DEVELOPMENT, ASIA; DAVID GABRIEL, SVP OF SALES & MARKETING, PUBLISHING; JEFF YOUNGQUIST, VP OF PRODUCTION & SPECIAL PROJECTS; DAN CARR, EXECUTIVE DIRECTOR OF PUBLISHING TECHNOLOGY; ALEX MORALES, DIRECTOR OF PUBLISHING OPERATIONS; SUSAN CRESPI, PRODUCTION MANAGER; STAN LEE, CHAIRMAN EMERITUS. FOR INFORMATION REGARDING ADVERTISING IN MARVEL COMICS OR ON MARVEL.COM, PLEASE CONTACT VIT DEBELLIS, INTEGRATED SALES MANAGER, AT VDEBELLIS@MARVEL.COM. FOR MARVEL SUBSCRIPTION INQUIRIES, PLEASE CALL 888-511-5480. **MANUFACTURED BETWEEN 3/18/2016 AND 4/25/2016 BY R.R. DONNELLEY, INC., SALEM, VA, USA.**

10 9 8 7 6 5 4 3 2 1

ADAPTED FROM THE NOVEL,
MAXIMUM RIDE: SCHOOL'S OUT FOREVER
BY **JAMES PATTERSON**

WRITER
JODY HOUSER

PENCILER
RB SILVA

INKERS
WALDEN WONG (#1 & #3-5) & **RB SILVA** (#2-3 & #5)
WITH **LE BEAU UNDERWOOD, SCOTT HANNA** & **LARRY WELCH** (#4)

COLORIST
RACHELLE ROSENBERG

LETTERER
VC'S TRAVIS LANHAM

COVER ARTIST
YASMINE PUTRI

EDITOR
EMILY SHAW

CONSULTING EDITOR
SANA AMANAT

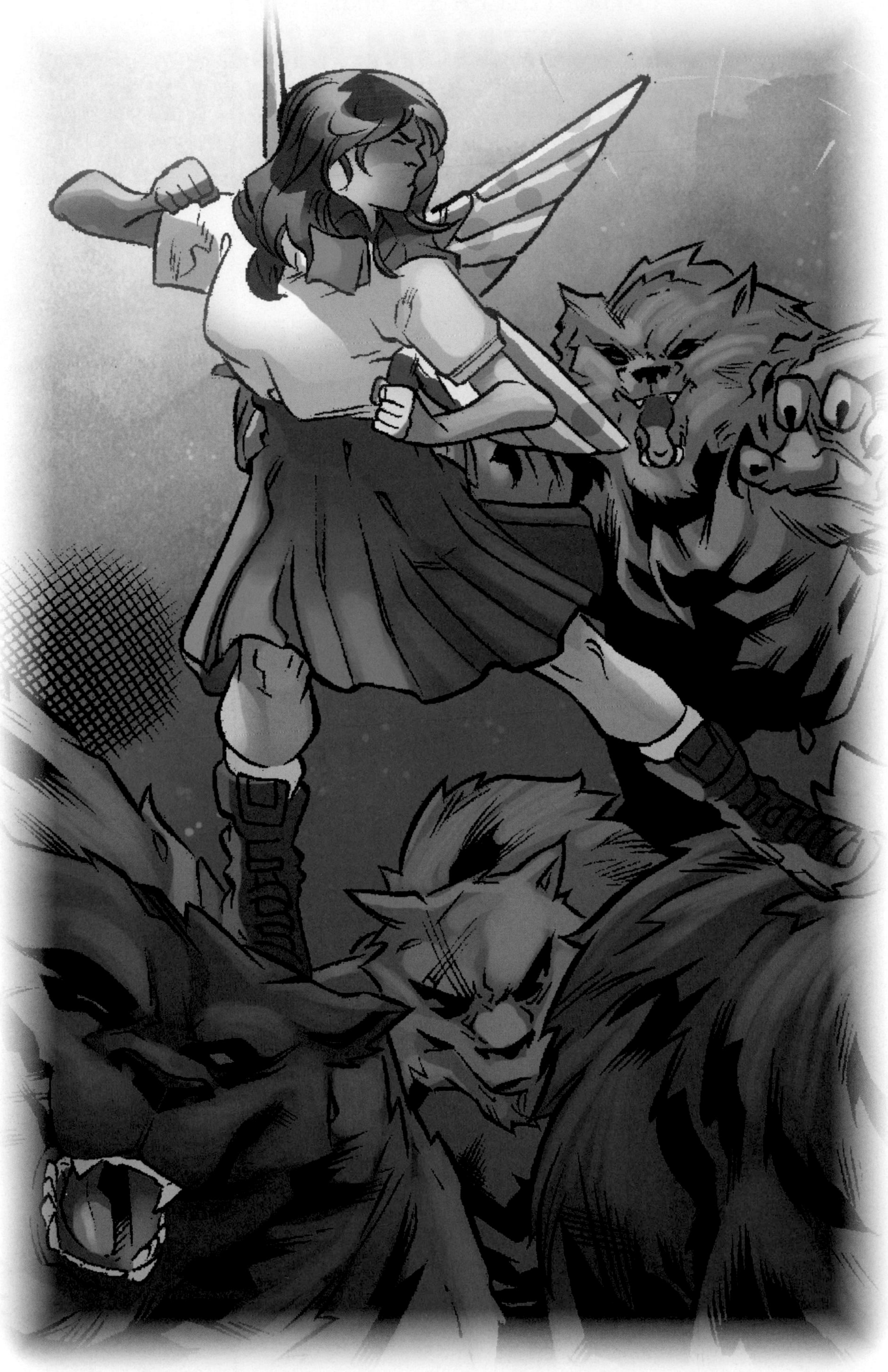

Welcome back! Or, if you're flying with us for the first time, welcome aloft! Max's adventure continues. Another flight. Another encounter with the Erasers (you didn't think they'd give up that easily, did you?).

I hate to break the news, but things aren't getting any easier for our beloved Flock. Having narrowly escaped from the Institute, Max, Fang, Iggy, Gazzy, Nudge, and Angel are off to Washington, D.C., in search of their parents. In addition to uncovering the secrets of her past, Max has to settle the little matter of who she will become. Will she answer the call to save the world? Or will she take Fang's advice and hide somewhere safe with the rest of the Flock?

There is a defining moment for every hero: run or fight. The artists at Marvel know this better than any other humans alive. Every single page overflows with action, color, and emotion. It is like we are with the Flock every step—and wing-stroke—of the way, cheering them on through fights *and* flights.

I've said it before and I'll say it again: it is you, the fans, who keep the Flock going. The world of Maximum Ride has one of the strongest followings of any of the series I've written. I never could have imagined that Maximum Ride would inspire so many fan fictions, videos, pieces of art, and adaptations like the thrilling graphic novel you are holding in your hands.

Anyhow, enough with these non-illustrated words. Please, turn the page and leap into the truly extraordinary world of Maximum Ride. The Flock's journey is far from over. You're in the creative and skilled hands of Marvel once again.

Wings out, my friends.

All my best,
JAMES PATTERSON

CHAPTER 1

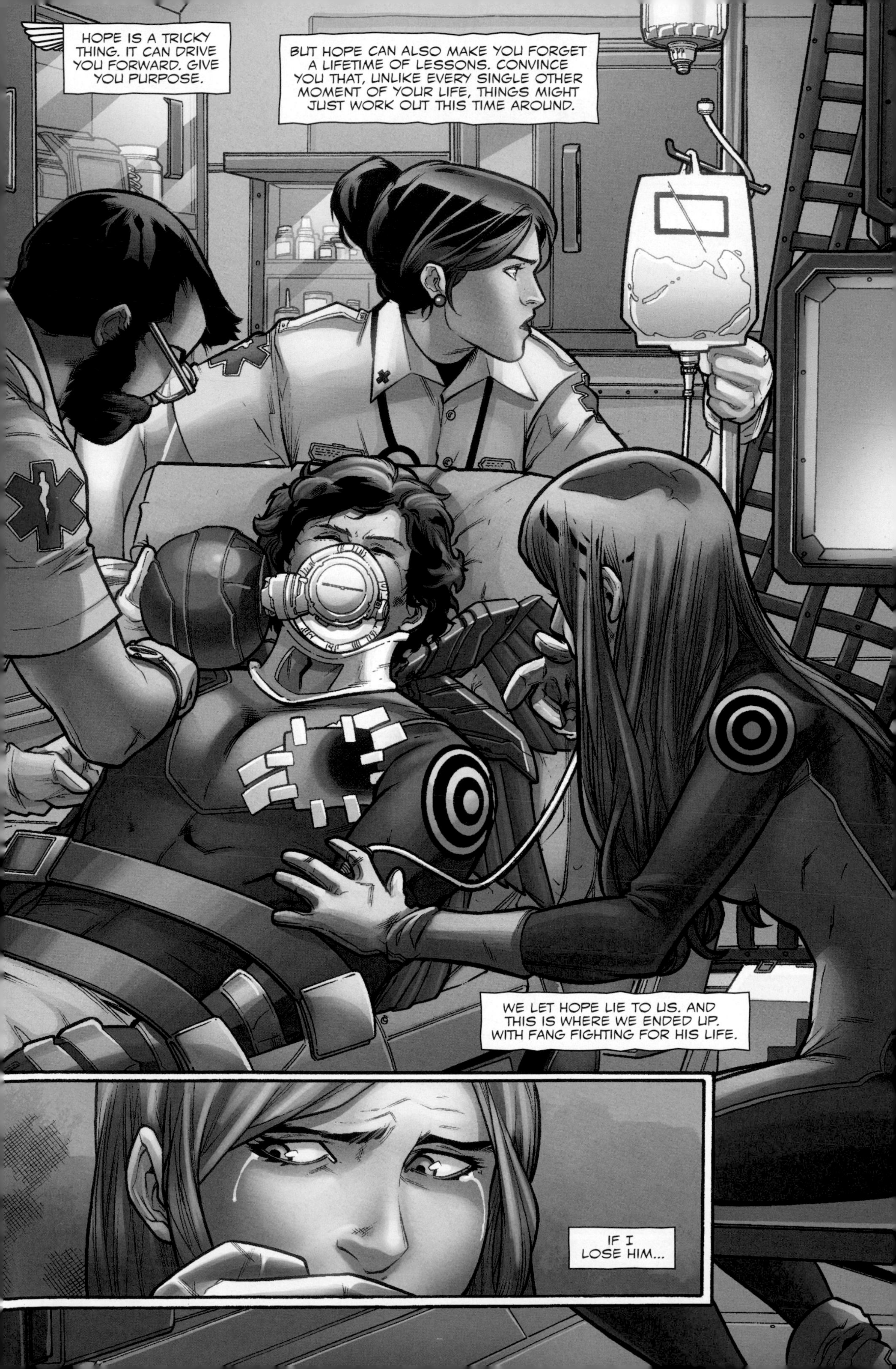
HOPE IS A TRICKY THING. IT CAN DRIVE YOU FORWARD. GIVE YOU PURPOSE.
BUT HOPE CAN ALSO MAKE YOU FORGET A LIFETIME OF LESSONS. CONVINCE YOU THAT, UNLIKE EVERY SINGLE OTHER MOMENT OF YOUR LIFE, THINGS MIGHT JUST WORK OUT THIS TIME AROUND.
WE LET HOPE LIE TO US. AND THIS IS WHERE WE ENDED UP. WITH FANG FIGHTING FOR HIS LIFE.
IF I LOSE HIM...

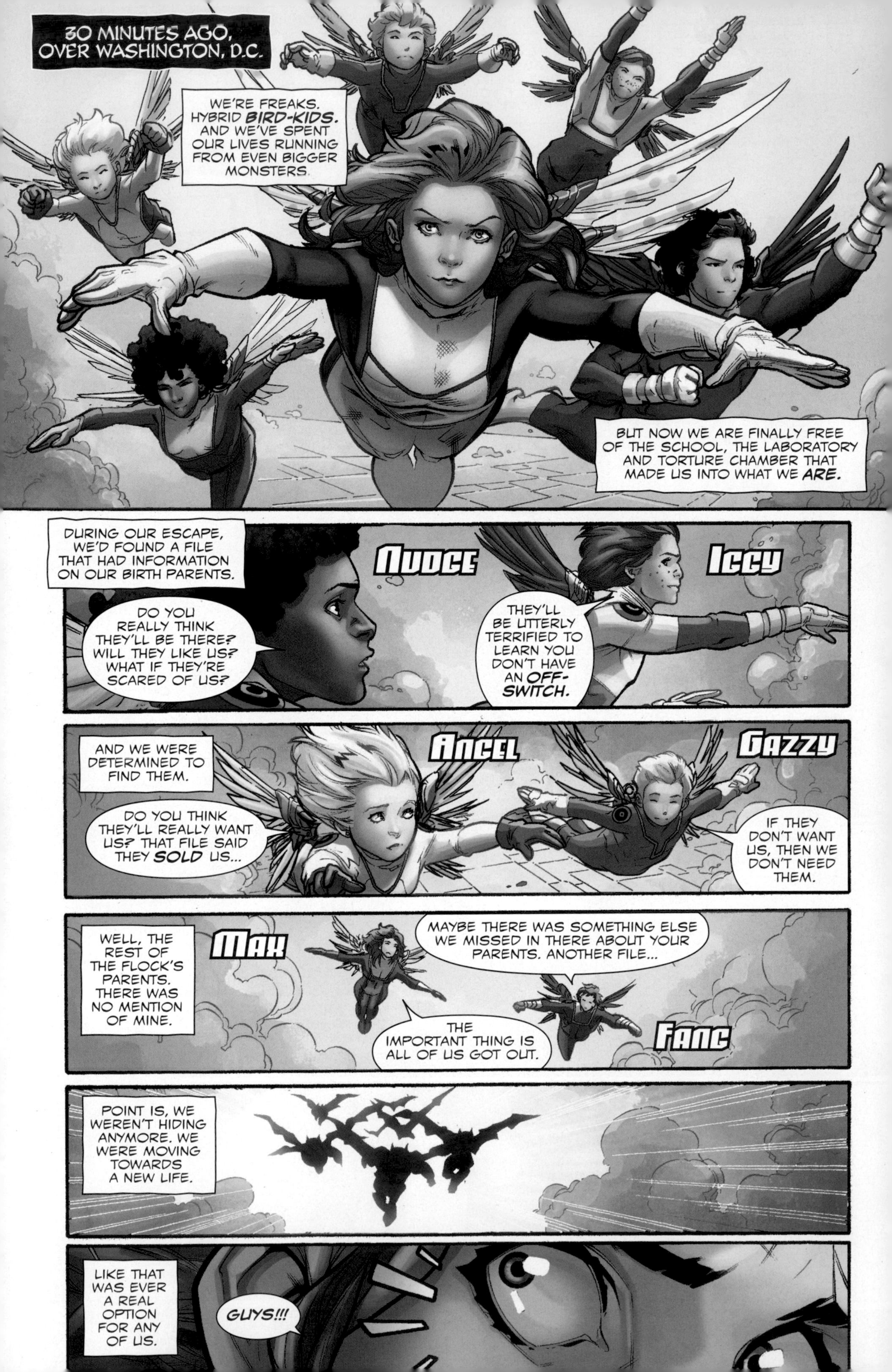
30 MINUTES AGO, OVER WASHINGTON, D.C.
WE'RE FREAKS. HYBRID BIRD-KIDS. AND WE'VE SPENT OUR LIVES RUNNING FROM EVEN BIGGER MONSTERS.
BUT NOW WE ARE FINALLY FREE OF THE SCHOOL, THE LABORATORY AND TORTURE CHAMBER THAT MADE US INTO WHAT WE ARE.
DURING OUR ESCAPE, WE'D FOUND A FILE THAT HAD INFORMATION ON OUR BIRTH PARENTS.
NUDGE
ICGY
DO YOU REALLY THINK THEY'LL BE THERE? WILL THEY LIKE US? WHAT IF THEY'RE SCARED OF US?
THEY'LL BE UTTERLY TERRIFIED TO LEARN YOU DON'T HAVE AN OFF-SWITCH.
AND WE WERE DETERMINED TO FIND THEM.
ANGEL
GAZZY
DO YOU THINK THEY'LL REALLY WANT US? THAT FILE SAID THEY SOLD US...
IF THEY DON'T WANT US, THEN WE DON'T NEED THEM.
WELL, THE REST OF THE FLOCK'S PARENTS. THERE WAS NO MENTION OF MINE.
MAX
MAYBE THERE WAS SOMETHING ELSE WE MISSED IN THERE ABOUT YOUR PARENTS. ANOTHER FILE...
THE IMPORTANT THING IS ALL OF US GOT OUT.
FANG
POINT IS, WE WEREN'T HIDING ANYMORE. WE WERE MOVING TOWARDS A NEW LIFE.
LIKE THAT WAS EVER A REAL OPTION FOR ANY OF US.
GUYS!!!

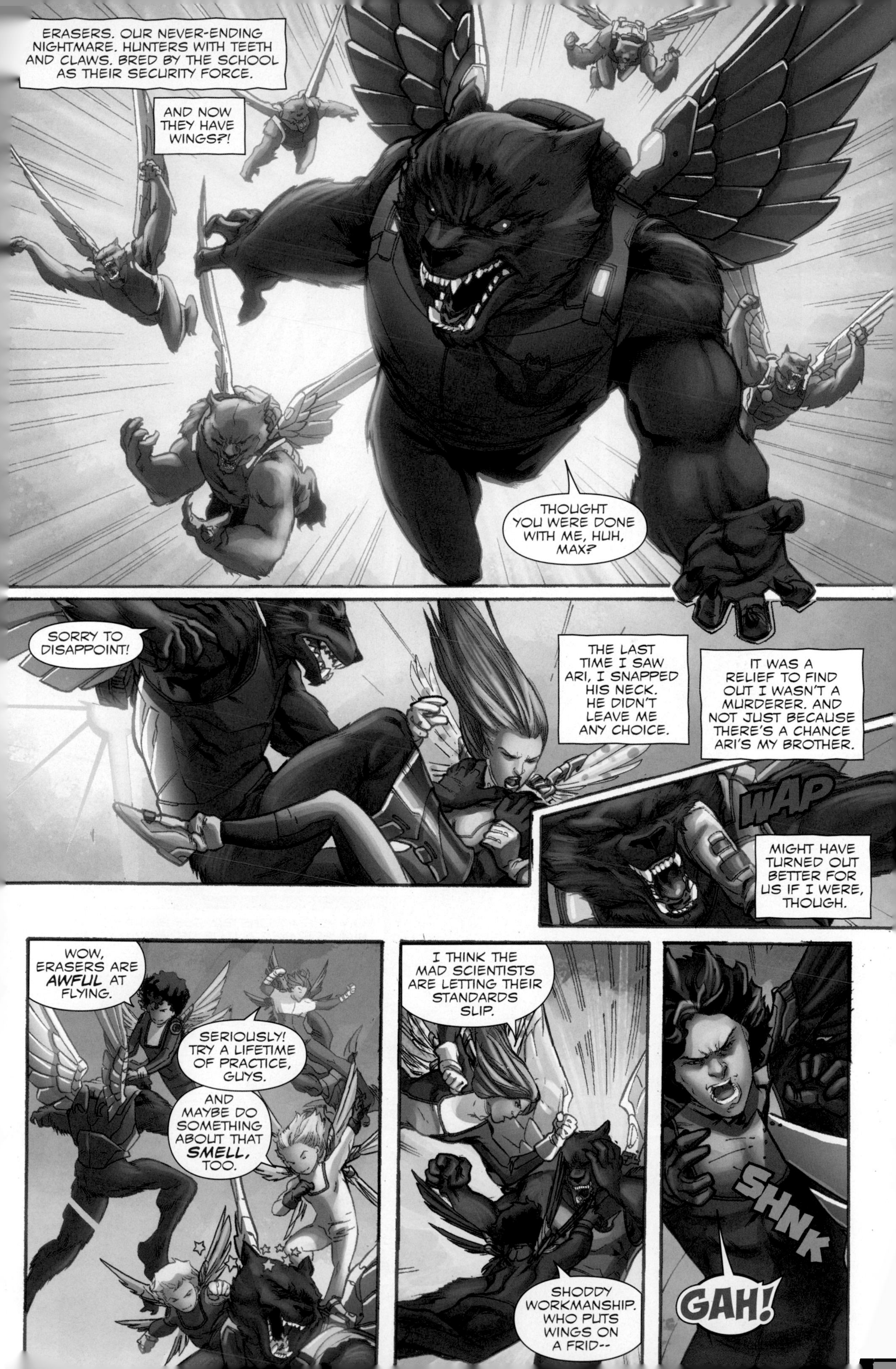
ERASERS. OUR NEVER-ENDING NIGHTMARE. HUNTERS WITH TEETH AND CLAWS. BRED BY THE SCHOOL AS THEIR SECURITY FORCE.
AND NOW THEY HAVE WINGS?!
THOUGHT YOU WERE DONE WITH ME, HUH, MAX?
SORRY TO DISAPPOINT!
THE LAST TIME I SAW ARI, I SNAPPED HIS NECK. HE DIDN'T LEAVE ME ANY CHOICE.
IT WAS A RELIEF TO FIND OUT I WASN'T A MURDERER. AND NOT JUST BECAUSE THERE'S A CHANCE ARI'S MY BROTHER.
WAP
MIGHT HAVE TURNED OUT BETTER FOR US IF I WERE, THOUGH.
WOW, ERASERS ARE AWFUL AT FLYING.
SERIOUSLY! TRY A LIFETIME OF PRACTICE, GUYS.
AND MAYBE DO SOMETHING ABOUT THAT SMELL, TOO.
I THINK THE MAD SCIENTISTS ARE LETTING THEIR STANDARDS SLIP.
SHODDY WORKMANSHIP. WHO PUTS WINGS ON A FRID--
SHNK
GAH!

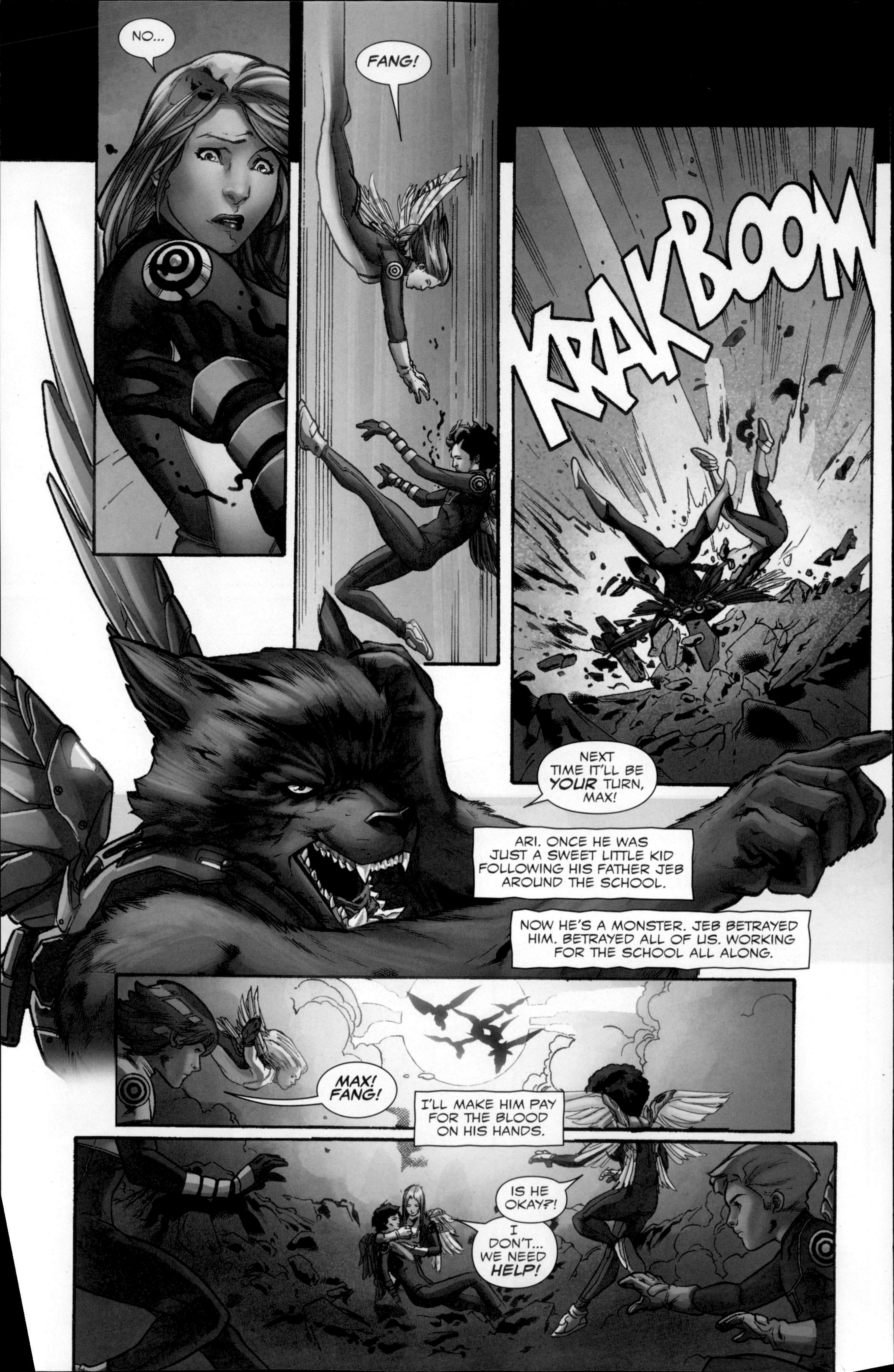
NO...
FANG!
KRAKBOOM
NEXT TIME IT'LL BE YOUR TURN, MAX!
ARI. ONCE HE WAS JUST A SWEET LITTLE KID FOLLOWING HIS FATHER JEB AROUND THE SCHOOL.
NOW HE'S A MONSTER. JEB BETRAYED HIM. BETRAYED ALL OF US. WORKING FOR THE SCHOOL ALL ALONG.
MAX! FANG!
I'LL MAKE HIM PAY FOR THE BLOOD ON HIS HANDS.
IS HE OKAY?!
I DON'T... WE NEED HELP!

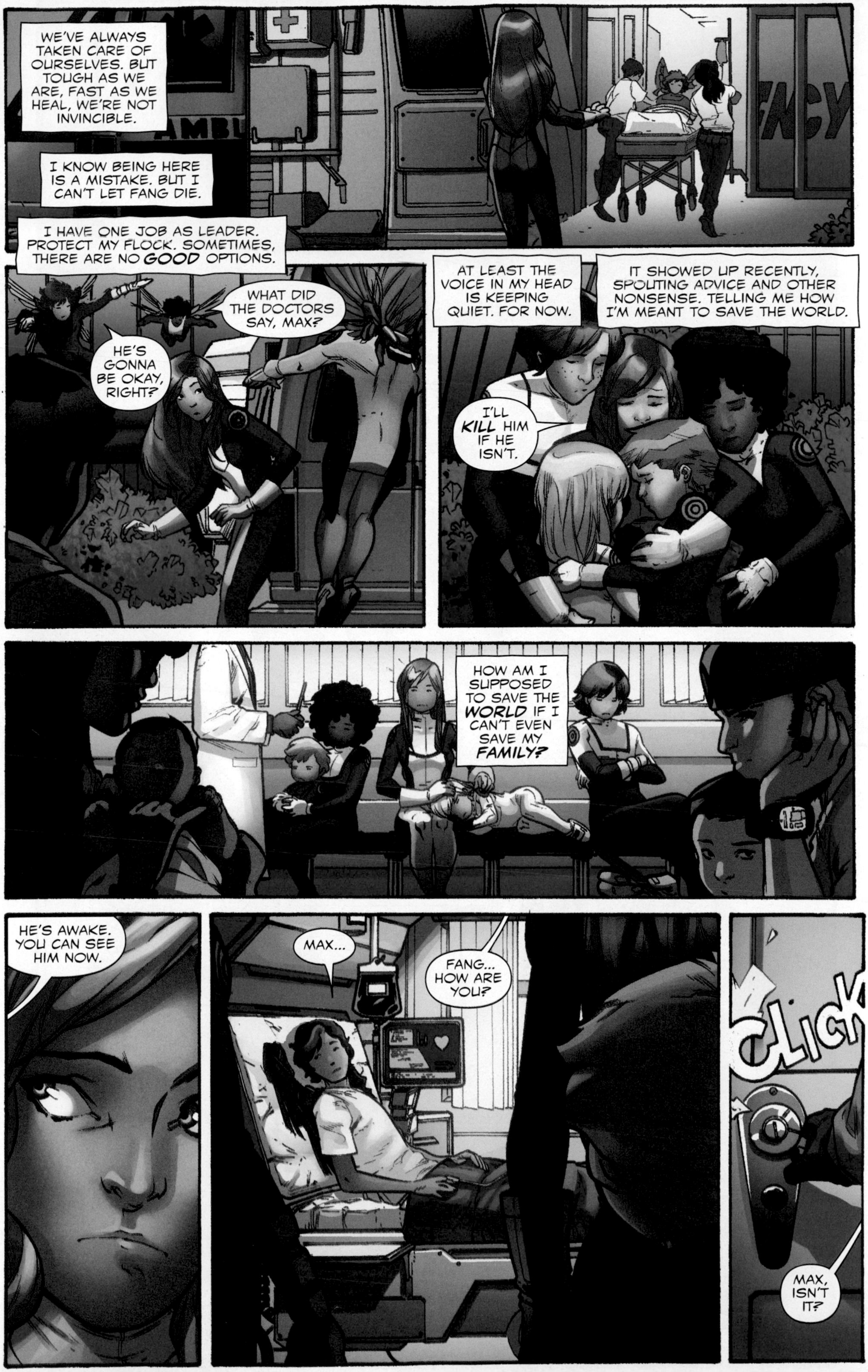

WE'VE ALWAYS TAKEN CARE OF OURSELVES. BUT TOUGH AS WE ARE, FAST AS WE HEAL, WE'RE NOT INVINCIBLE.
I KNOW BEING HERE IS A MISTAKE. BUT I CAN'T LET FANG DIE.
I HAVE ONE JOB AS LEADER. PROTECT MY FLOCK. SOMETIMES, THERE ARE NO GOOD OPTIONS.
WHAT DID THE DOCTORS SAY, MAX?
HE'S GONNA BE OKAY, RIGHT?
AT LEAST THE VOICE IN MY HEAD IS KEEPING QUIET. FOR NOW.
IT SHOWED UP RECENTLY, SPOUTING ADVICE AND OTHER NONSENSE. TELLING ME HOW I'M MEANT TO SAVE THE WORLD.
I'LL KILL HIM IF HE ISN'T.
HOW AM I SUPPOSED TO SAVE THE WORLD IF I CAN'T EVEN SAVE MY FAMILY?
HE'S AWAKE. YOU CAN SEE HIM NOW.
MAX...
FANG... HOW ARE YOU?
CLICK
MAX, ISN'T IT?

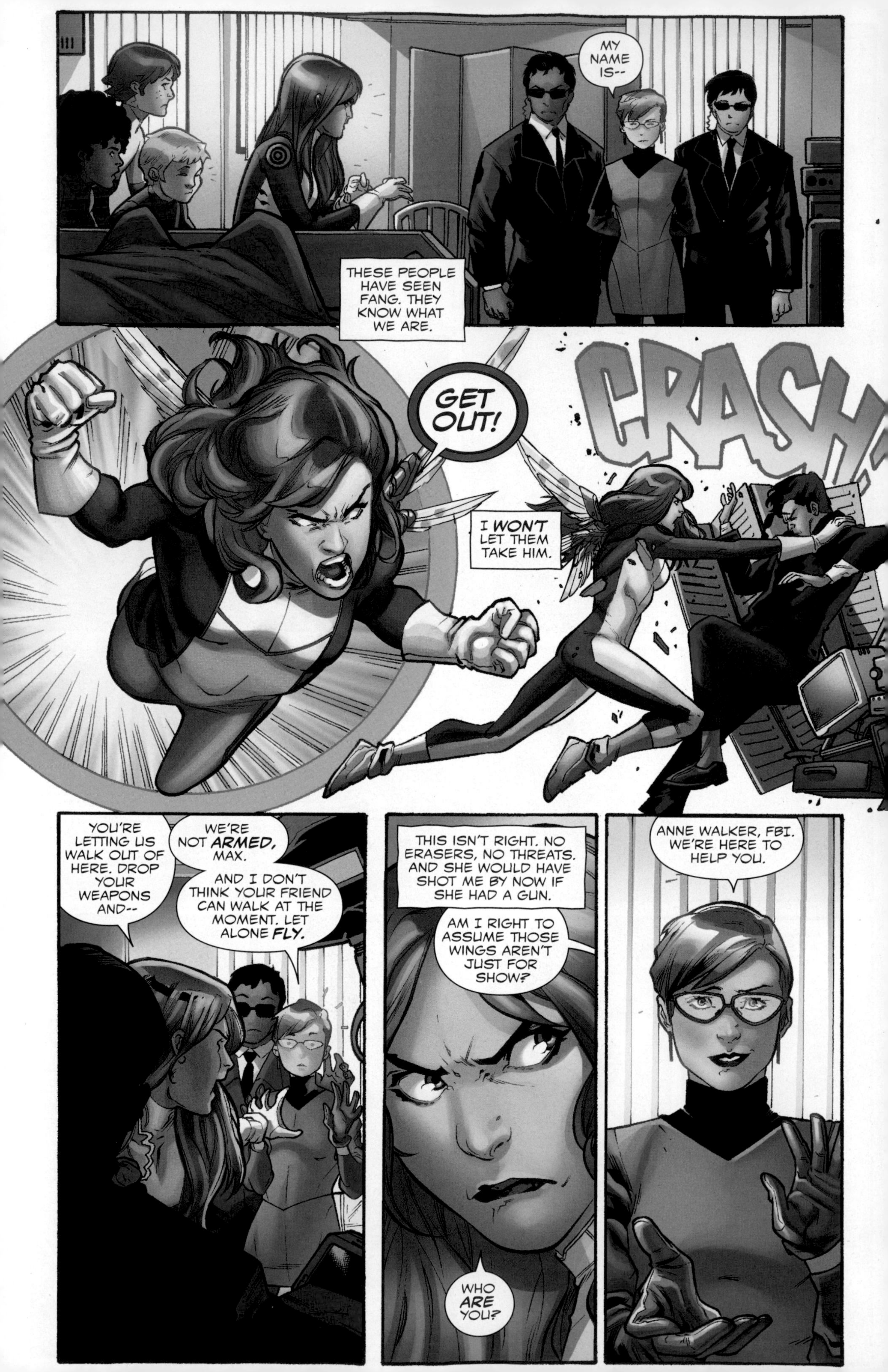
MY NAME IS--
THESE PEOPLE HAVE SEEN FANG. THEY KNOW WHAT WE ARE.
GET OUT!
CRASH!
I WON'T LET THEM TAKE HIM.
YOU'RE LETTING US WALK OUT OF HERE. DROP YOUR WEAPONS AND--
WE'RE NOT ARMED, MAX.
AND I DON'T THINK YOUR FRIEND CAN WALK AT THE MOMENT. LET ALONE FLY.
THIS ISN'T RIGHT. NO ERASERS, NO THREATS. AND SHE WOULD HAVE SHOT ME BY NOW IF SHE HAD A GUN.
AM I RIGHT TO ASSUME THOSE WINGS AREN'T JUST FOR SHOW?
WHO ARE YOU?
ANNE WALKER, FBI. WE'RE HERE TO HELP YOU.

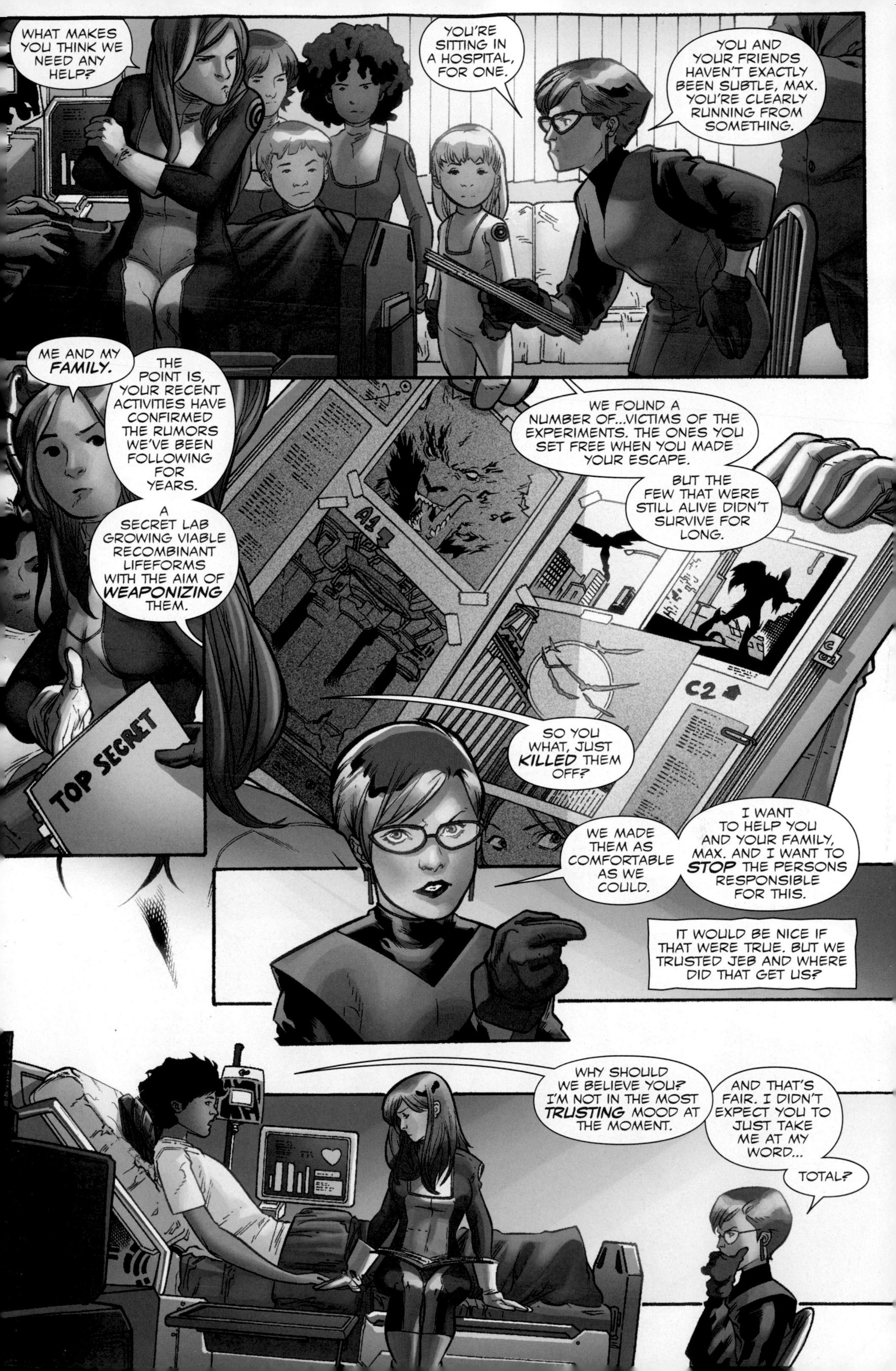
WHAT MAKES YOU THINK WE NEED ANY HELP?
YOU'RE SITTING IN A HOSPITAL, FOR ONE.
YOU AND YOUR FRIENDS HAVEN'T EXACTLY BEEN SUBTLE, MAX. YOU'RE CLEARLY RUNNING FROM SOMETHING.
ME AND MY FAMILY.
THE POINT IS, YOUR RECENT ACTIVITIES HAVE CONFIRMED THE RUMORS WE'VE BEEN FOLLOWING FOR YEARS.
A SECRET LAB GROWING VIABLE RECOMBINANT LIFEFORMS WITH THE AIM OF WEAPONIZING THEM.
TOP SECRET
WE FOUND A NUMBER OF...VICTIMS OF THE EXPERIMENTS. THE ONES YOU SET FREE WHEN YOU MADE YOUR ESCAPE.
BUT THE FEW THAT WERE STILL ALIVE DIDN'T SURVIVE FOR LONG.
A1
C2
SO YOU WHAT, JUST KILLED THEM OFF?
WE MADE THEM AS COMFORTABLE AS WE COULD.
I WANT TO HELP YOU AND YOUR FAMILY, MAX. AND I WANT TO STOP THE PERSONS RESPONSIBLE FOR THIS.
IT WOULD BE NICE IF THAT WERE TRUE. BUT WE TRUSTED JEB AND WHERE DID THAT GET US?
WHY SHOULD WE BELIEVE YOU? I'M NOT IN THE MOST TRUSTING MOOD AT THE MOMENT.
AND THAT'S FAIR. I DIDN'T EXPECT YOU TO JUST TAKE ME AT MY WORD...
TOTAL?

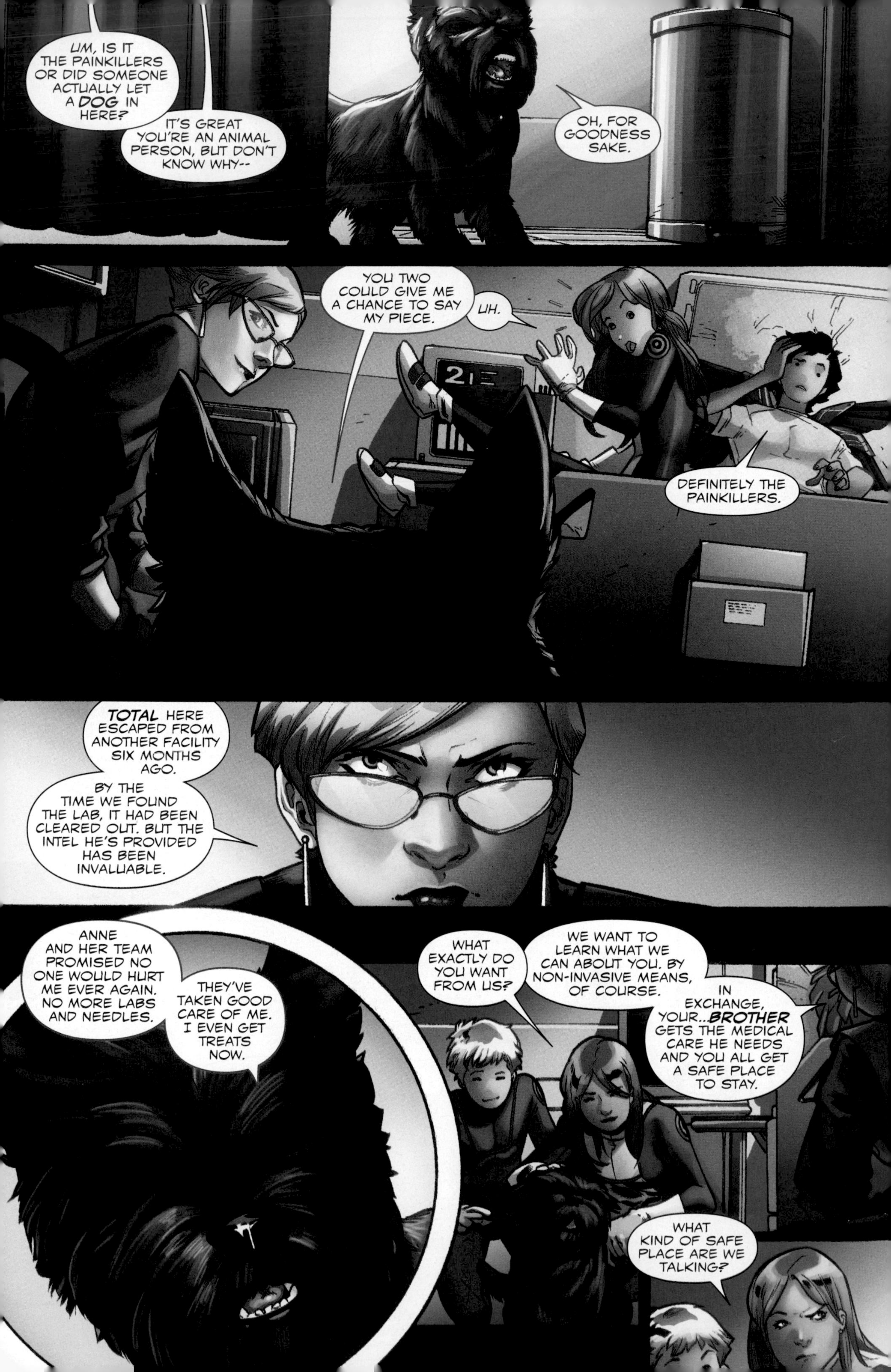
UM, IS IT THE PAINKILLERS OR DID SOMEONE ACTUALLY LET A DOG IN HERE?
IT'S GREAT YOU'RE AN ANIMAL PERSON, BUT DON'T KNOW WHY--
OH, FOR GOODNESS SAKE.
YOU TWO COULD GIVE ME A CHANCE TO SAY MY PIECE.
UH.
DEFINITELY THE PAINKILLERS.
TOTAL HERE ESCAPED FROM ANOTHER FACILITY SIX MONTHS AGO.
BY THE TIME WE FOUND THE LAB, IT HAD BEEN CLEARED OUT. BUT THE INTEL HE'S PROVIDED HAS BEEN INVALUABLE.
ANNE AND HER TEAM PROMISED NO ONE WOULD HURT ME EVER AGAIN. NO MORE LABS AND NEEDLES.
THEY'VE TAKEN GOOD CARE OF ME. I EVEN GET TREATS NOW.
WHAT EXACTLY DO YOU WANT FROM US?
WE WANT TO LEARN WHAT WE CAN ABOUT YOU. BY NON-INVASIVE MEANS, OF COURSE.
IN EXCHANGE, YOUR...BROTHER GETS THE MEDICAL CARE HE NEEDS AND YOU ALL GET A SAFE PLACE TO STAY.
WHAT KIND OF SAFE PLACE ARE WE TALKING?

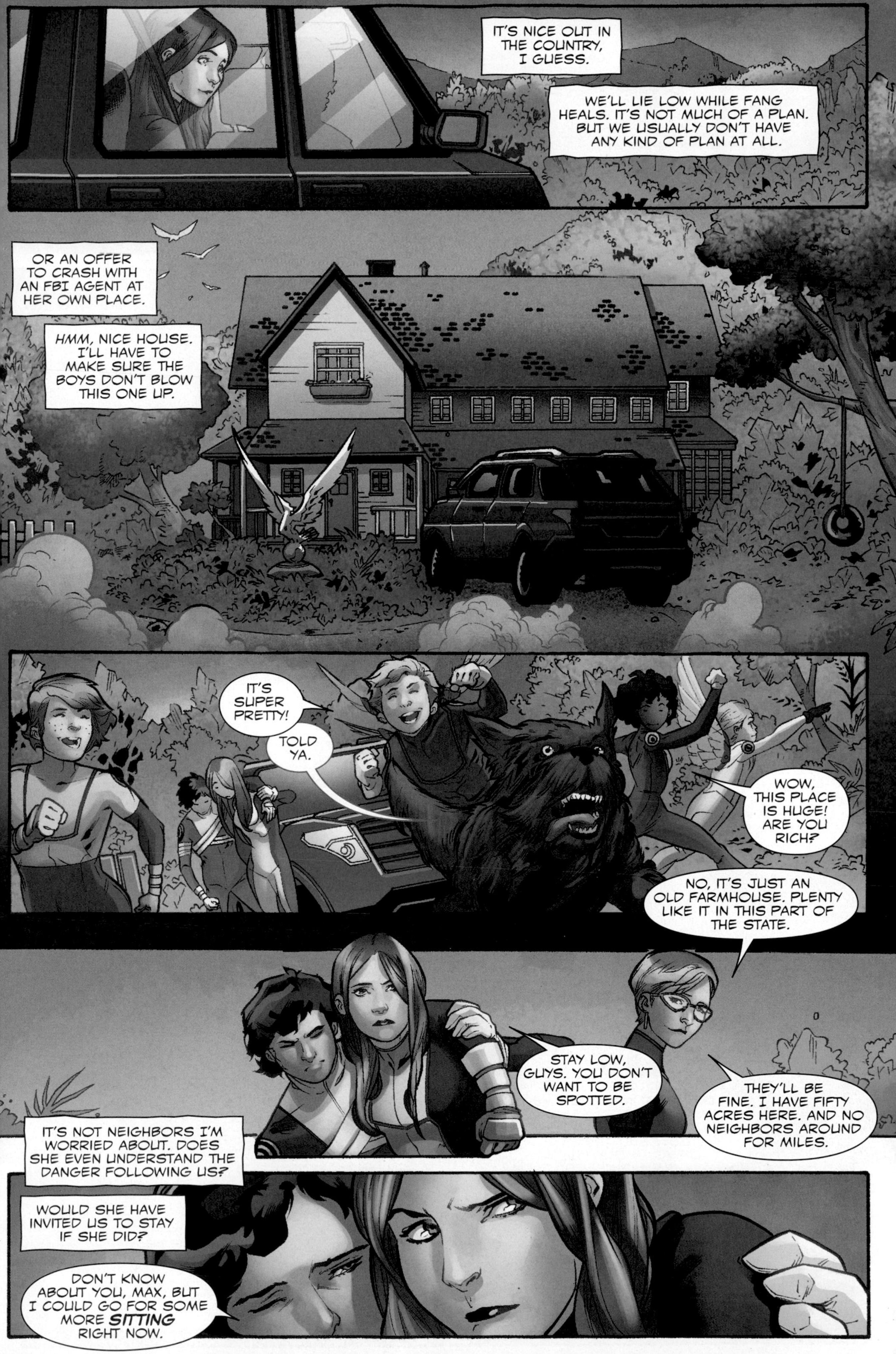
IT'S NICE OUT IN THE COUNTRY, I GUESS.
WE'LL LIE LOW WHILE FANG HEALS. IT'S NOT MUCH OF A PLAN. BUT WE USUALLY DON'T HAVE ANY KIND OF PLAN AT ALL.
OR AN OFFER TO CRASH WITH AN FBI AGENT AT HER OWN PLACE.
HMM, NICE HOUSE. I'LL HAVE TO MAKE SURE THE BOYS DON'T BLOW THIS ONE UP.
IT'S SUPER PRETTY!
TOLD YA.
WOW, THIS PLACE IS HUGE! ARE YOU RICH?
NO, IT'S JUST AN OLD FARMHOUSE. PLENTY LIKE IT IN THIS PART OF THE STATE.
STAY LOW, GUYS. YOU DON'T WANT TO BE SPOTTED.
THEY'LL BE FINE. I HAVE FIFTY ACRES HERE. AND NO NEIGHBORS AROUND FOR MILES.
IT'S NOT NEIGHBORS I'M WORRIED ABOUT. DOES SHE EVEN UNDERSTAND THE DANGER FOLLOWING US?
WOULD SHE HAVE INVITED US TO STAY IF SHE DID?
DON'T KNOW ABOUT YOU, MAX, BUT I COULD GO FOR SOME MORE ***SITTING*** RIGHT NOW.

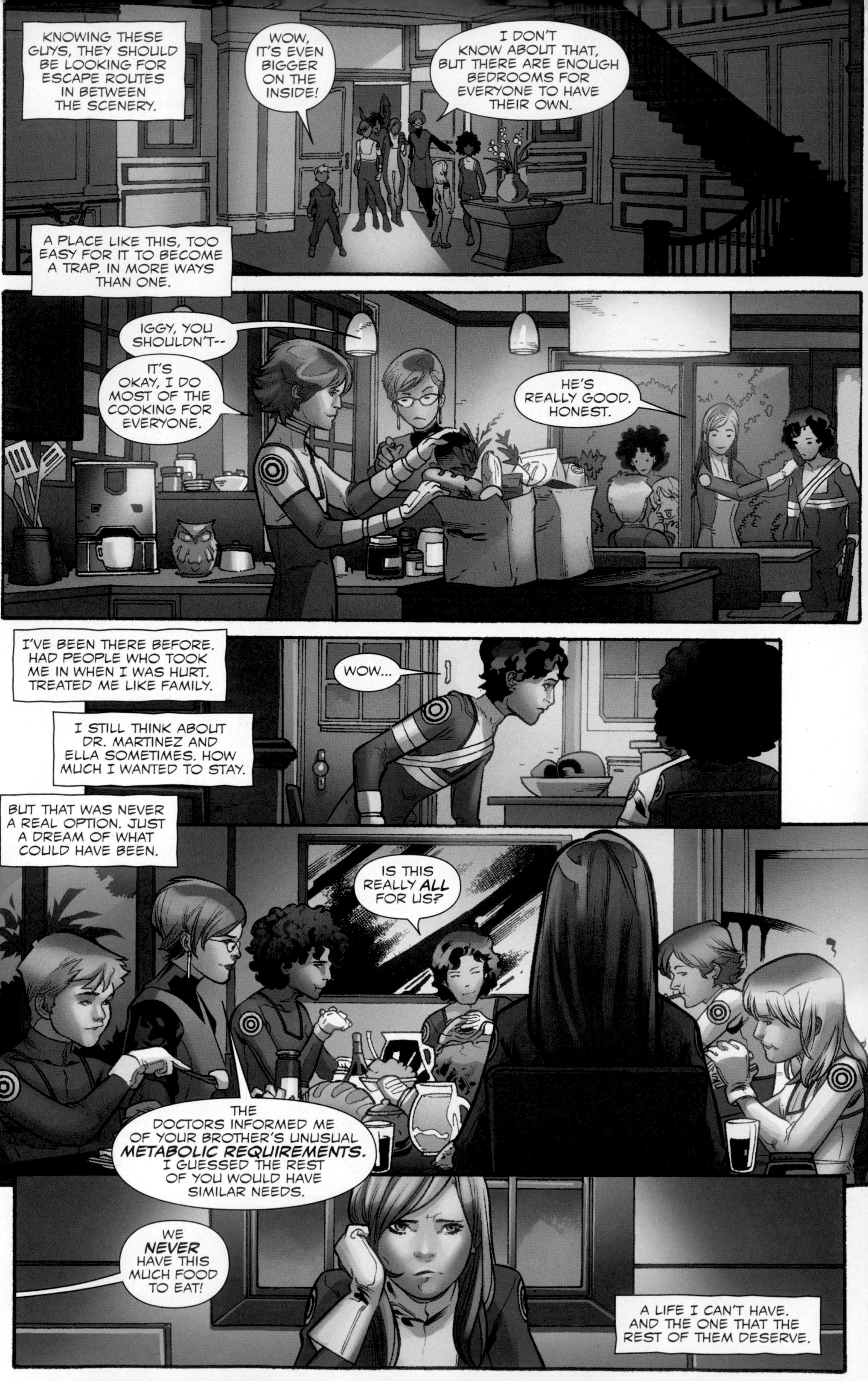

KNOWING THESE GUYS, THEY SHOULD BE LOOKING FOR ESCAPE ROUTES IN BETWEEN THE SCENERY.
WOW, IT'S EVEN BIGGER ON THE INSIDE!
I DON'T KNOW ABOUT THAT, BUT THERE ARE ENOUGH BEDROOMS FOR EVERYONE TO HAVE THEIR OWN.
A PLACE LIKE THIS, TOO EASY FOR IT TO BECOME A TRAP. IN MORE WAYS THAN ONE.
IGGY, YOU SHOULDN'T--
IT'S OKAY, I DO MOST OF THE COOKING FOR EVERYONE.
HE'S REALLY GOOD. HONEST.
I'VE BEEN THERE BEFORE. HAD PEOPLE WHO TOOK ME IN WHEN I WAS HURT. TREATED ME LIKE FAMILY.
WOW...
I STILL THINK ABOUT DR. MARTINEZ AND ELLA SOMETIMES. HOW MUCH I WANTED TO STAY.
BUT THAT WAS NEVER A REAL OPTION. JUST A DREAM OF WHAT COULD HAVE BEEN.
IS THIS REALLY ALL FOR US?
THE DOCTORS INFORMED ME OF YOUR BROTHER'S UNUSUAL METABOLIC REQUIREMENTS. I GUESSED THE REST OF YOU WOULD HAVE SIMILAR NEEDS.
WE NEVER HAVE THIS MUCH FOOD TO EAT!
A LIFE I CAN'T HAVE. AND THE ONE THAT THE REST OF THEM DESERVE.

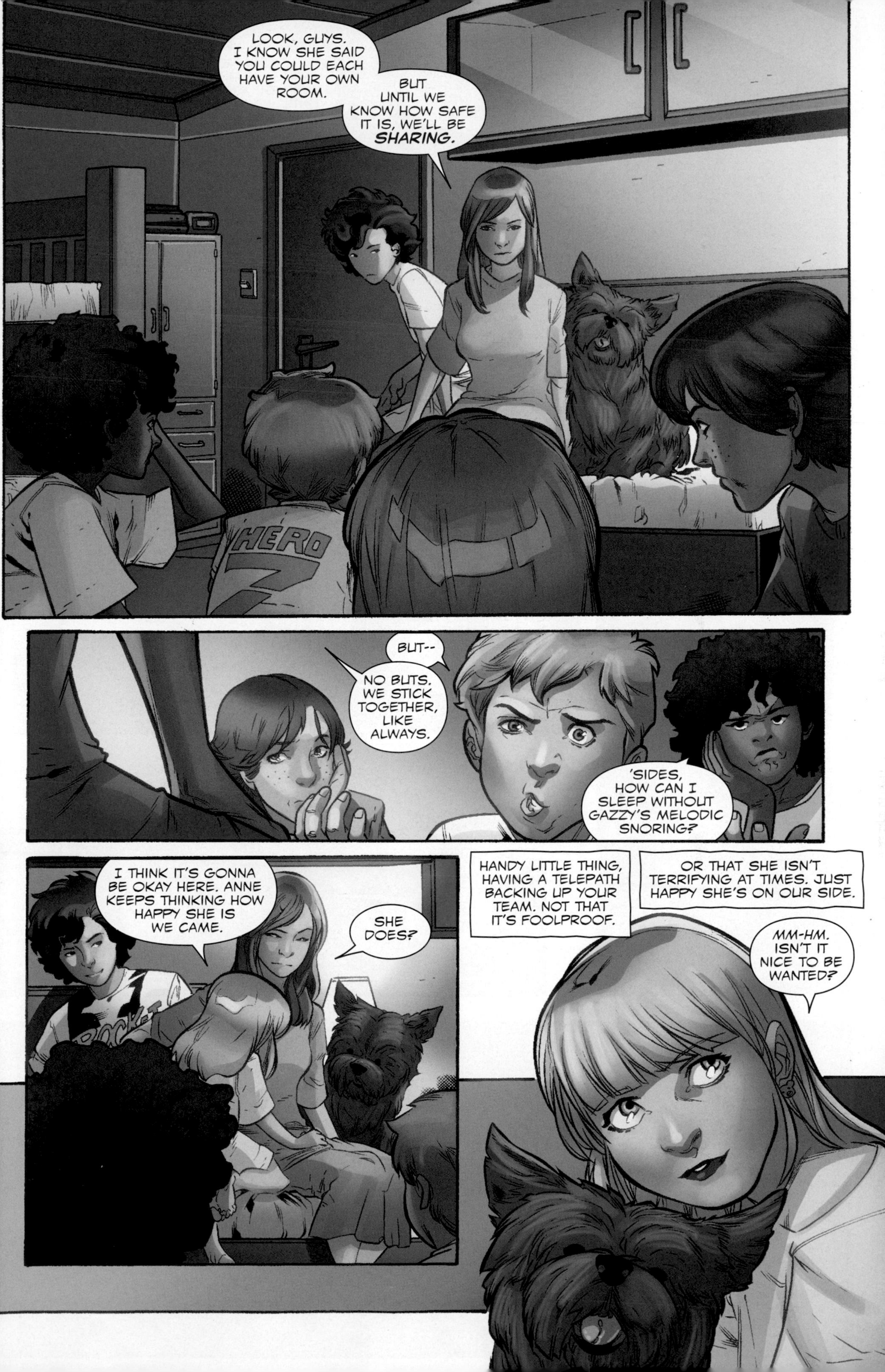
LOOK, GUYS. I KNOW SHE SAID YOU COULD EACH HAVE YOUR OWN ROOM.
BUT UNTIL WE KNOW HOW SAFE IT IS, WE'LL BE **SHARING.**
HERO
7
BUT--
NO BUTS. WE STICK TOGETHER, LIKE ALWAYS.
'SIDES, HOW CAN I SLEEP WITHOUT GAZZY'S MELODIC SNORING?
I THINK IT'S GONNA BE OKAY HERE. ANNE KEEPS THINKING HOW HAPPY SHE IS WE CAME.
SHE DOES?
HANDY LITTLE THING, HAVING A TELEPATH BACKING UP YOUR TEAM. NOT THAT IT'S FOOLPROOF.
OR THAT SHE ISN'T TERRIFYING AT TIMES. JUST HAPPY SHE'S ON OUR SIDE.
MM-HM. ISN'T IT NICE TO BE WANTED?

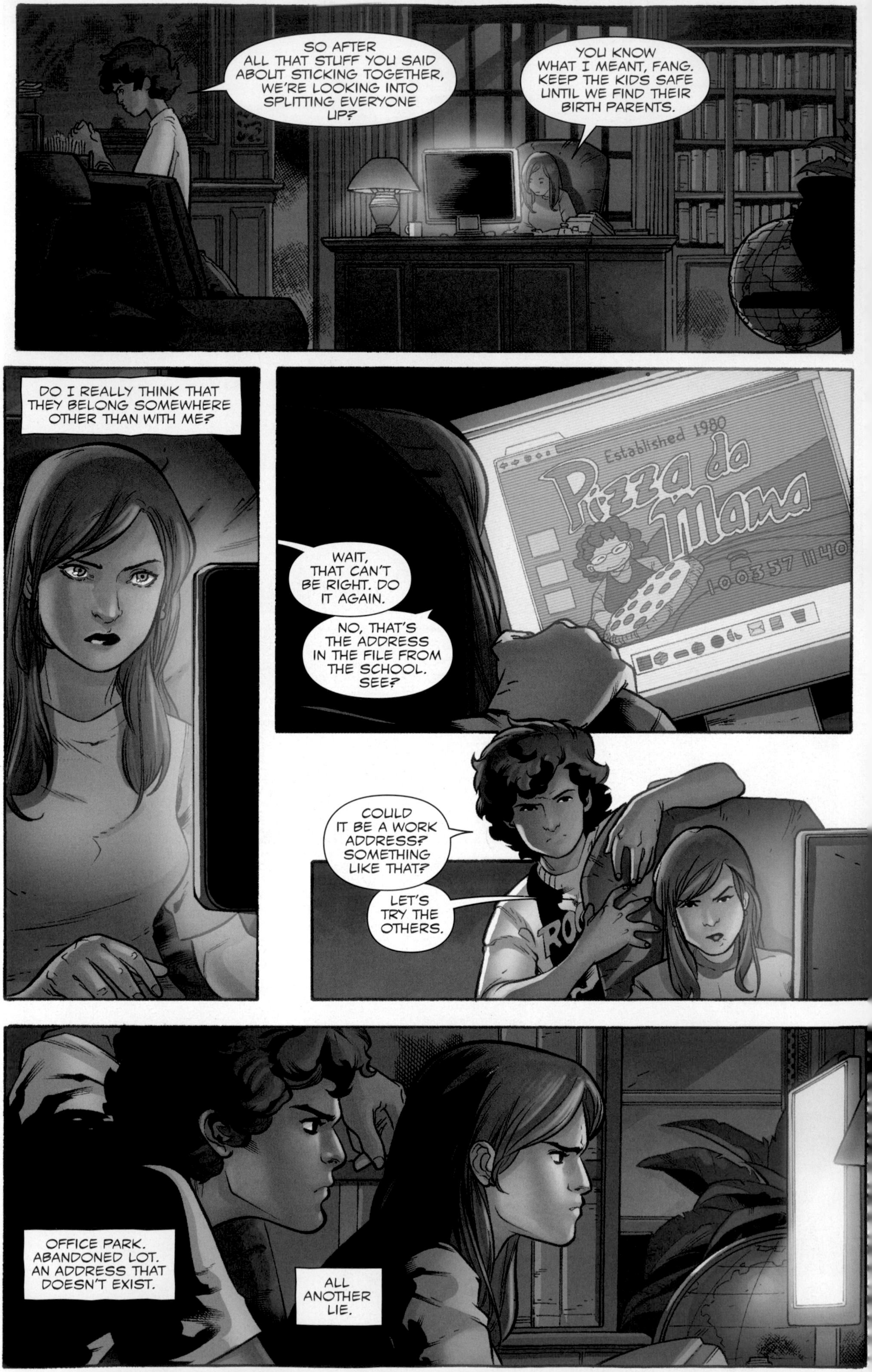
SO AFTER ALL THAT STUFF YOU SAID ABOUT STICKING TOGETHER, WE'RE LOOKING INTO SPLITTING EVERYONE UP?
YOU KNOW WHAT I MEANT, FANG. KEEP THE KIDS SAFE UNTIL WE FIND THEIR BIRTH PARENTS.
DO I REALLY THINK THAT THEY BELONG SOMEWHERE OTHER THAN WITH ME?
Established 1980
Pizza da Mama
WAIT, THAT CAN'T BE RIGHT. DO IT AGAIN.
NO, THAT'S THE ADDRESS IN THE FILE FROM THE SCHOOL. SEE?
COULD IT BE A WORK ADDRESS? SOMETHING LIKE THAT?
LET'S TRY THE OTHERS.
OFFICE PARK. ABANDONED LOT. AN ADDRESS THAT DOESN'T EXIST.
ALL ANOTHER LIE.

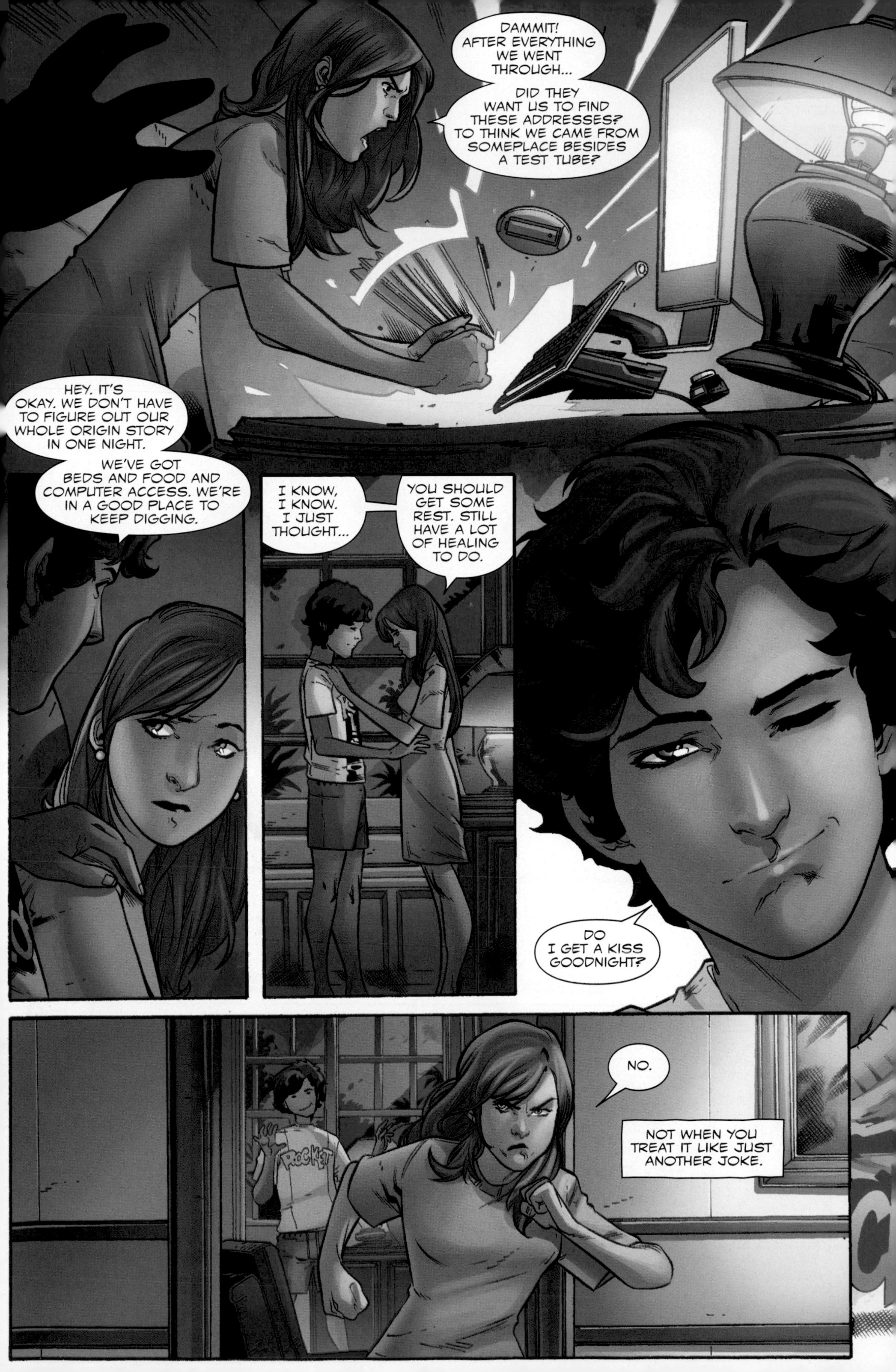
DAMMIT! AFTER EVERYTHING WE WENT THROUGH...
DID THEY WANT US TO FIND THESE ADDRESSES? TO THINK WE CAME FROM SOMEPLACE BESIDES A TEST TUBE?
HEY. IT'S OKAY. WE DON'T HAVE TO FIGURE OUT OUR WHOLE ORIGIN STORY IN ONE NIGHT.
WE'VE GOT BEDS AND FOOD AND COMPUTER ACCESS. WE'RE IN A GOOD PLACE TO KEEP DIGGING.
I KNOW, I KNOW. I JUST THOUGHT...
YOU SHOULD GET SOME REST. STILL HAVE A LOT OF HEALING TO DO.
DO I GET A KISS GOODNIGHT?
NO.
NOT WHEN YOU TREAT IT LIKE JUST ANOTHER JOKE.

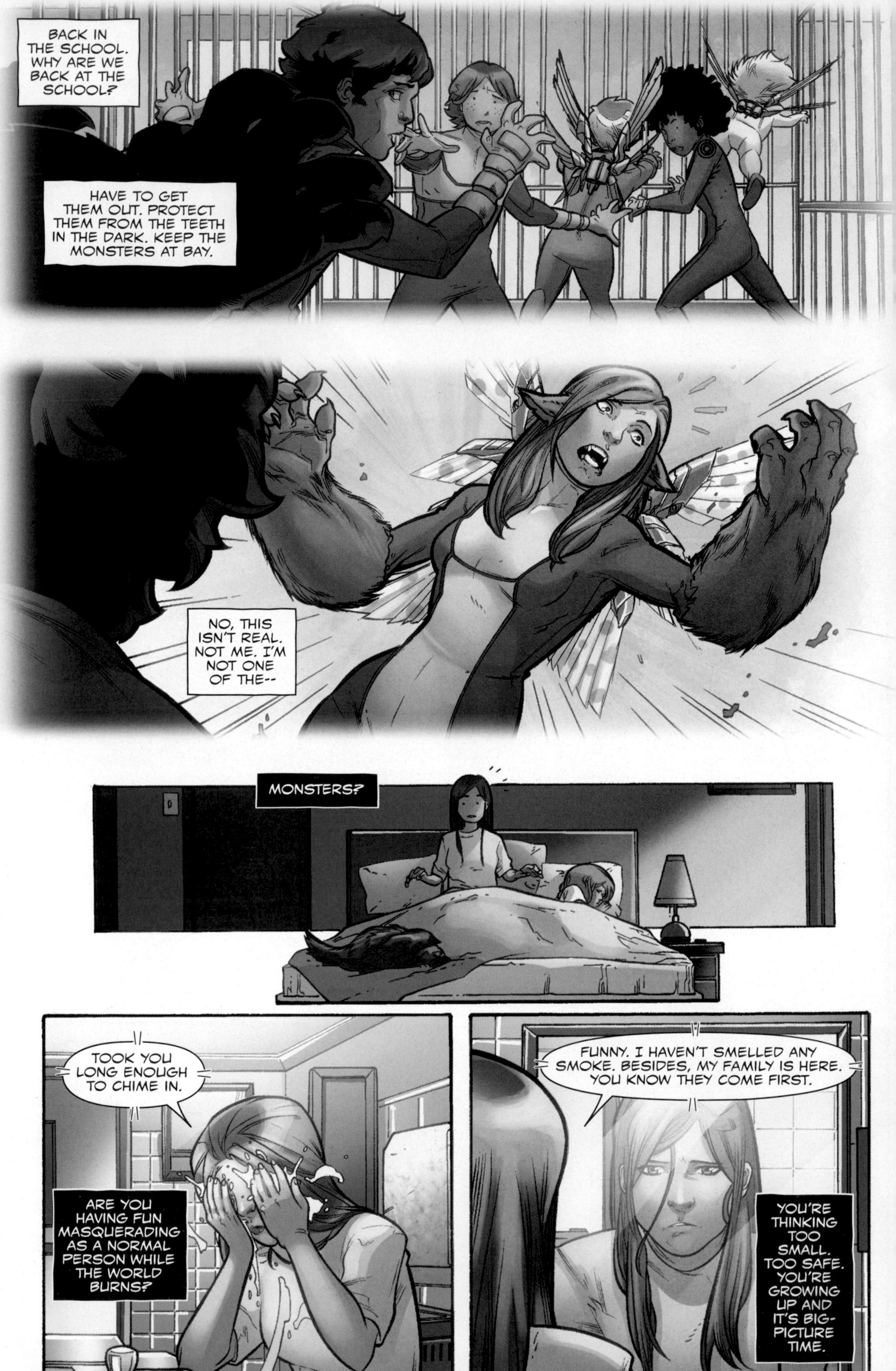
BACK IN THE SCHOOL. WHY ARE WE BACK AT THE SCHOOL?
HAVE TO GET THEM OUT. PROTECT THEM FROM THE TEETH IN THE DARK. KEEP THE MONSTERS AT BAY.
NO, THIS ISN'T REAL. NOT ME. I'M NOT ONE OF THE--
MONSTERS?
TOOK YOU LONG ENOUGH TO CHIME IN.
ARE YOU HAVING FUN MASQUERADING AS A NORMAL PERSON WHILE THE WORLD BURNS?
FUNNY. I HAVEN'T SMELLED ANY SMOKE. BESIDES, MY FAMILY IS HERE. YOU KNOW THEY COME FIRST.
YOU'RE THINKING TOO SMALL. TOO SAFE. YOU'RE GROWING UP AND IT'S BIG-PICTURE TIME.

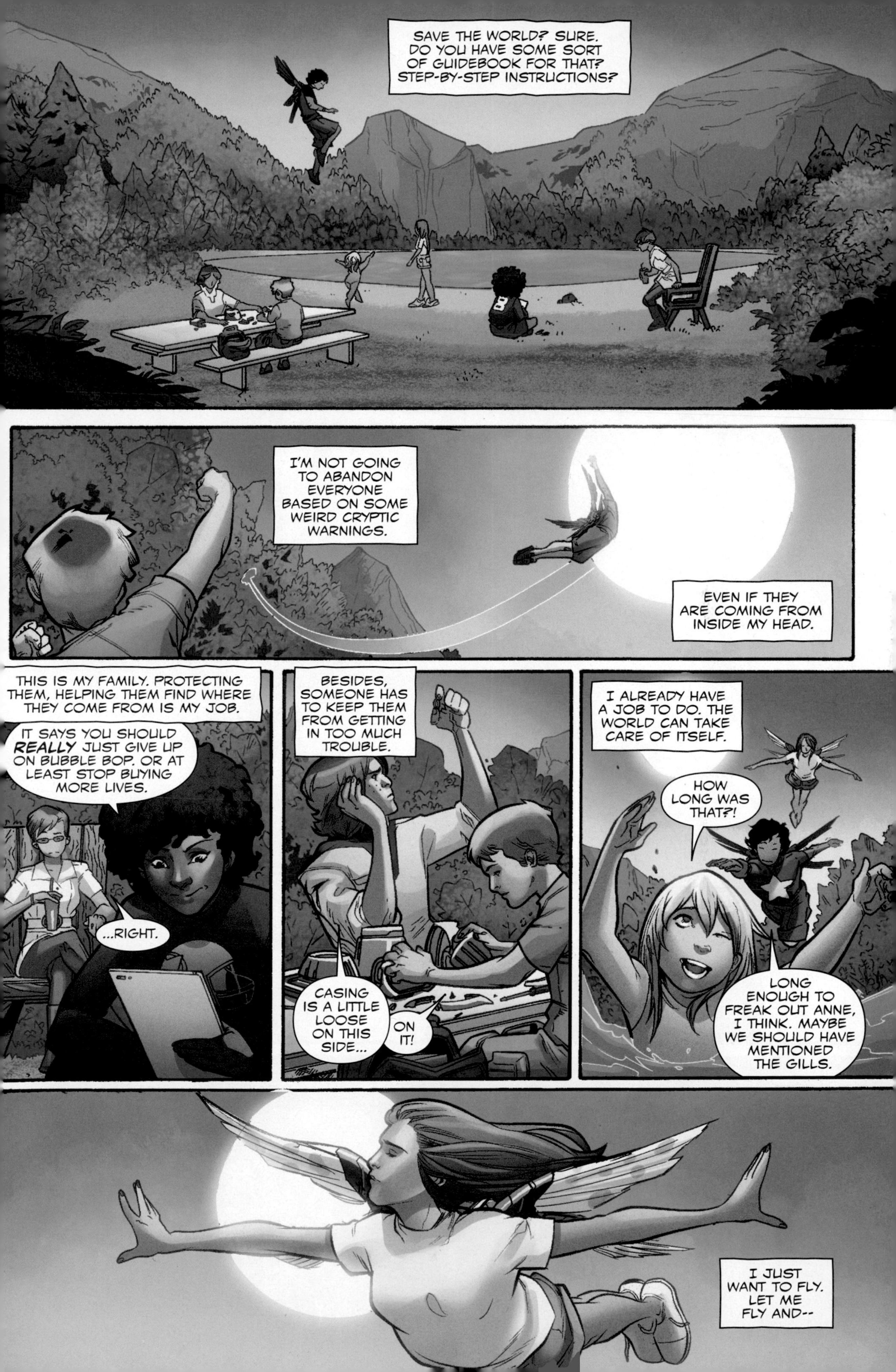
SAVE THE WORLD? SURE. DO YOU HAVE SOME SORT OF GUIDEBOOK FOR THAT? STEP-BY-STEP INSTRUCTIONS?
I'M NOT GOING TO ABANDON EVERYONE BASED ON SOME WEIRD CRYPTIC WARNINGS.
EVEN IF THEY ARE COMING FROM INSIDE MY HEAD.
THIS IS MY FAMILY. PROTECTING THEM, HELPING THEM FIND WHERE THEY COME FROM IS MY JOB.
IT SAYS YOU SHOULD **REALLY** JUST GIVE UP ON BUBBLE BOP. OR AT LEAST STOP BUYING MORE LIVES.
...RIGHT.
BESIDES, SOMEONE HAS TO KEEP THEM FROM GETTING IN TOO MUCH TROUBLE.
CASING IS A LITTLE LOOSE ON THIS SIDE...
ON IT!
I ALREADY HAVE A JOB TO DO. THE WORLD CAN TAKE CARE OF ITSELF.
HOW LONG WAS THAT?!
LONG ENOUGH TO FREAK OUT ANNE, I THINK. MAYBE WE SHOULD HAVE MENTIONED THE GILLS.
I JUST WANT TO FLY. LET ME FLY AND--

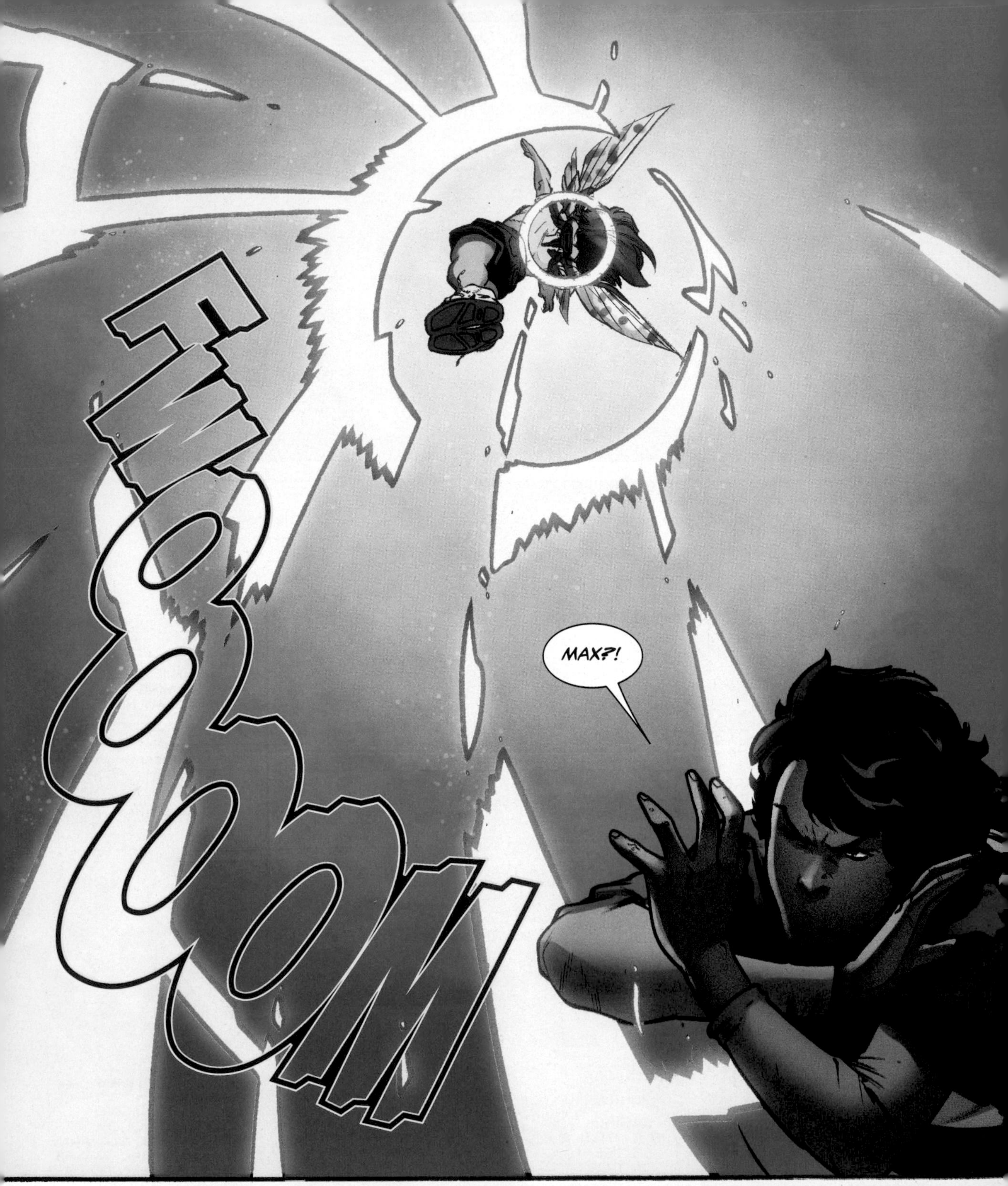
FWOOOOOM
MAX?!

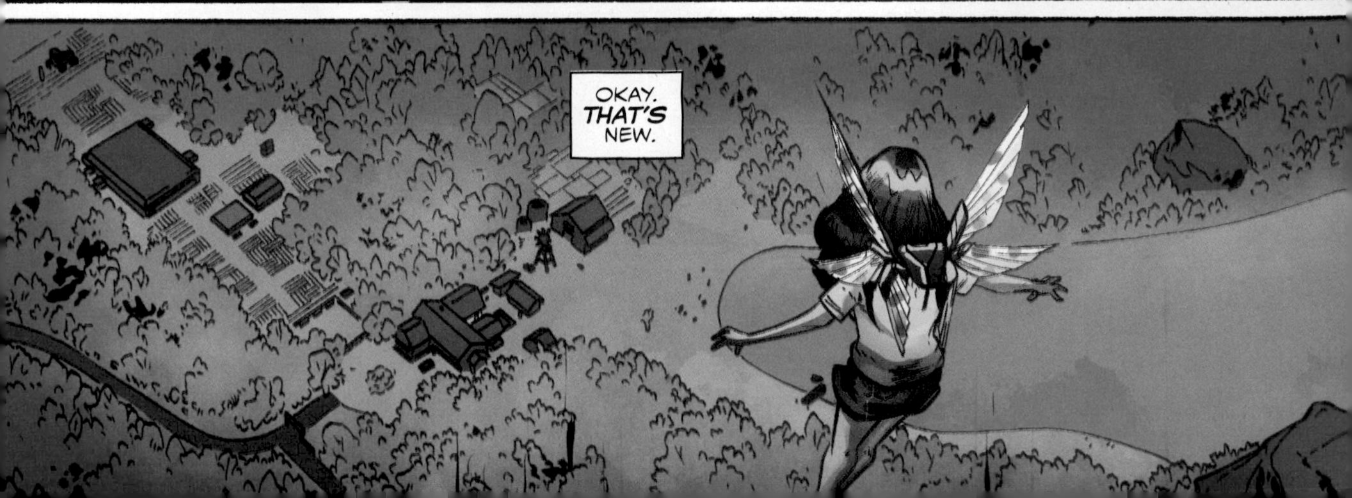
OKAY. THAT'S NEW.

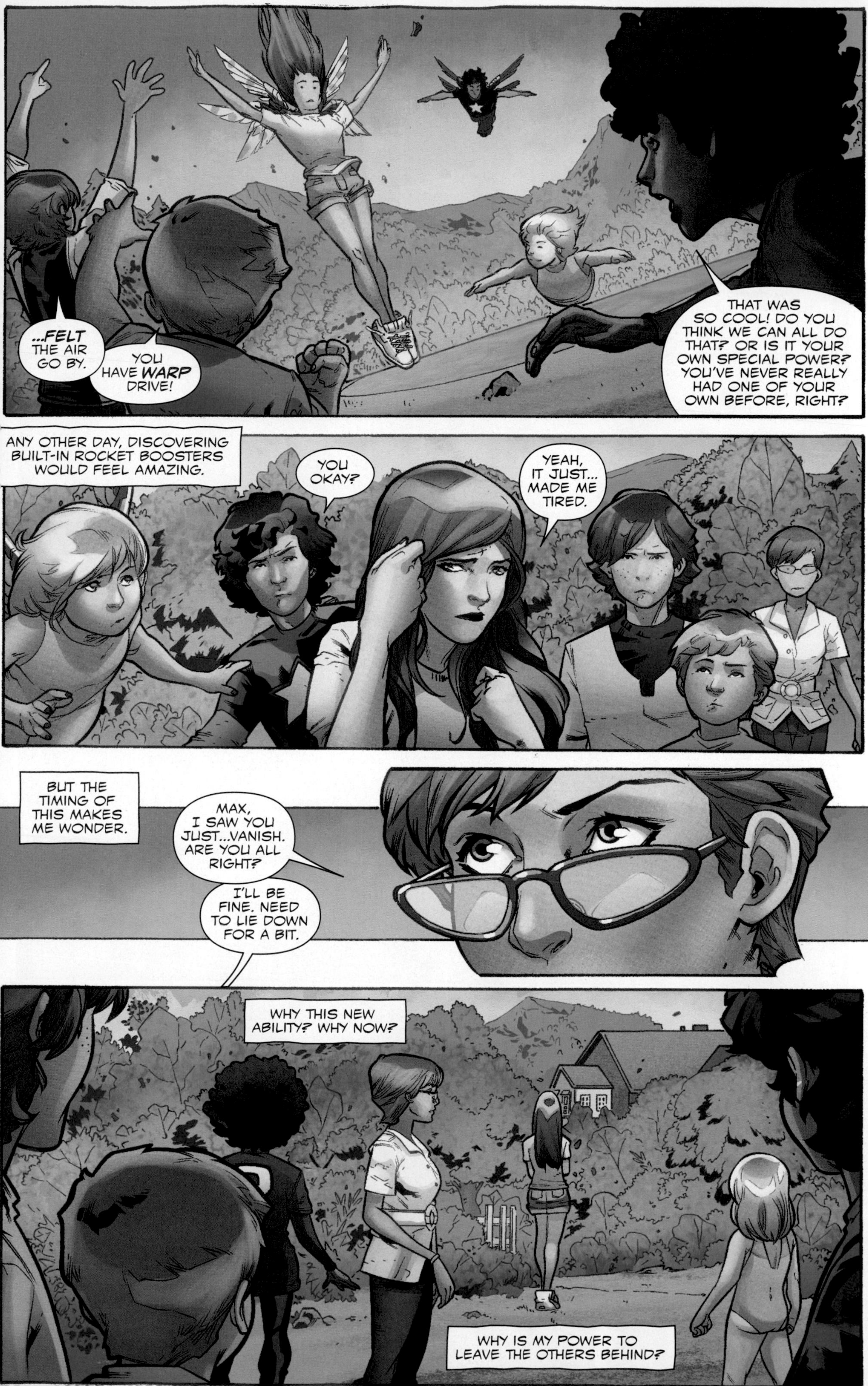
...FELT THE AIR GO BY.
YOU HAVE WARP DRIVE!
THAT WAS SO COOL! DO YOU THINK WE CAN ALL DO THAT? OR IS IT YOUR OWN SPECIAL POWER? YOU'VE NEVER REALLY HAD ONE OF YOUR OWN BEFORE, RIGHT?
ANY OTHER DAY, DISCOVERING BUILT-IN ROCKET BOOSTERS WOULD FEEL AMAZING.
YOU OKAY?
YEAH, IT JUST... MADE ME TIRED.
BUT THE TIMING OF THIS MAKES ME WONDER.
MAX, I SAW YOU JUST...VANISH. ARE YOU ALL RIGHT?
I'LL BE FINE. NEED TO LIE DOWN FOR A BIT.
WHY THIS NEW ABILITY? WHY NOW?
WHY IS MY POWER TO LEAVE THE OTHERS BEHIND?

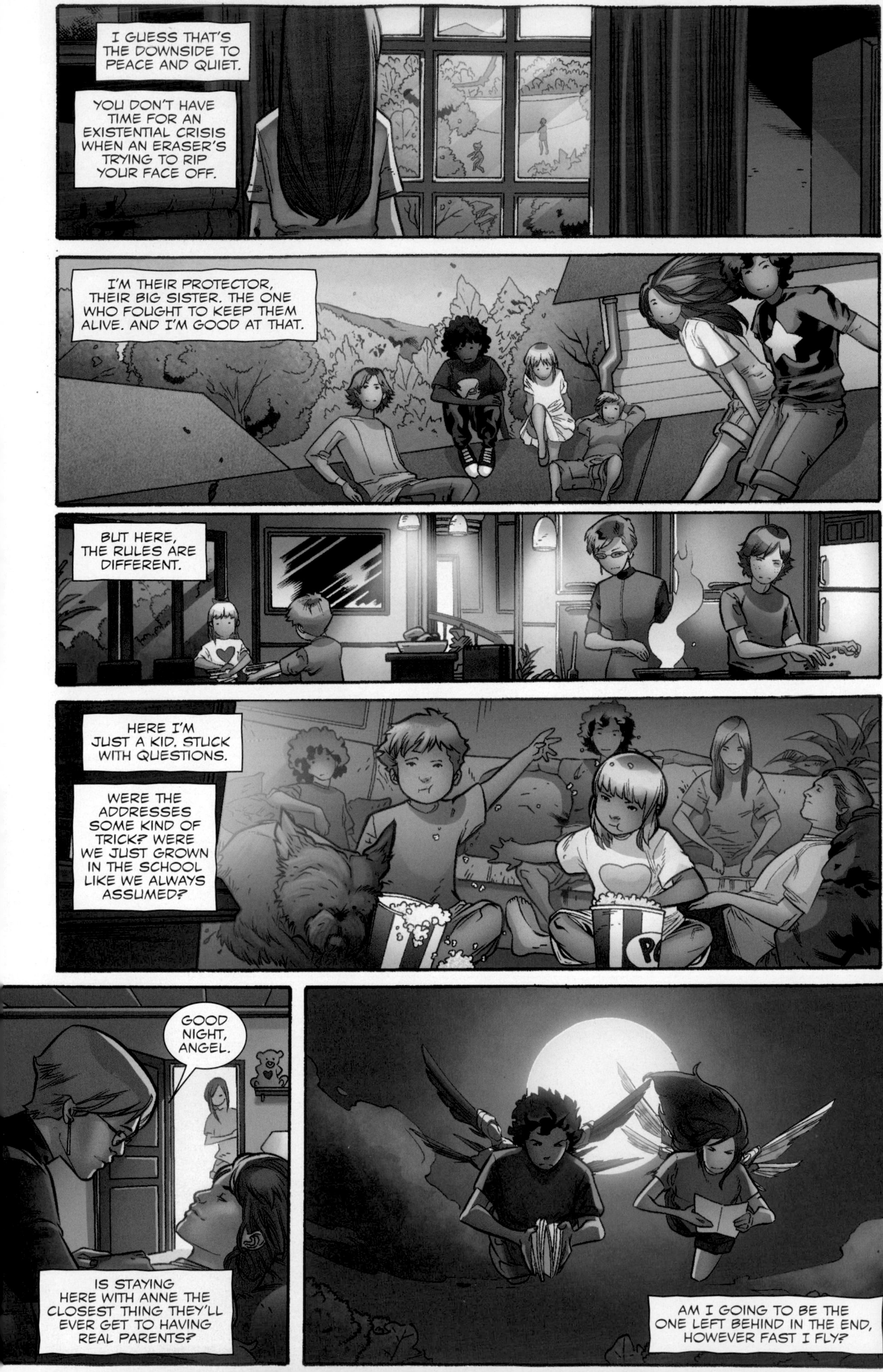
I GUESS THAT'S THE DOWNSIDE TO PEACE AND QUIET.
YOU DON'T HAVE TIME FOR AN EXISTENTIAL CRISIS WHEN AN ERASER'S TRYING TO RIP YOUR FACE OFF.
I'M THEIR PROTECTOR, THEIR BIG SISTER. THE ONE WHO FOUGHT TO KEEP THEM ALIVE. AND I'M GOOD AT THAT.
BUT HERE, THE RULES ARE DIFFERENT.
HERE I'M JUST A KID. STUCK WITH QUESTIONS.
WERE THE ADDRESSES SOME KIND OF TRICK? WERE WE JUST GROWN IN THE SCHOOL LIKE WE ALWAYS ASSUMED?
GOOD NIGHT, ANGEL.
IS STAYING HERE WITH ANNE THE CLOSEST THING THEY'LL EVER GET TO HAVING REAL PARENTS?
AM I GOING TO BE THE ONE LEFT BEHIND IN THE END, HOWEVER FAST I FLY?

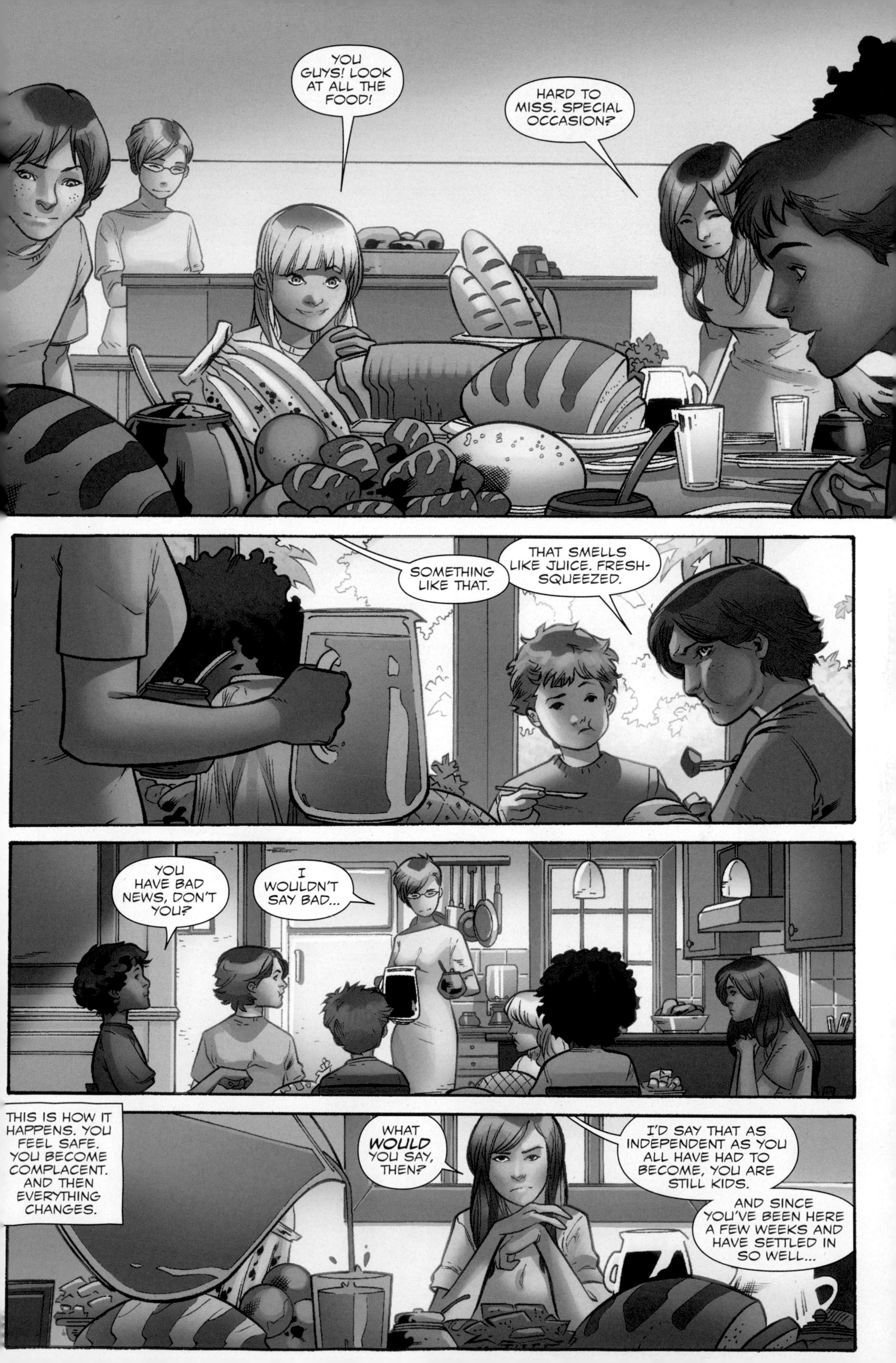

YOU GUYS! LOOK AT ALL THE FOOD!
HARD TO MISS. SPECIAL OCCASION?
SOMETHING LIKE THAT.
THAT SMELLS LIKE JUICE. FRESH-SQUEEZED.
YOU HAVE BAD NEWS, DON'T YOU?
I WOULDN'T SAY BAD...
THIS IS HOW IT HAPPENS. YOU FEEL SAFE. YOU BECOME COMPLACENT. AND THEN EVERYTHING CHANGES.
WHAT **WOULD** YOU SAY, THEN?
I'D SAY THAT AS INDEPENDENT AS YOU ALL HAVE HAD TO BECOME, YOU ARE STILL KIDS.
AND SINCE YOU'VE BEEN HERE A FEW WEEKS AND HAVE SETTLED IN SO WELL...

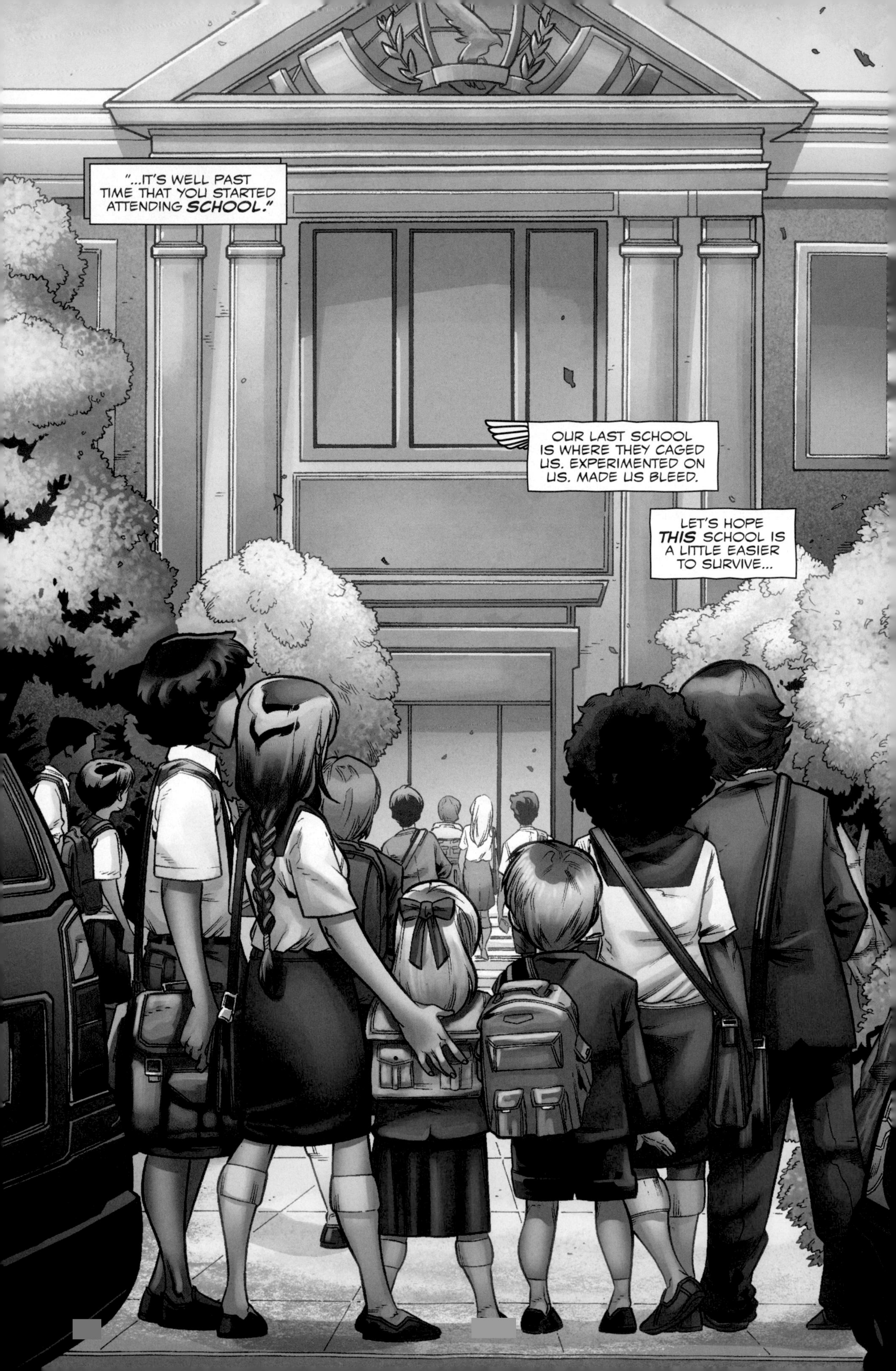
"...IT'S WELL PAST TIME THAT YOU STARTED ATTENDING SCHOOL."
OUR LAST SCHOOL IS WHERE THEY CAGED US. EXPERIMENTED ON US. MADE US BLEED.
LET'S HOPE THIS SCHOOL IS A LITTLE EASIER TO SURVIVE...

CHAPTER 2

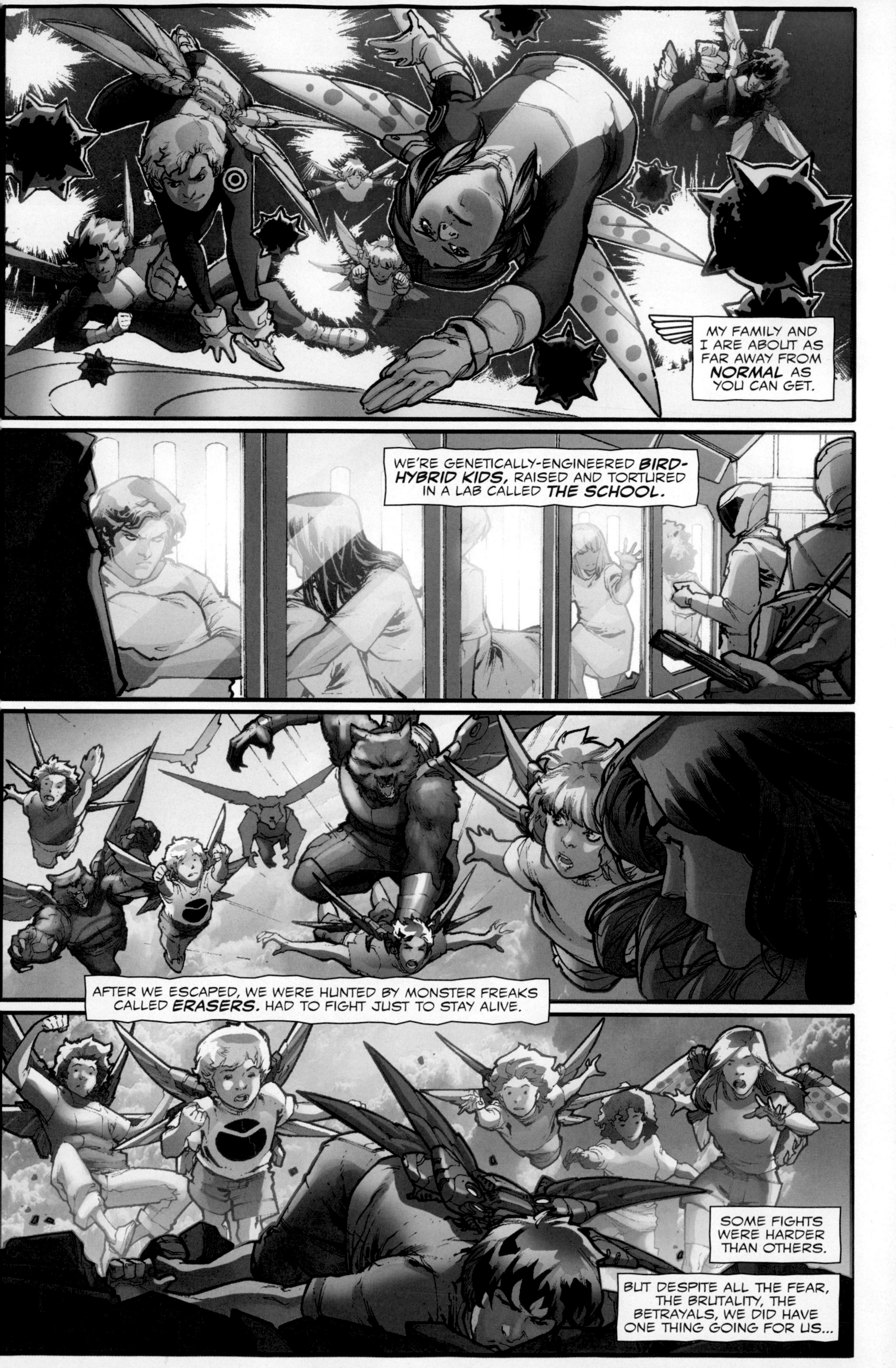
MY FAMILY AND I ARE ABOUT AS FAR AWAY FROM NORMAL AS YOU CAN GET.
WE'RE GENETICALLY-ENGINEERED BIRD-HYBRID KIDS, RAISED AND TORTURED IN A LAB CALLED THE SCHOOL.
AFTER WE ESCAPED, WE WERE HUNTED BY MONSTER FREAKS CALLED ERASERS. HAD TO FIGHT JUST TO STAY ALIVE.
SOME FIGHTS WERE HARDER THAN OTHERS.
BUT DESPITE ALL THE FEAR, THE BRUTALITY, THE BETRAYALS, WE DID HAVE ONE THING GOING FOR US...

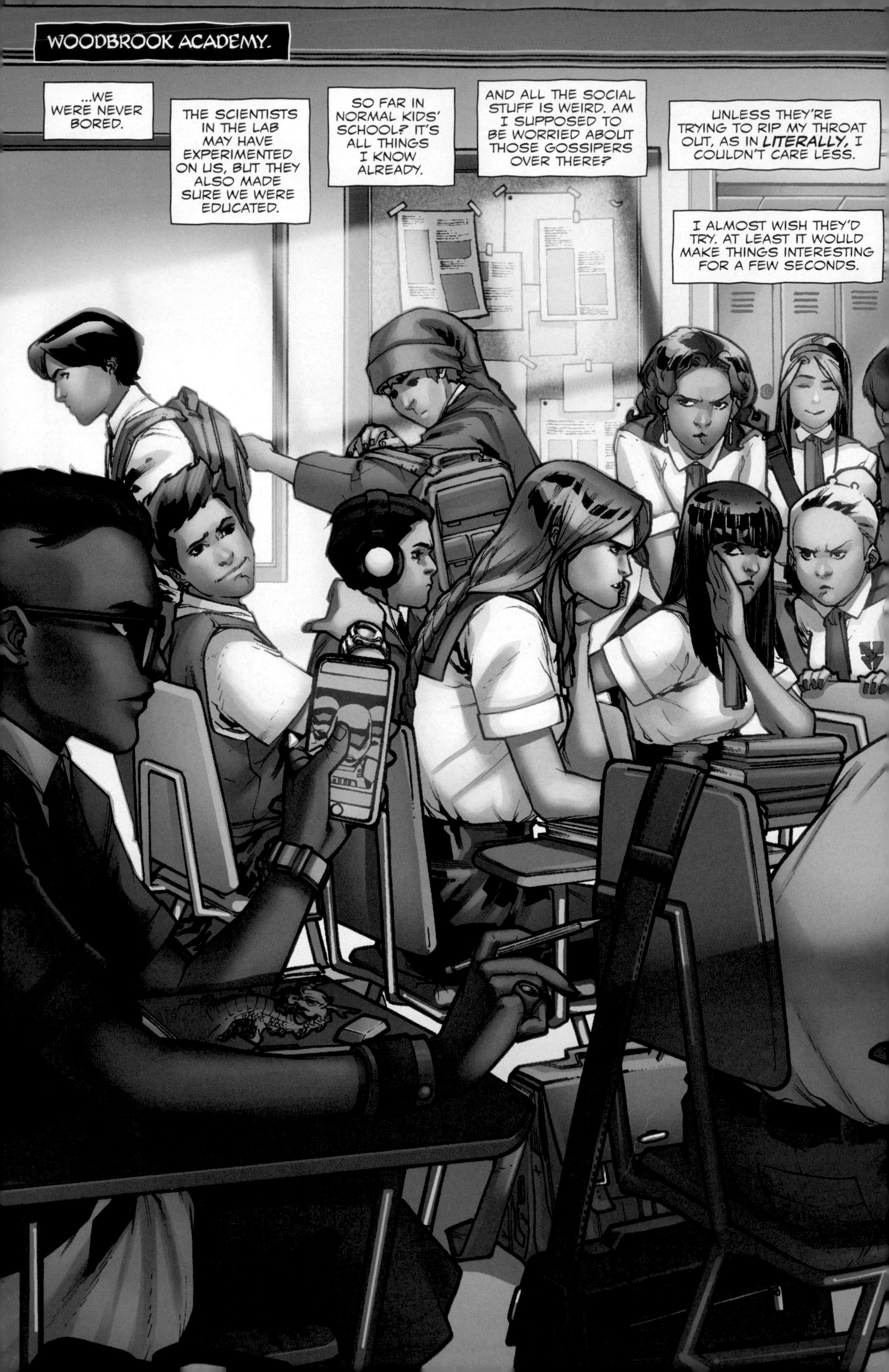
WOODBROOK ACADEMY.
...WE WERE NEVER BORED.
THE SCIENTISTS IN THE LAB MAY HAVE EXPERIMENTED ON US, BUT THEY ALSO MADE SURE WE WERE EDUCATED.
SO FAR IN NORMAL KIDS' SCHOOL? IT'S ALL THINGS I KNOW ALREADY.
AND ALL THE SOCIAL STUFF IS WEIRD. AM I SUPPOSED TO BE WORRIED ABOUT THOSE GOSSIPERS OVER THERE?
UNLESS THEY'RE TRYING TO RIP MY THROAT OUT, AS IN LITERALLY, I COULDN'T CARE LESS.
I ALMOST WISH THEY'D TRY. AT LEAST IT WOULD MAKE THINGS INTERESTING FOR A FEW SECONDS.

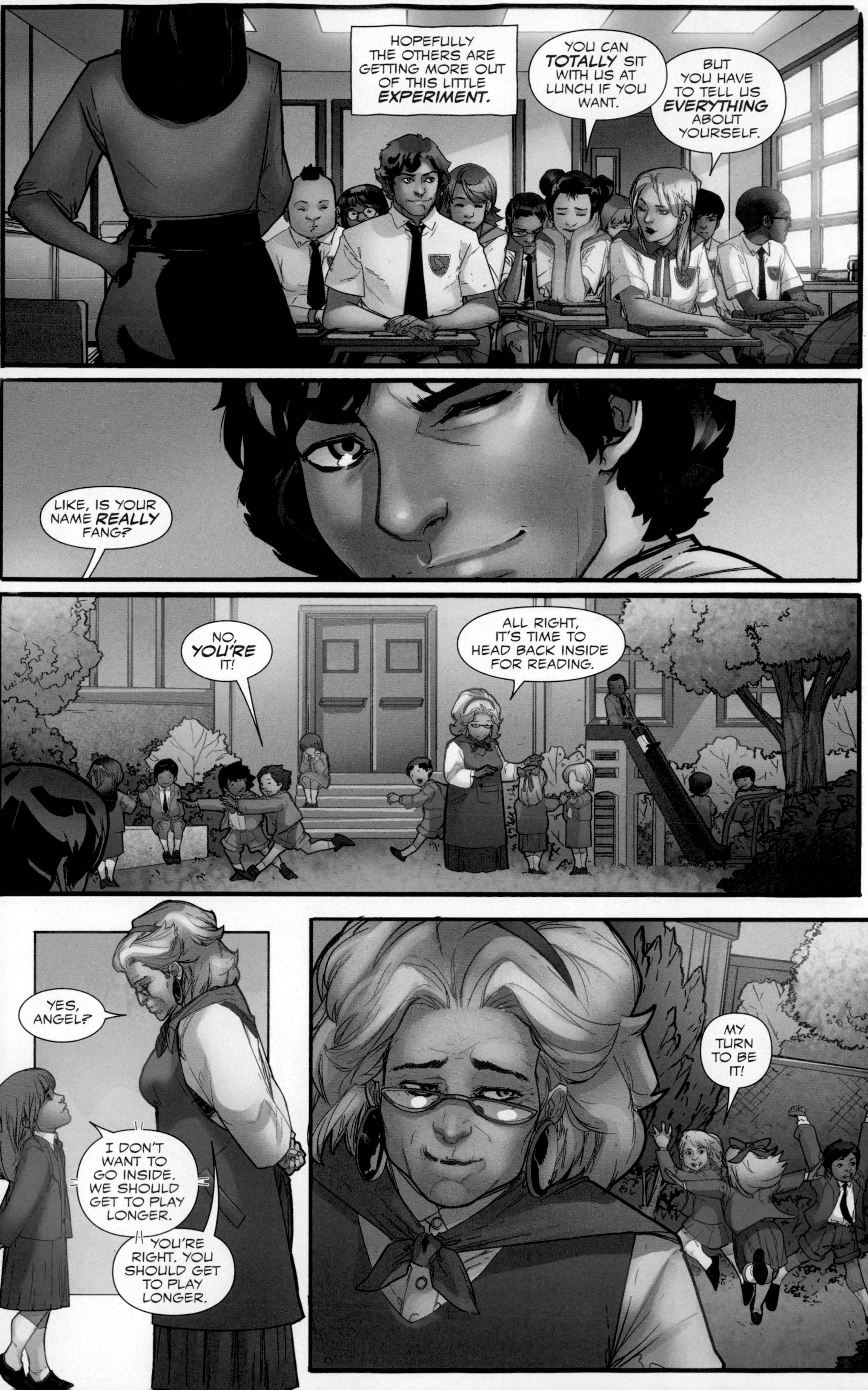
HOPEFULLY THE OTHERS ARE GETTING MORE OUT OF THIS LITTLE EXPERIMENT.
YOU CAN TOTALLY SIT WITH US AT LUNCH IF YOU WANT.
BUT YOU HAVE TO TELL US EVERYTHING ABOUT YOURSELF.
LIKE, IS YOUR NAME REALLY FANG?
NO, YOU'RE IT!
ALL RIGHT, IT'S TIME TO HEAD BACK INSIDE FOR READING.
YES, ANGEL?
I DON'T WANT TO GO INSIDE. WE SHOULD GET TO PLAY LONGER.
YOU'RE RIGHT. YOU SHOULD GET TO PLAY LONGER.
MY TURN TO BE IT!

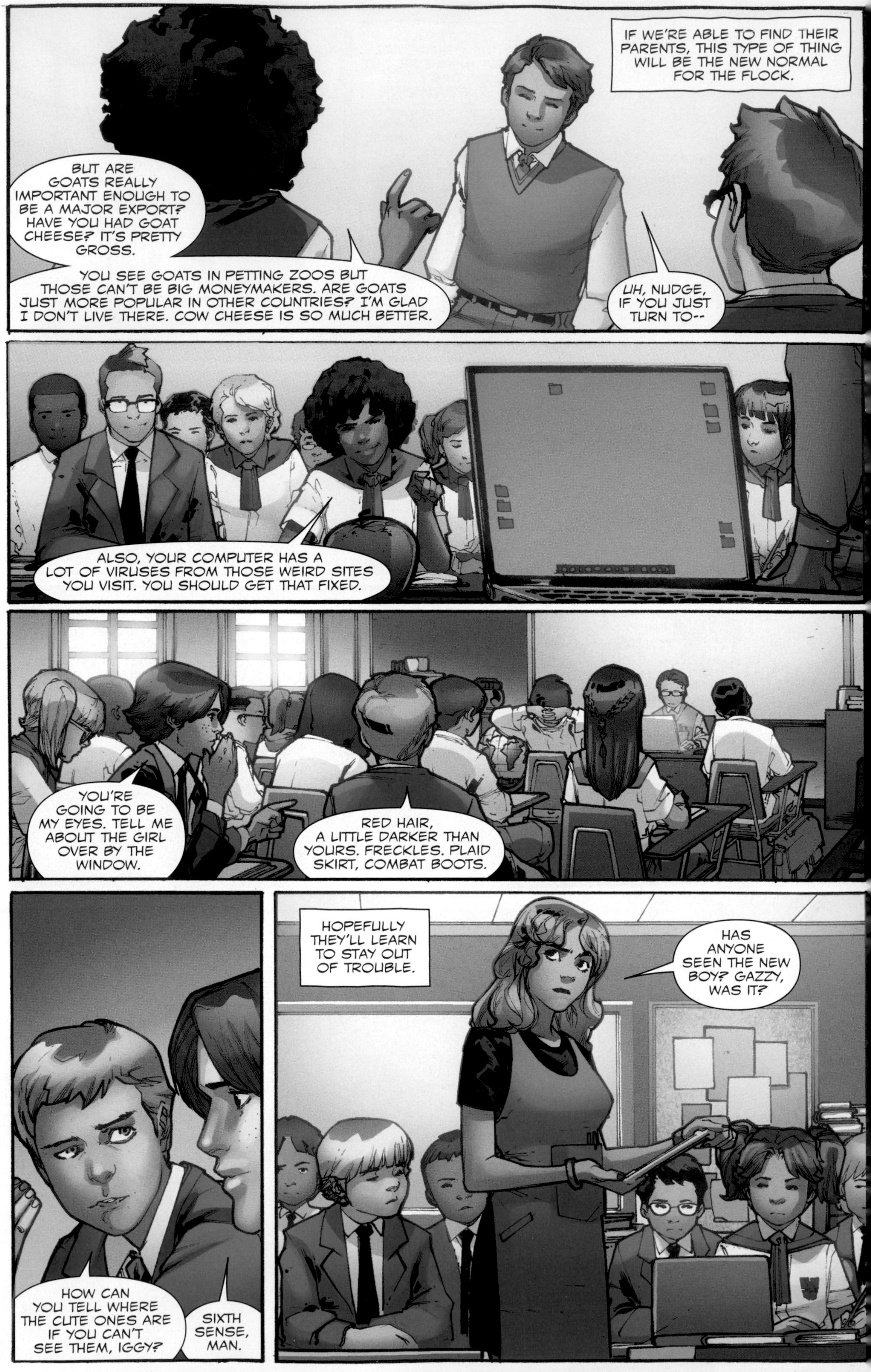
IF WE'RE ABLE TO FIND THEIR PARENTS, THIS TYPE OF THING WILL BE THE NEW NORMAL FOR THE FLOCK.
BUT ARE GOATS REALLY IMPORTANT ENOUGH TO BE A MAJOR EXPORT? HAVE YOU HAD GOAT CHEESE? IT'S PRETTY GROSS.
YOU SEE GOATS IN PETTING ZOOS BUT THOSE CAN'T BE BIG MONEYMAKERS. ARE GOATS JUST MORE POPULAR IN OTHER COUNTRIES? I'M GLAD I DON'T LIVE THERE. COW CHEESE IS SO MUCH BETTER.
UH, NUDGE, IF YOU JUST TURN TO--
ALSO, YOUR COMPUTER HAS A LOT OF VIRUSES FROM THOSE WEIRD SITES YOU VISIT. YOU SHOULD GET THAT FIXED.
YOU'RE GOING TO BE MY EYES. TELL ME ABOUT THE GIRL OVER BY THE WINDOW.
RED HAIR, A LITTLE DARKER THAN YOURS. FRECKLES. PLAID SKIRT, COMBAT BOOTS.
HOW CAN YOU TELL WHERE THE CUTE ONES ARE IF YOU CAN'T SEE THEM, IGGY?
SIXTH SENSE, MAN.
HOPEFULLY THEY'LL LEARN TO STAY OUT OF TROUBLE.
HAS ANYONE SEEN THE NEW BOY? GAZZY, WAS IT?

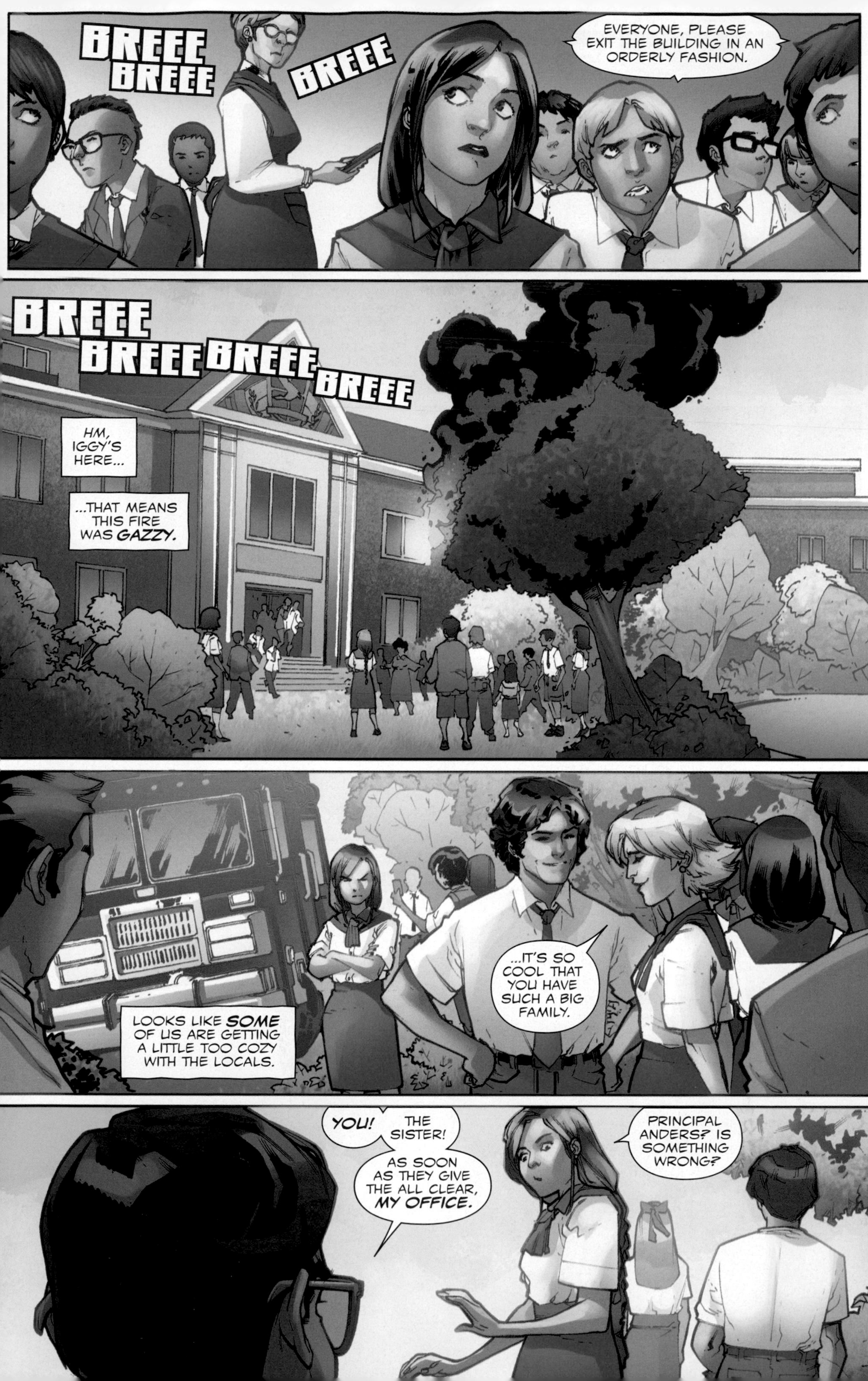

BREEE BREEE
BREEE
EVERYONE, PLEASE EXIT THE BUILDING IN AN ORDERLY FASHION.
BREEE BREEE BREEE BREEE
HM, IGGY'S HERE...
...THAT MEANS THIS FIRE WAS GAZZY.
LOOKS LIKE SOME OF US ARE GETTING A LITTLE TOO COZY WITH THE LOCALS.
...IT'S SO COOL THAT YOU HAVE SUCH A BIG FAMILY.
YOU!
THE SISTER!
AS SOON AS THEY GIVE THE ALL CLEAR, MY OFFICE.
PRINCIPAL ANDERS? IS SOMETHING WRONG?

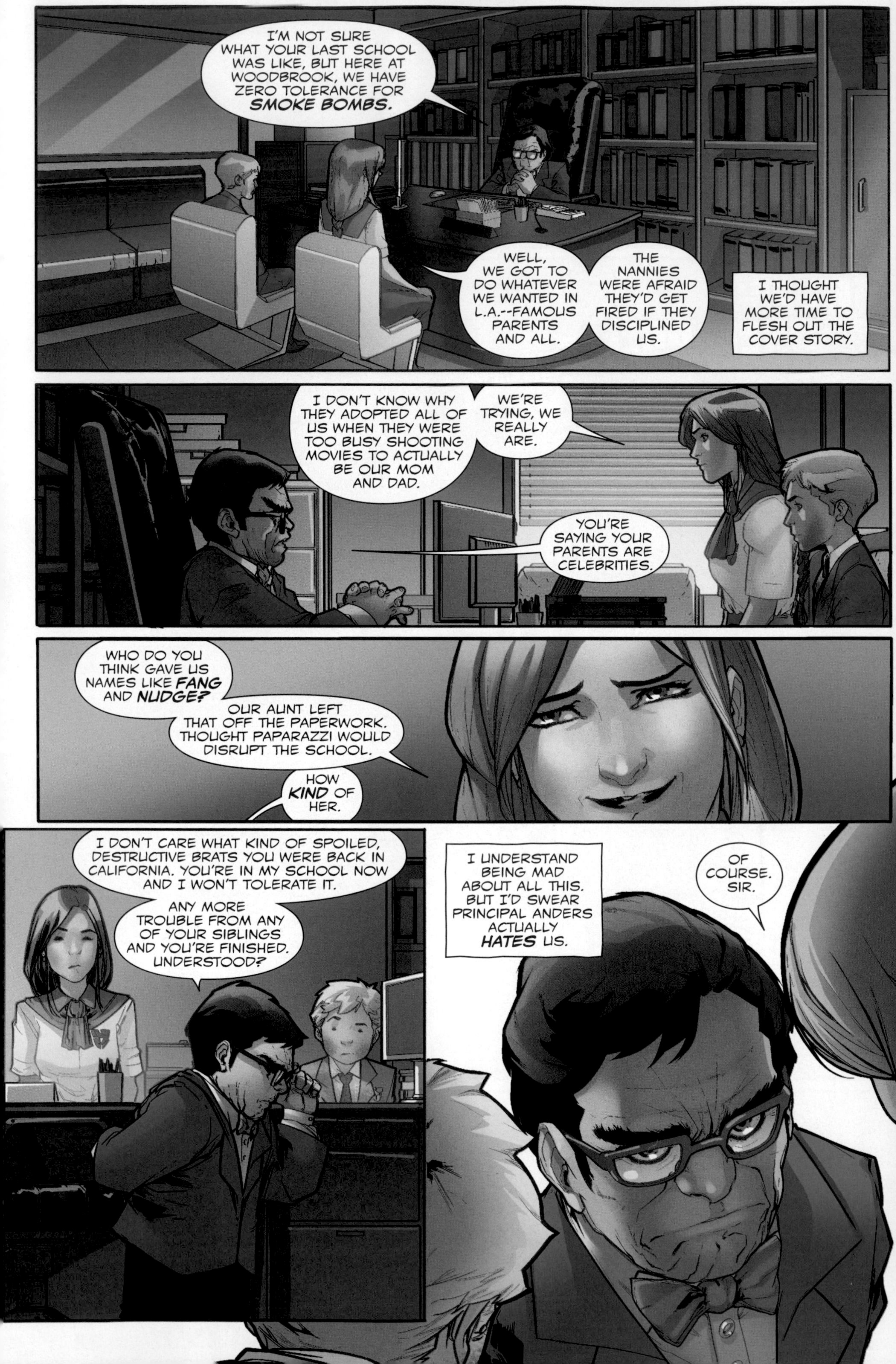
I'M NOT SURE WHAT YOUR LAST SCHOOL WAS LIKE, BUT HERE AT WOODBROOK, WE HAVE ZERO TOLERANCE FOR SMOKE BOMBS.
WELL, WE GOT TO DO WHATEVER WE WANTED IN L.A.--FAMOUS PARENTS AND ALL.
THE NANNIES WERE AFRAID THEY'D GET FIRED IF THEY DISCIPLINED US.
I THOUGHT WE'D HAVE MORE TIME TO FLESH OUT THE COVER STORY.
I DON'T KNOW WHY THEY ADOPTED ALL OF US WHEN THEY WERE TOO BUSY SHOOTING MOVIES TO ACTUALLY BE OUR MOM AND DAD.
WE'RE TRYING, WE REALLY ARE.
YOU'RE SAYING YOUR PARENTS ARE CELEBRITIES.
WHO DO YOU THINK GAVE US NAMES LIKE FANG AND NUDGE?
OUR AUNT LEFT THAT OFF THE PAPERWORK. THOUGHT PAPARAZZI WOULD DISRUPT THE SCHOOL.
HOW KIND OF HER.
I DON'T CARE WHAT KIND OF SPOILED, DESTRUCTIVE BRATS YOU WERE BACK IN CALIFORNIA. YOU'RE IN MY SCHOOL NOW AND I WON'T TOLERATE IT.
ANY MORE TROUBLE FROM ANY OF YOUR SIBLINGS AND YOU'RE FINISHED. UNDERSTOOD?
I UNDERSTAND BEING MAD ABOUT ALL THIS. BUT I'D SWEAR PRINCIPAL ANDERS ACTUALLY HATES US.
OF COURSE. SIR.

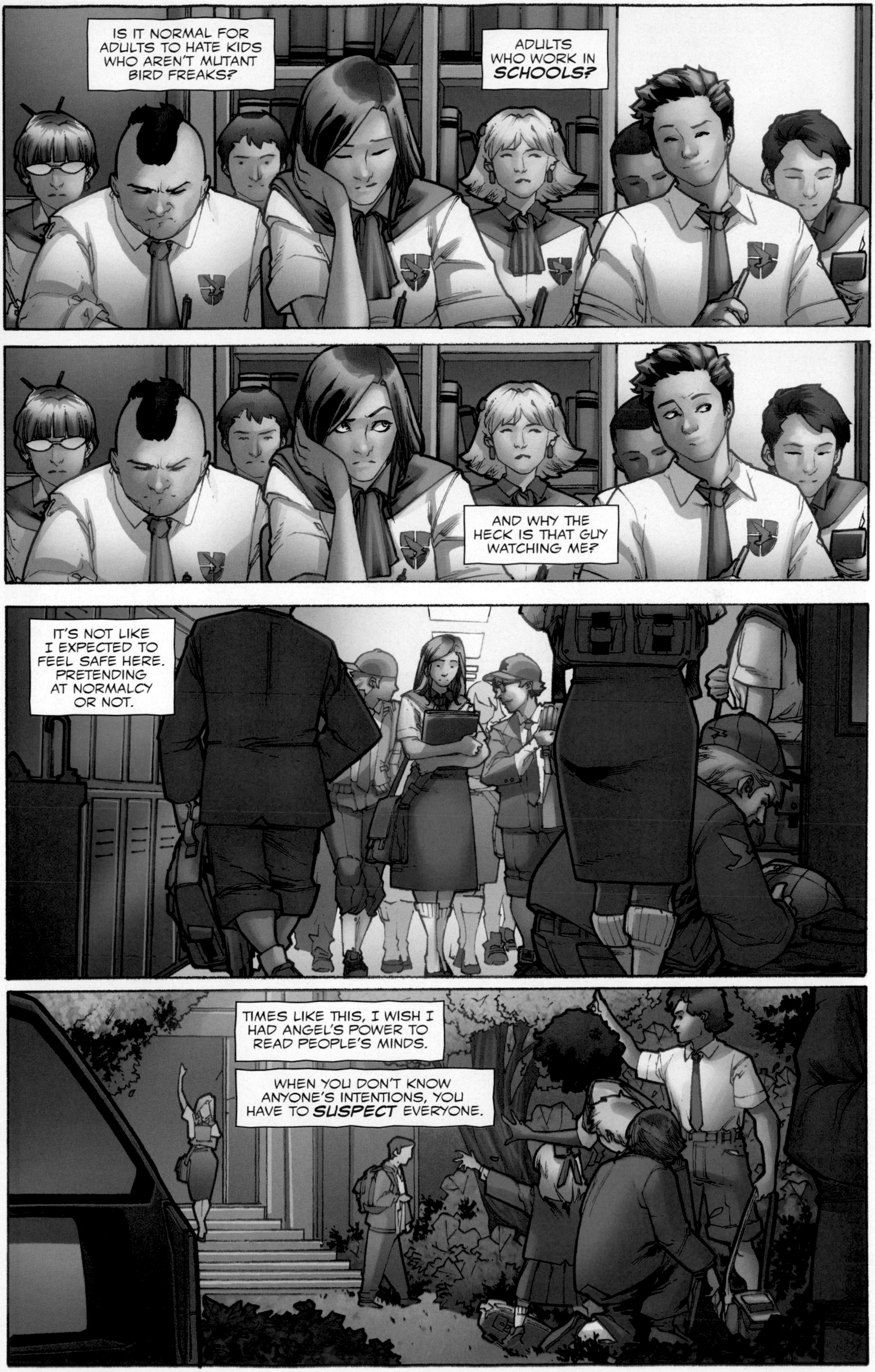
IS IT NORMAL FOR ADULTS TO HATE KIDS WHO AREN'T MUTANT BIRD FREAKS?
ADULTS WHO WORK IN SCHOOLS?
AND WHY THE HECK IS THAT GUY WATCHING ME?
IT'S NOT LIKE I EXPECTED TO FEEL SAFE HERE. PRETENDING AT NORMALCY OR NOT.
TIMES LIKE THIS, I WISH I HAD ANGEL'S POWER TO READ PEOPLE'S MINDS.
WHEN YOU DON'T KNOW ANYONE'S INTENTIONS, YOU HAVE TO SUSPECT EVERYONE.

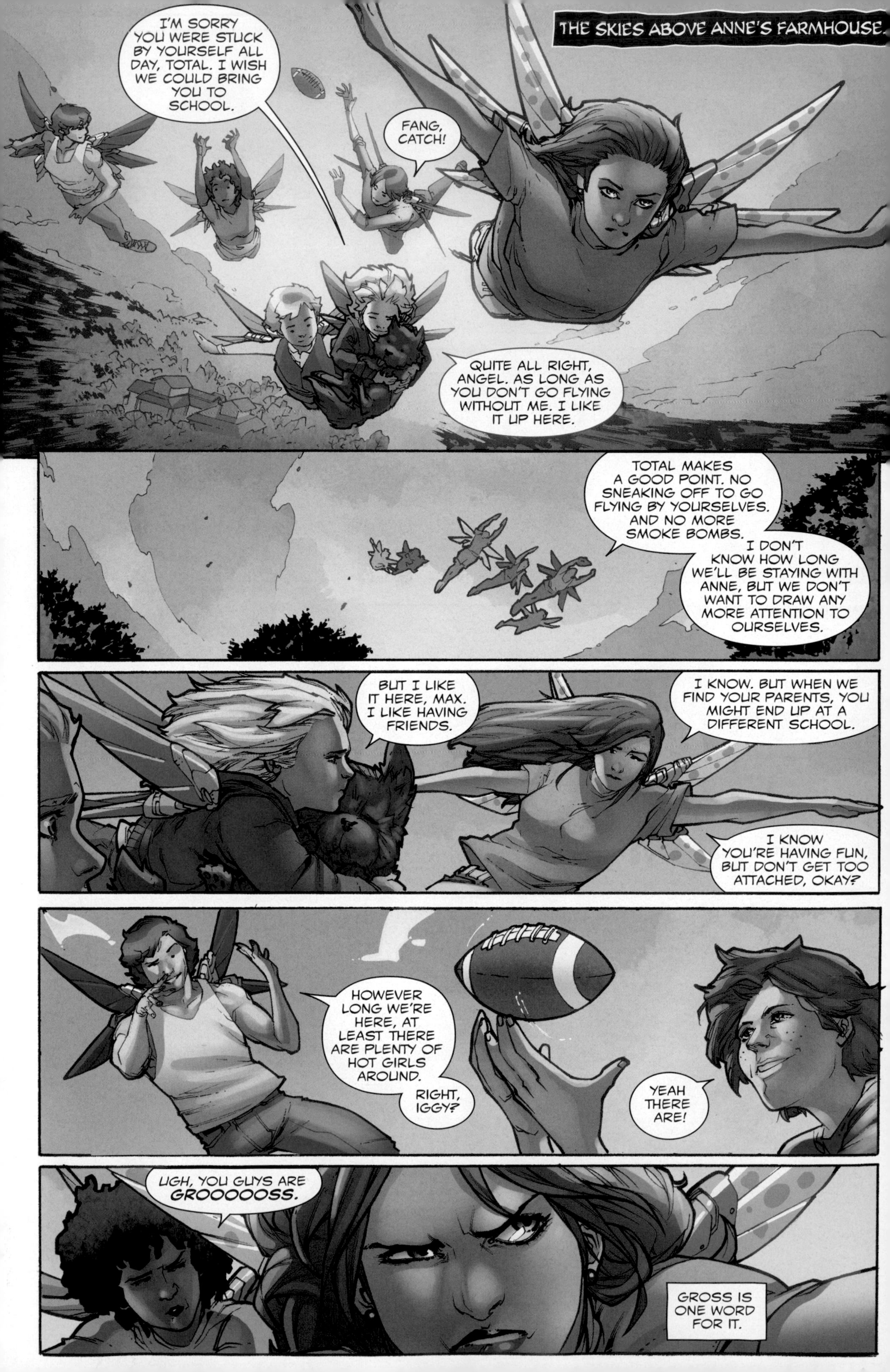
THE SKIES ABOVE ANNE'S FARMHOUSE.
I'M SORRY YOU WERE STUCK BY YOURSELF ALL DAY, TOTAL. I WISH WE COULD BRING YOU TO SCHOOL.
FANG, CATCH!
QUITE ALL RIGHT, ANGEL. AS LONG AS YOU DON'T GO FLYING WITHOUT ME. I LIKE IT UP HERE.
TOTAL MAKES A GOOD POINT. NO SNEAKING OFF TO GO FLYING BY YOURSELVES. AND NO MORE SMOKE BOMBS.
I DON'T KNOW HOW LONG WE'LL BE STAYING WITH ANNE, BUT WE DON'T WANT TO DRAW ANY MORE ATTENTION TO OURSELVES.
BUT I LIKE IT HERE, MAX. I LIKE HAVING FRIENDS.
I KNOW. BUT WHEN WE FIND YOUR PARENTS, YOU MIGHT END UP AT A DIFFERENT SCHOOL.
I KNOW YOU'RE HAVING FUN, BUT DON'T GET TOO ATTACHED, OKAY?
HOWEVER LONG WE'RE HERE, AT LEAST THERE ARE PLENTY OF HOT GIRLS AROUND.
RIGHT, IGGY?
YEAH THERE ARE!
UGH, YOU GUYS ARE GROOOOOSS.
GROSS IS ONE WORD FOR IT.

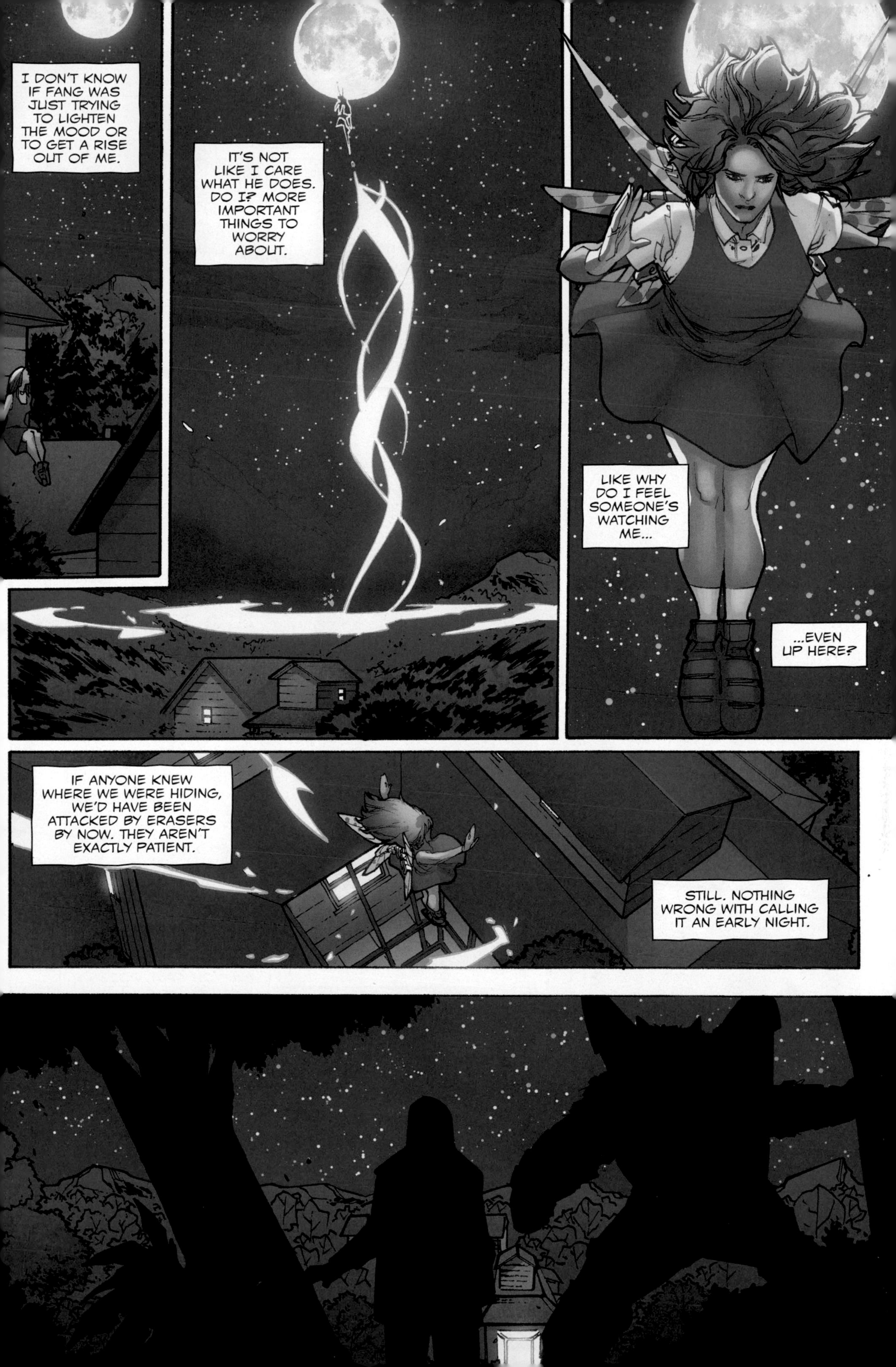

I DON'T KNOW IF FANG WAS JUST TRYING TO LIGHTEN THE MOOD OR TO GET A RISE OUT OF ME.
IT'S NOT LIKE I CARE WHAT HE DOES. DO I? MORE IMPORTANT THINGS TO WORRY ABOUT.
LIKE WHY DO I FEEL SOMEONE'S WATCHING ME...
...EVEN UP HERE?
IF ANYONE KNEW WHERE WE WERE HIDING, WE'D HAVE BEEN ATTACKED BY ERASERS BY NOW. THEY AREN'T EXACTLY PATIENT.
STILL. NOTHING WRONG WITH CALLING IT AN EARLY NIGHT.

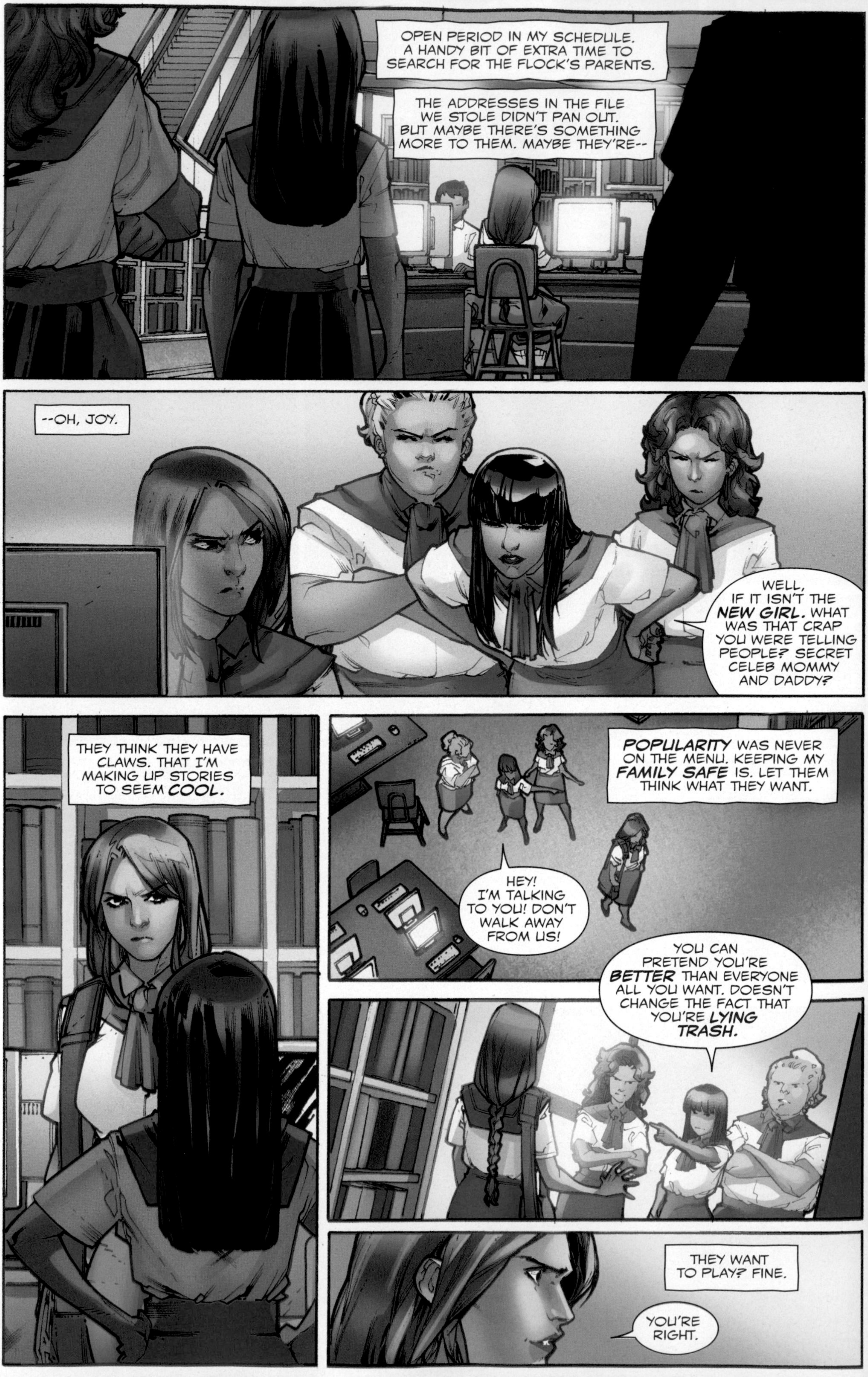
OPEN PERIOD IN MY SCHEDULE. A HANDY BIT OF EXTRA TIME TO SEARCH FOR THE FLOCK'S PARENTS.
THE ADDRESSES IN THE FILE WE STOLE DIDN'T PAN OUT. BUT MAYBE THERE'S SOMETHING MORE TO THEM. MAYBE THEY'RE--
--OH, JOY.
WELL, IF IT ISN'T THE **NEW GIRL.** WHAT WAS THAT CRAP YOU WERE TELLING PEOPLE? SECRET CELEB MOMMY AND DADDY?
THEY THINK THEY HAVE CLAWS. THAT I'M MAKING UP STORIES TO SEEM **COOL.**
POPULARITY WAS NEVER ON THE MENU. KEEPING MY ***FAMILY SAFE*** IS. LET THEM THINK WHAT THEY WANT.
HEY! I'M TALKING TO YOU! DON'T WALK AWAY FROM US!
YOU CAN PRETEND YOU'RE ***BETTER*** THAN EVERYONE ALL YOU WANT. DOESN'T CHANGE THE FACT THAT YOU'RE ***LYING TRASH.***
THEY WANT TO PLAY? FINE.
YOU'RE RIGHT.

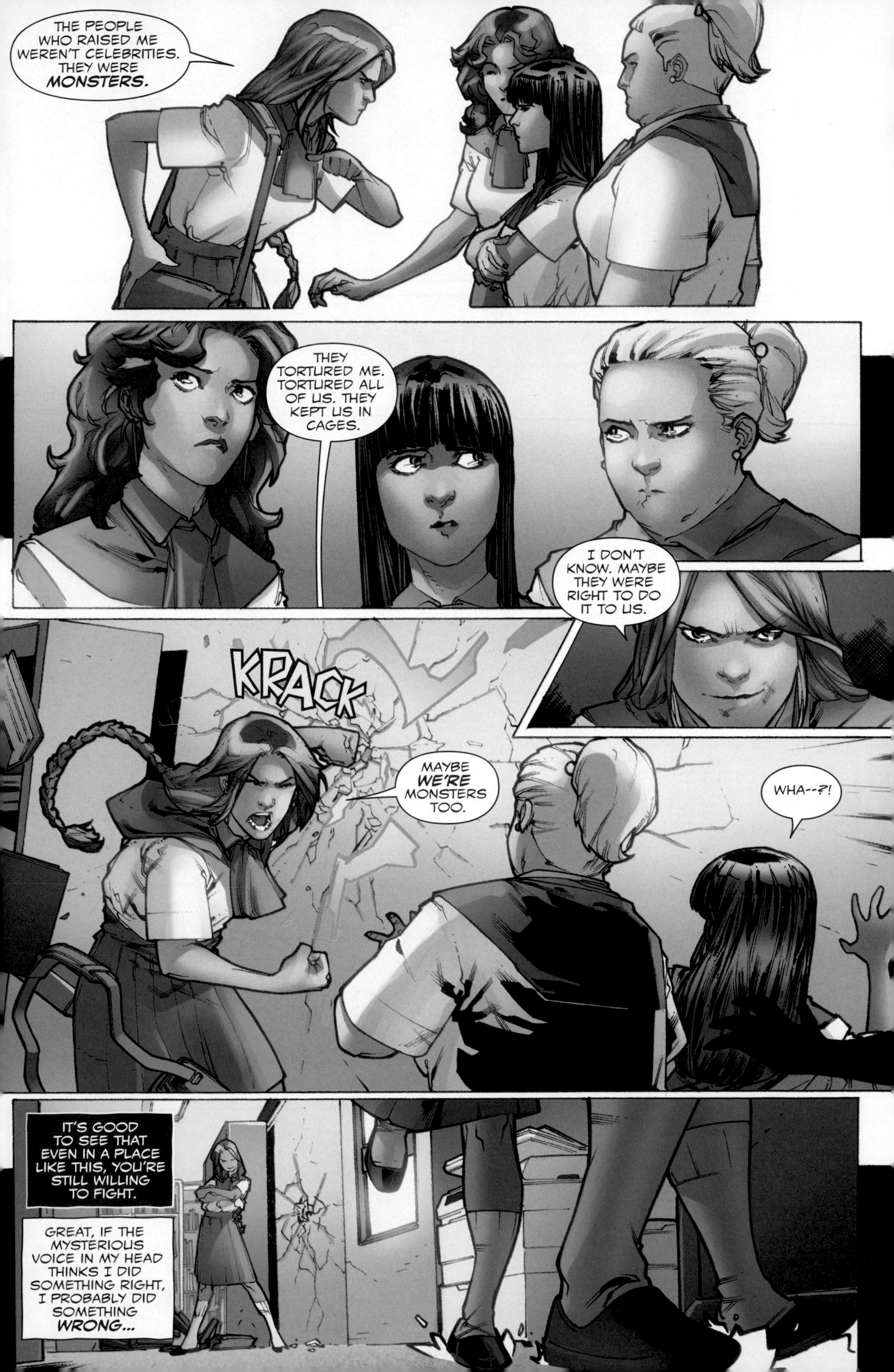
THE PEOPLE WHO RAISED ME WEREN'T CELEBRITIES. THEY WERE MONSTERS.
THEY TORTURED ME. TORTURED ALL OF US. THEY KEPT US IN CAGES.
I DON'T KNOW. MAYBE THEY WERE RIGHT TO DO IT TO US.
KRACK
MAYBE WE'RE MONSTERS TOO.
WHA--?!
IT'S GOOD TO SEE THAT EVEN IN A PLACE LIKE THIS, YOU'RE STILL WILLING TO FIGHT.
GREAT, IF THE MYSTERIOUS VOICE IN MY HEAD THINKS I DID SOMETHING RIGHT, I PROBABLY DID SOMETHING WRONG...

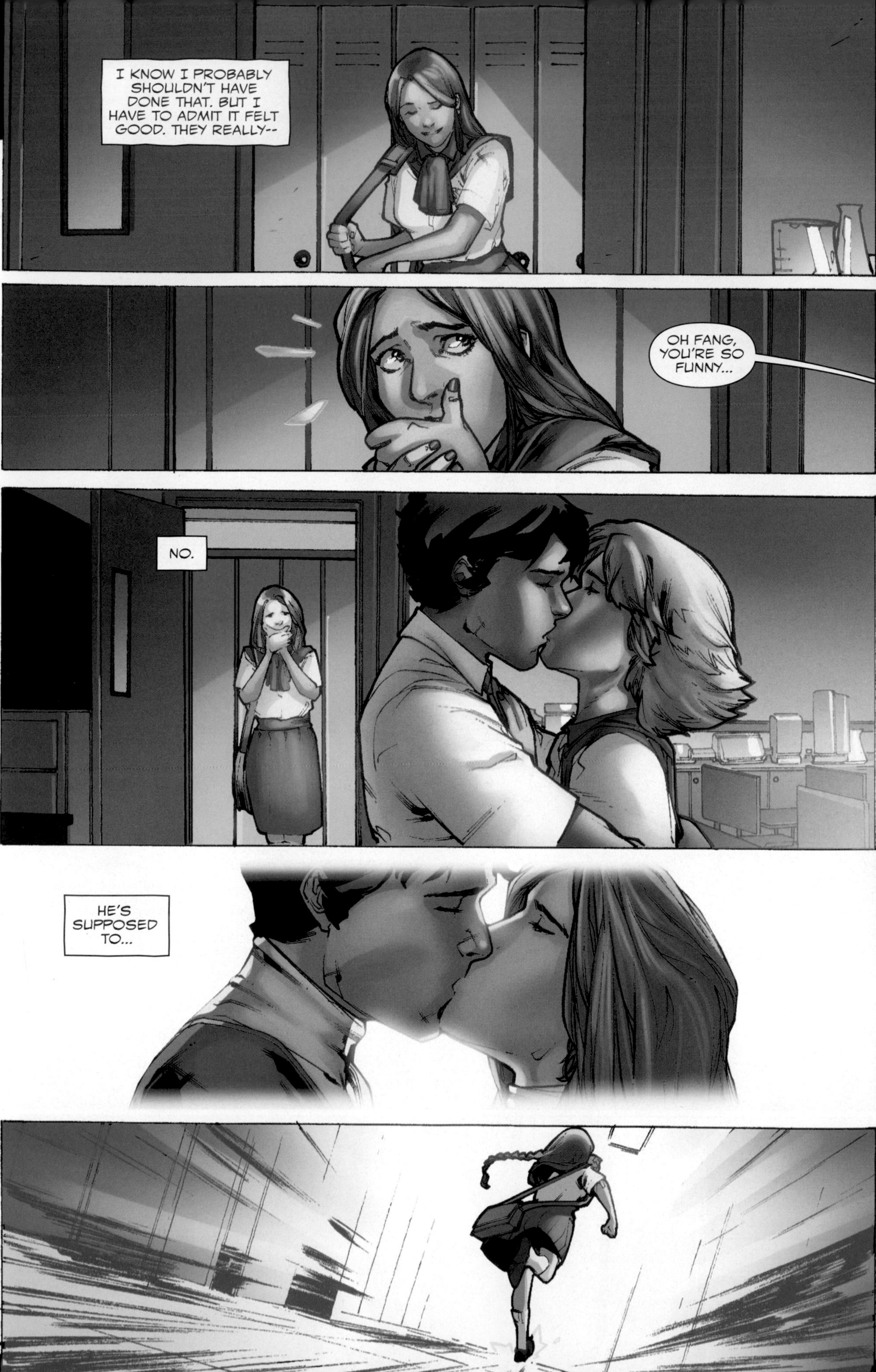
I KNOW I PROBABLY SHOULDN'T HAVE DONE THAT. BUT I HAVE TO ADMIT IT FELT GOOD. THEY REALLY--
OH FANG, YOU'RE SO FUNNY...
NO.
HE'S SUPPOSED TO...

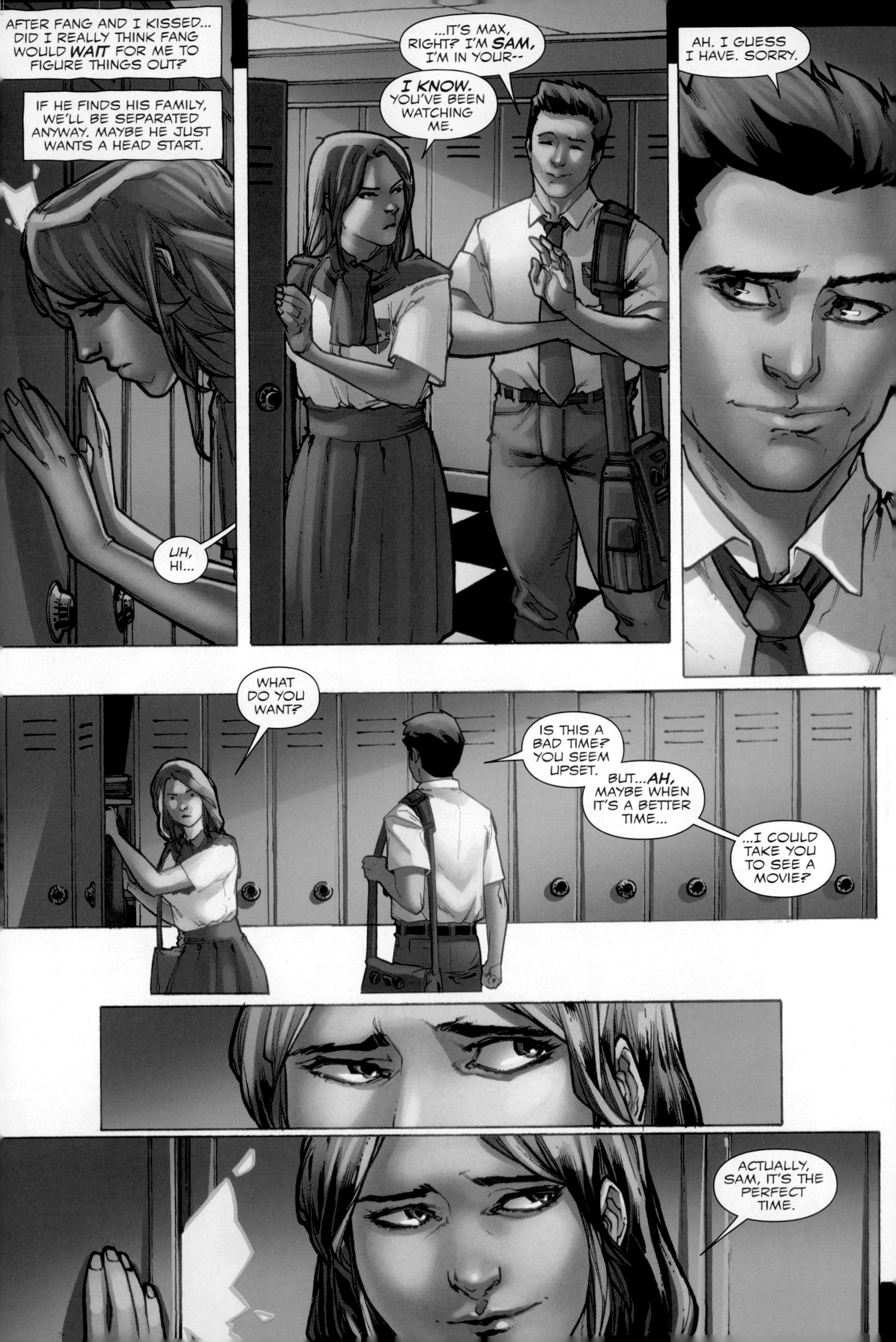
AFTER FANG AND I KISSED... DID I REALLY THINK FANG WOULD **WAIT** FOR ME TO FIGURE THINGS OUT?
IF HE FINDS HIS FAMILY, WE'LL BE SEPARATED ANYWAY. MAYBE HE JUST WANTS A HEAD START.
UH, HI...
...IT'S MAX, RIGHT? I'M **SAM,** I'M IN YOUR--
I KNOW. YOU'VE BEEN WATCHING ME.
AH. I GUESS I HAVE. SORRY.
WHAT DO YOU WANT?
IS THIS A BAD TIME? YOU SEEM UPSET.
BUT...**AH,** MAYBE WHEN IT'S A BETTER TIME...
...I COULD TAKE YOU TO SEE A MOVIE?
ACTUALLY, SAM, IT'S THE PERFECT TIME.

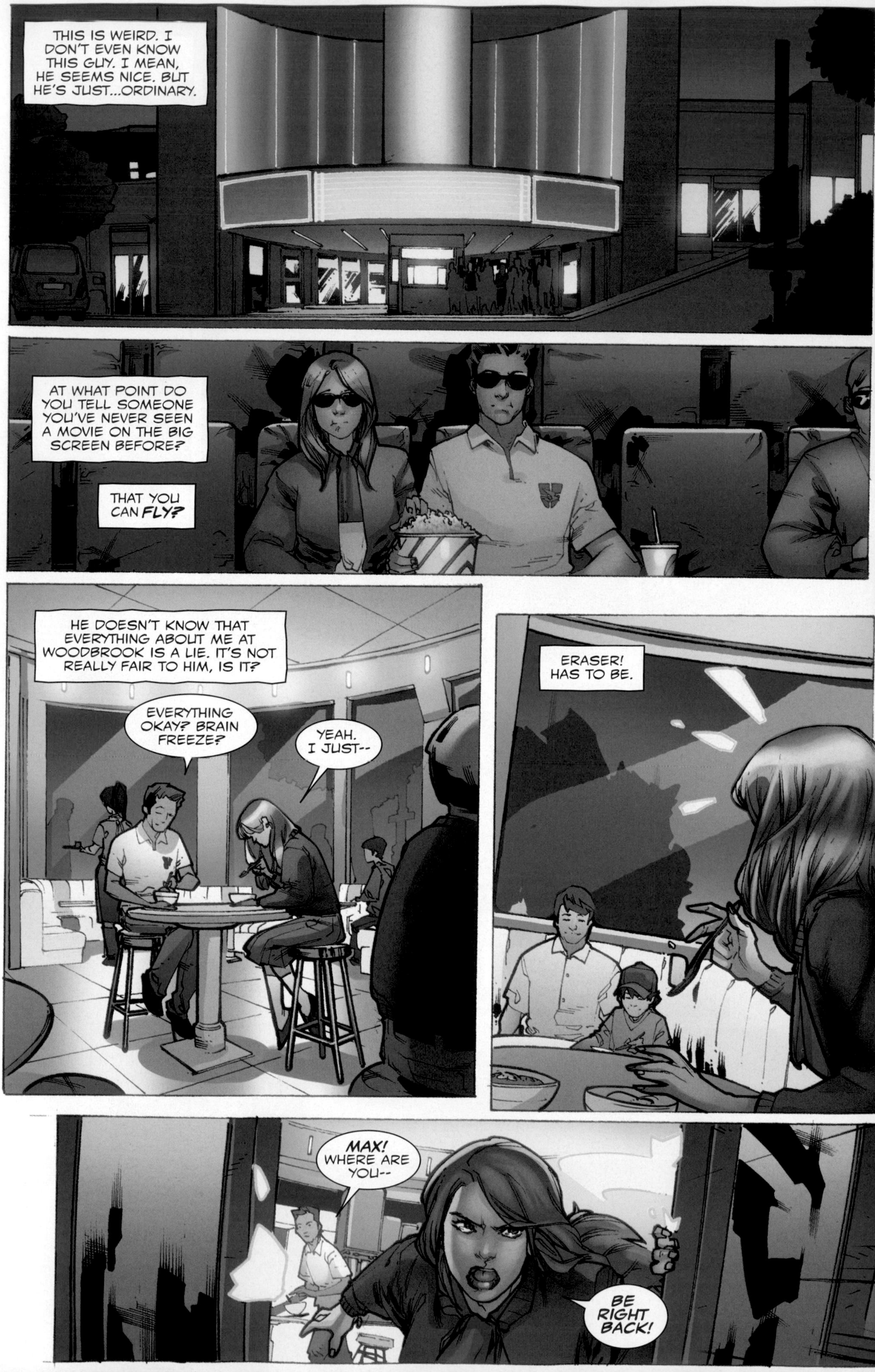

THIS IS WEIRD. I DON'T EVEN KNOW THIS GUY. I MEAN, HE SEEMS NICE. BUT HE'S JUST...ORDINARY.
AT WHAT POINT DO YOU TELL SOMEONE YOU'VE NEVER SEEN A MOVIE ON THE BIG SCREEN BEFORE?
THAT YOU CAN FLY?
HE DOESN'T KNOW THAT EVERYTHING ABOUT ME AT WOODBROOK IS A LIE. IT'S NOT REALLY FAIR TO HIM, IS IT?
EVERYTHING OKAY? BRAIN FREEZE?
YEAH. I JUST--
ERASER! HAS TO BE.
MAX! WHERE ARE YOU--
BE RIGHT BACK!

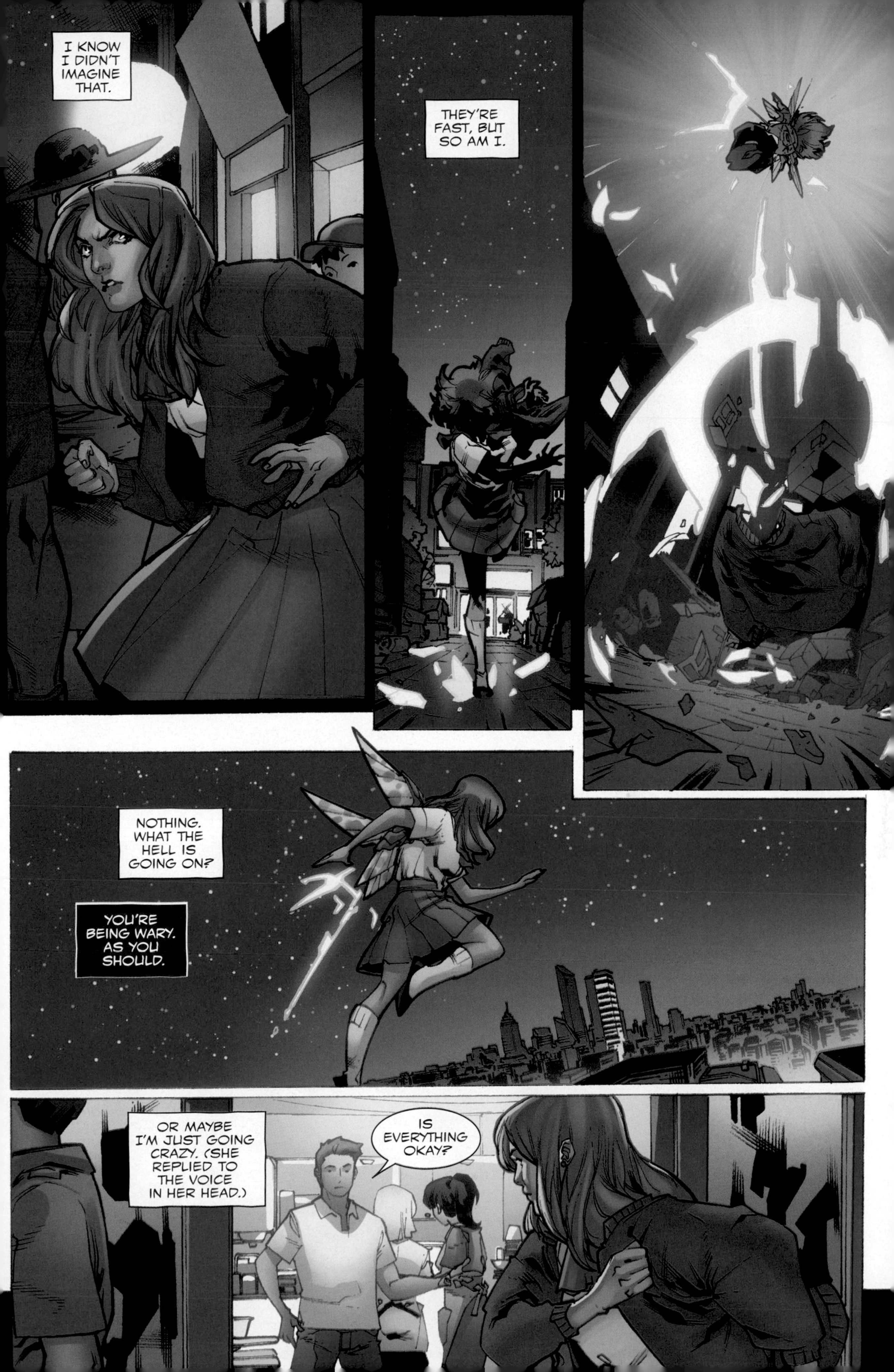
I KNOW I DIDN'T IMAGINE THAT.
THEY'RE FAST, BUT SO AM I.
NOTHING. WHAT THE HELL IS GOING ON?
YOU'RE BEING WARY. AS YOU SHOULD.
OR MAYBE I'M JUST GOING CRAZY. (SHE REPLIED TO THE VOICE IN HER HEAD.)
IS EVERYTHING OKAY?

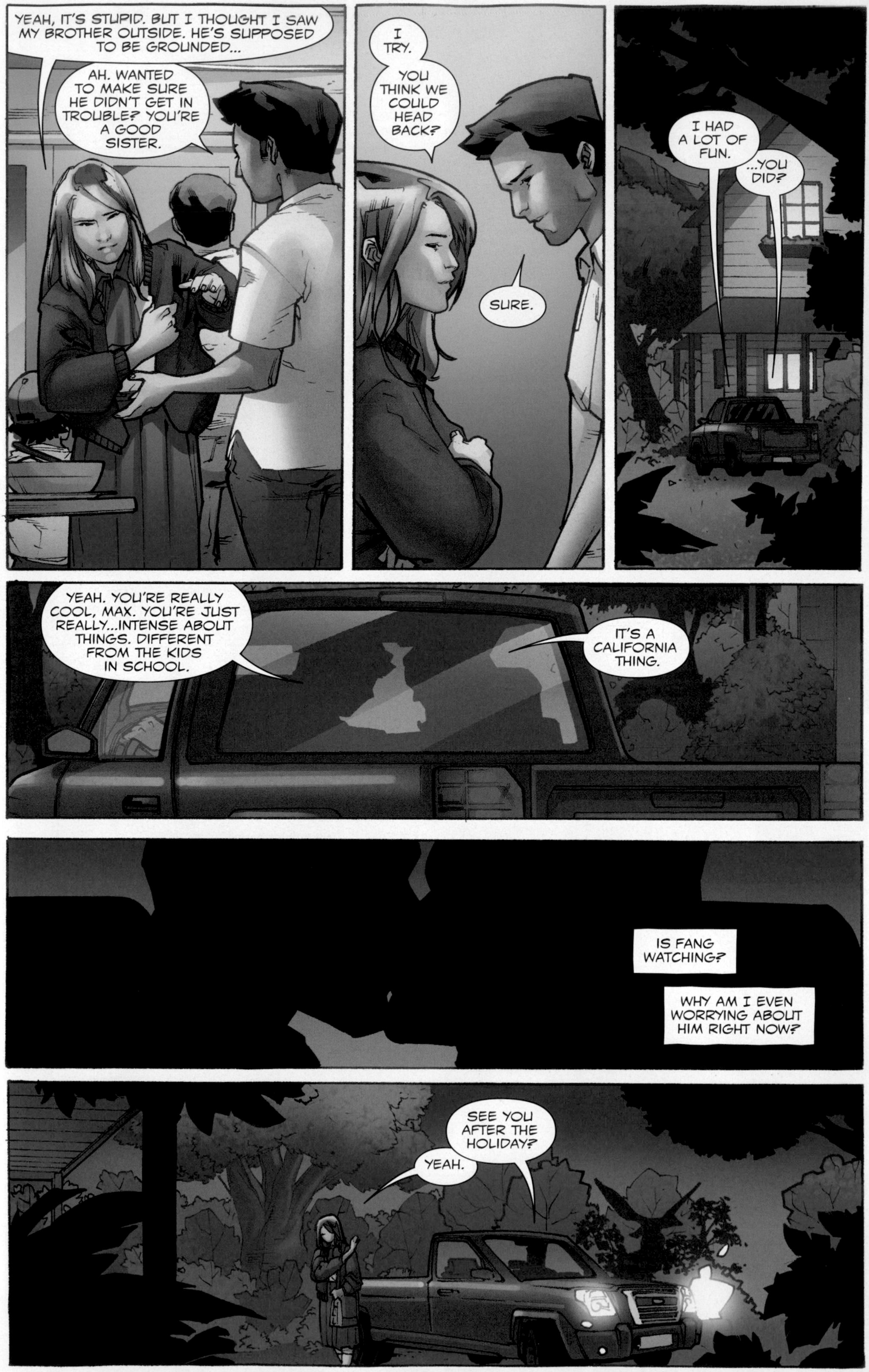
YEAH, IT'S STUPID. BUT I THOUGHT I SAW MY BROTHER OUTSIDE. HE'S SUPPOSED TO BE GROUNDED...
AH. WANTED TO MAKE SURE HE DIDN'T GET IN TROUBLE? YOU'RE A GOOD SISTER.
I TRY.
YOU THINK WE COULD HEAD BACK?
SURE.
I HAD A LOT OF FUN.
...YOU DID?
YEAH. YOU'RE REALLY COOL, MAX. YOU'RE JUST REALLY...INTENSE ABOUT THINGS. DIFFERENT FROM THE KIDS IN SCHOOL.
IT'S A CALIFORNIA THING.
IS FANG WATCHING?
WHY AM I EVEN WORRYING ABOUT HIM RIGHT NOW?
SEE YOU AFTER THE HOLIDAY?
YEAH.

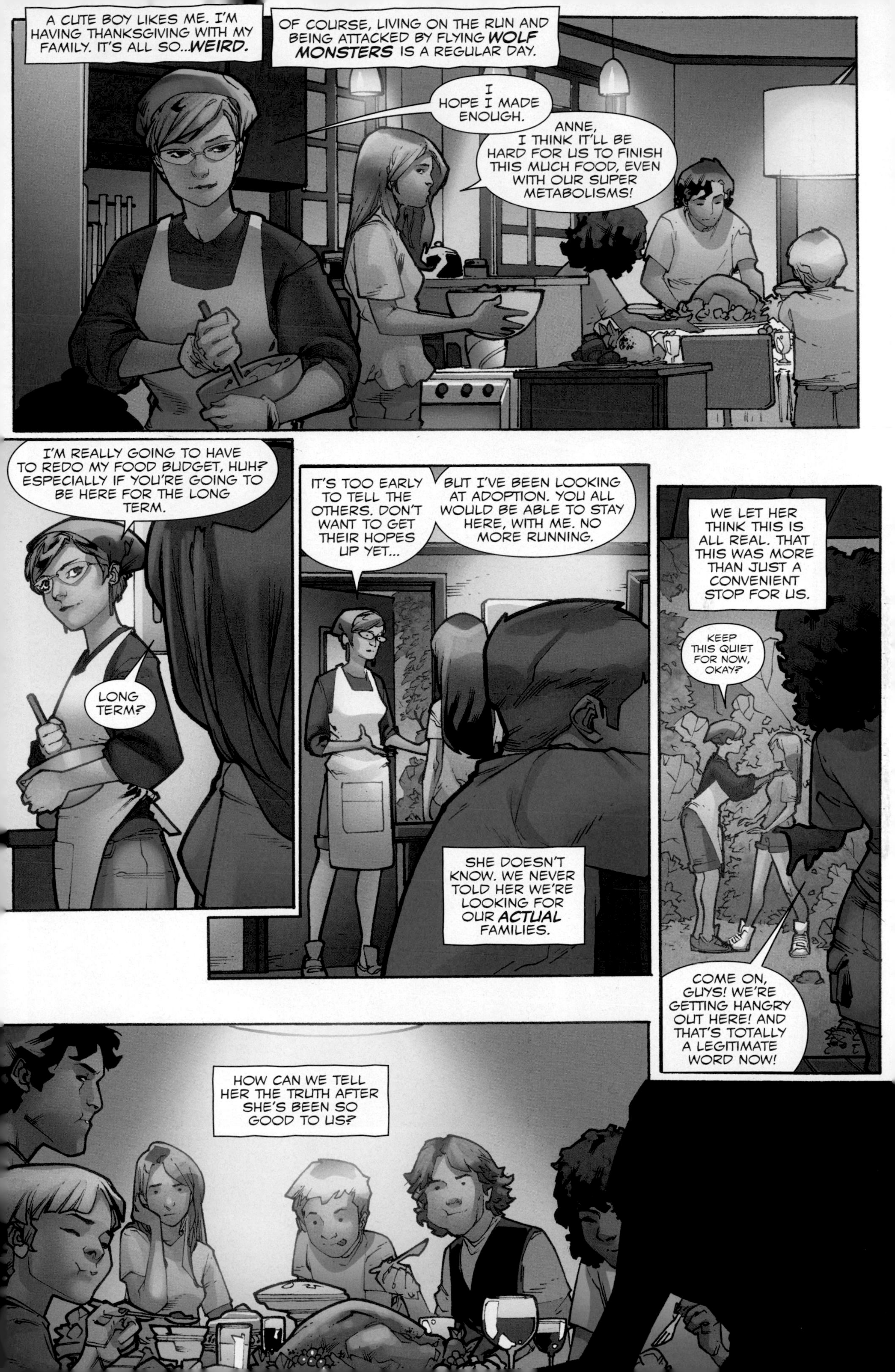
A CUTE BOY LIKES ME. I'M HAVING THANKSGIVING WITH MY FAMILY. IT'S ALL SO...WEIRD.
OF COURSE, LIVING ON THE RUN AND BEING ATTACKED BY FLYING WOLF MONSTERS IS A REGULAR DAY.
I HOPE I MADE ENOUGH.
ANNE, I THINK IT'LL BE HARD FOR US TO FINISH THIS MUCH FOOD, EVEN WITH OUR SUPER METABOLISMS!
I'M REALLY GOING TO HAVE TO REDO MY FOOD BUDGET, HUH? ESPECIALLY IF YOU'RE GOING TO BE HERE FOR THE LONG TERM.
LONG TERM?
IT'S TOO EARLY TO TELL THE OTHERS. DON'T WANT TO GET THEIR HOPES UP YET...
BUT I'VE BEEN LOOKING AT ADOPTION. YOU ALL WOULD BE ABLE TO STAY HERE, WITH ME. NO MORE RUNNING.
SHE DOESN'T KNOW. WE NEVER TOLD HER WE'RE LOOKING FOR OUR ACTUAL FAMILIES.
WE LET HER THINK THIS IS ALL REAL. THAT THIS WAS MORE THAN JUST A CONVENIENT STOP FOR US.
KEEP THIS QUIET FOR NOW, OKAY?
COME ON, GUYS! WE'RE GETTING HANGRY OUT HERE! AND THAT'S TOTALLY A LEGITIMATE WORD NOW!
HOW CAN WE TELL HER THE TRUTH AFTER SHE'S BEEN SO GOOD TO US?

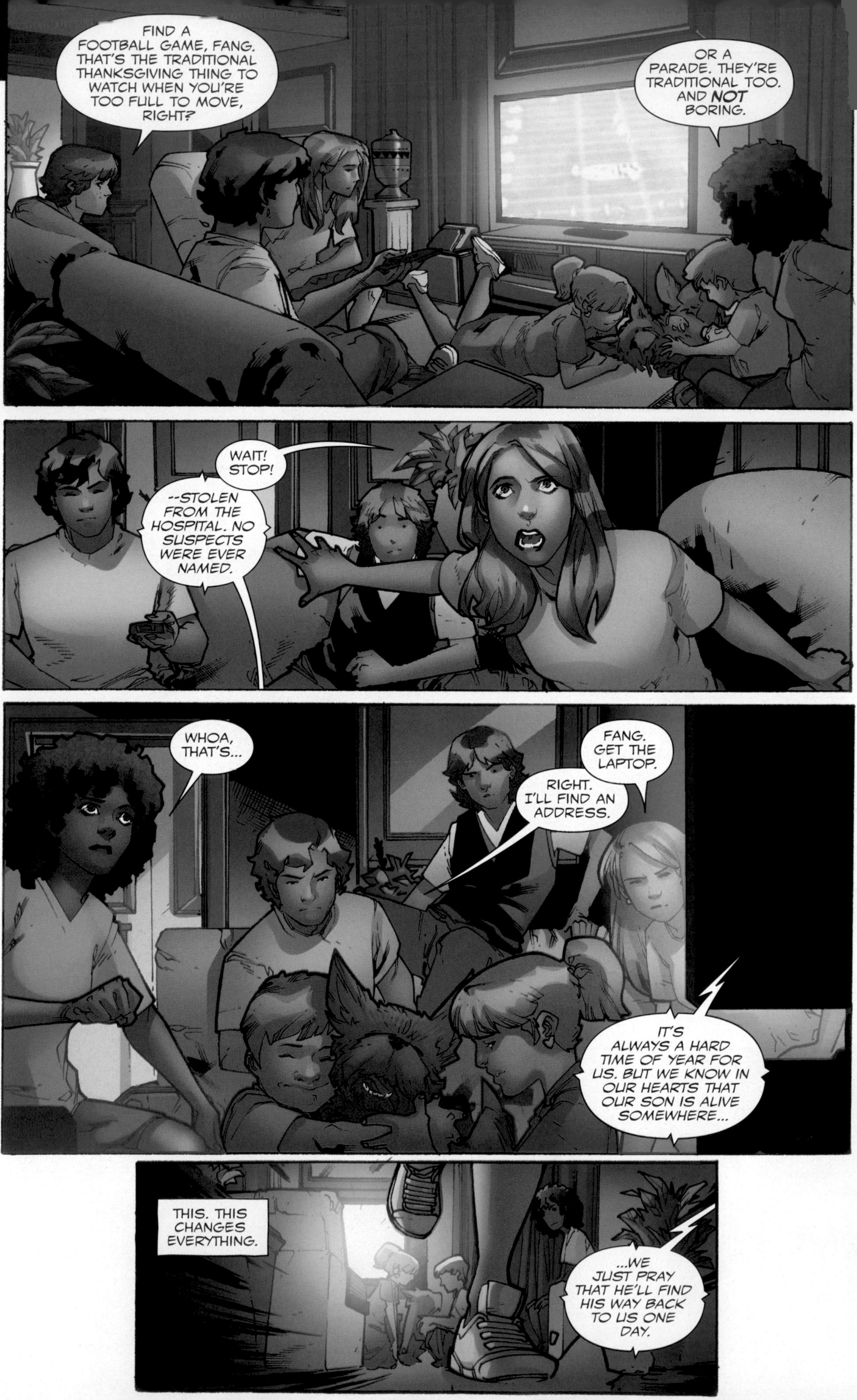
FIND A FOOTBALL GAME, FANG. THAT'S THE TRADITIONAL THANKSGIVING THING TO WATCH WHEN YOU'RE TOO FULL TO MOVE, RIGHT?
OR A PARADE. THEY'RE TRADITIONAL TOO. AND NOT BORING.
WAIT! STOP!
--STOLEN FROM THE HOSPITAL. NO SUSPECTS WERE EVER NAMED.
WHOA, THAT'S...
FANG. GET THE LAPTOP.
RIGHT. I'LL FIND AN ADDRESS.
IT'S ALWAYS A HARD TIME OF YEAR FOR US. BUT WE KNOW IN OUR HEARTS THAT OUR SON IS ALIVE SOMEWHERE...
THIS. THIS CHANGES EVERYTHING.
...WE JUST PRAY THAT HE'LL FIND HIS WAY BACK TO US ONE DAY.

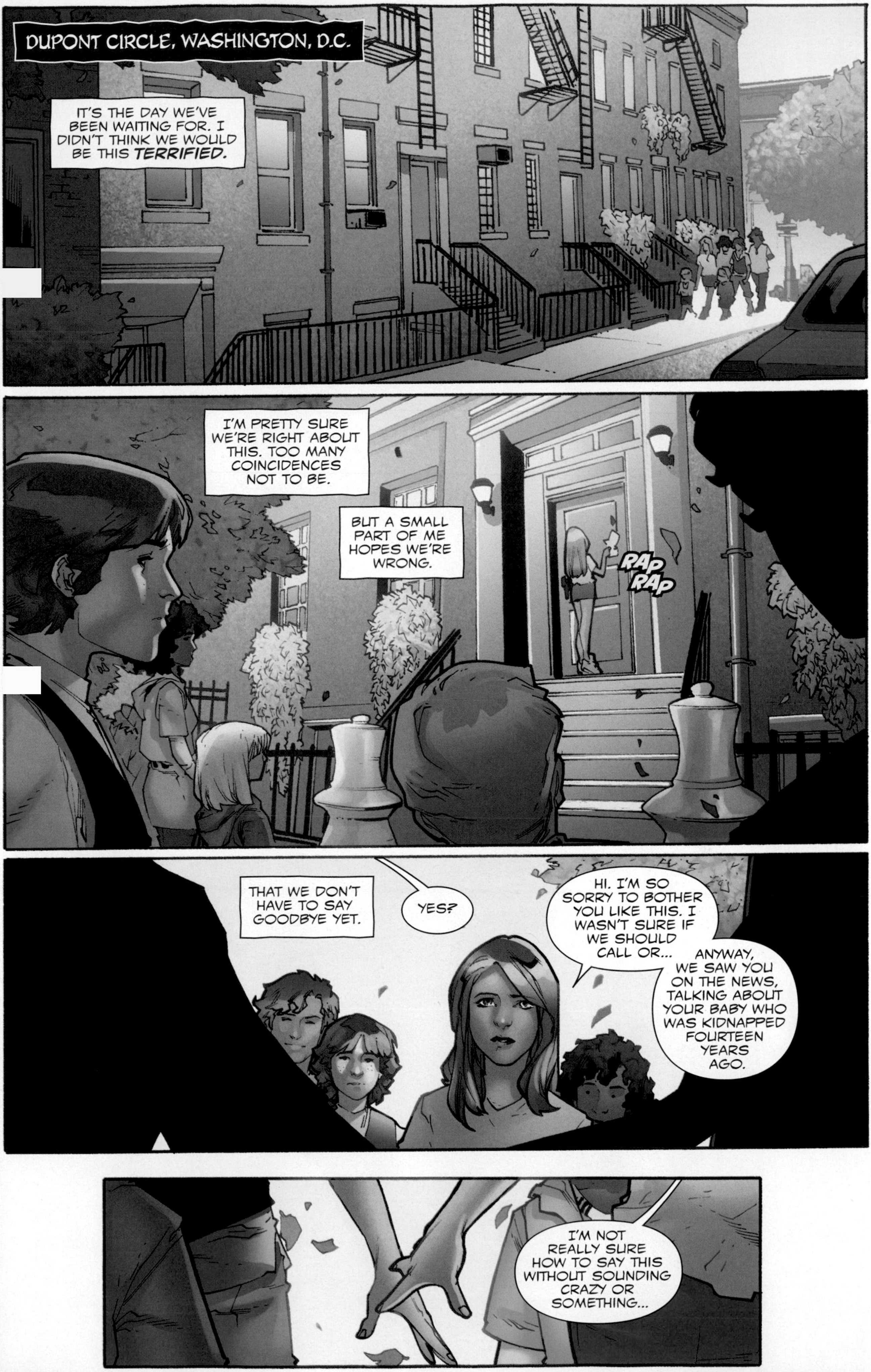
DUPONT CIRCLE, WASHINGTON, D.C.
IT'S THE DAY WE'VE BEEN WAITING FOR. I DIDN'T THINK WE WOULD BE THIS TERRIFIED.
I'M PRETTY SURE WE'RE RIGHT ABOUT THIS. TOO MANY COINCIDENCES NOT TO BE.
BUT A SMALL PART OF ME HOPES WE'RE WRONG.
RAP RAP
THAT WE DON'T HAVE TO SAY GOODBYE YET.
YES?
HI. I'M SO SORRY TO BOTHER YOU LIKE THIS. I WASN'T SURE IF WE SHOULD CALL OR...
ANYWAY, WE SAW YOU ON THE NEWS, TALKING ABOUT YOUR BABY WHO WAS KIDNAPPED FOURTEEN YEARS AGO.
I'M NOT REALLY SURE HOW TO SAY THIS WITHOUT SOUNDING CRAZY OR SOMETHING...

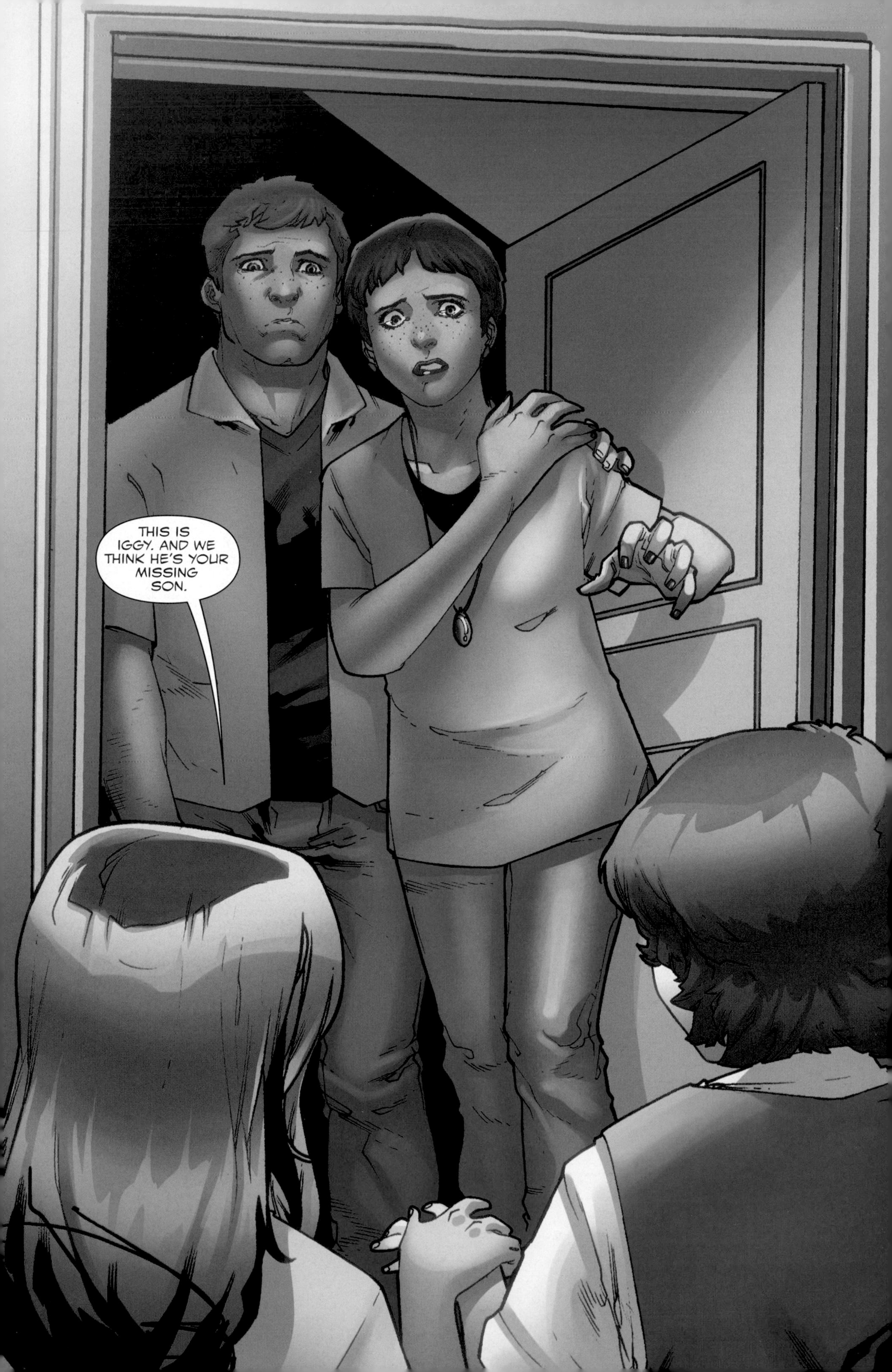
THIS IS IGGY. AND WE THINK HE'S YOUR MISSING SON.

CHAPTER 3

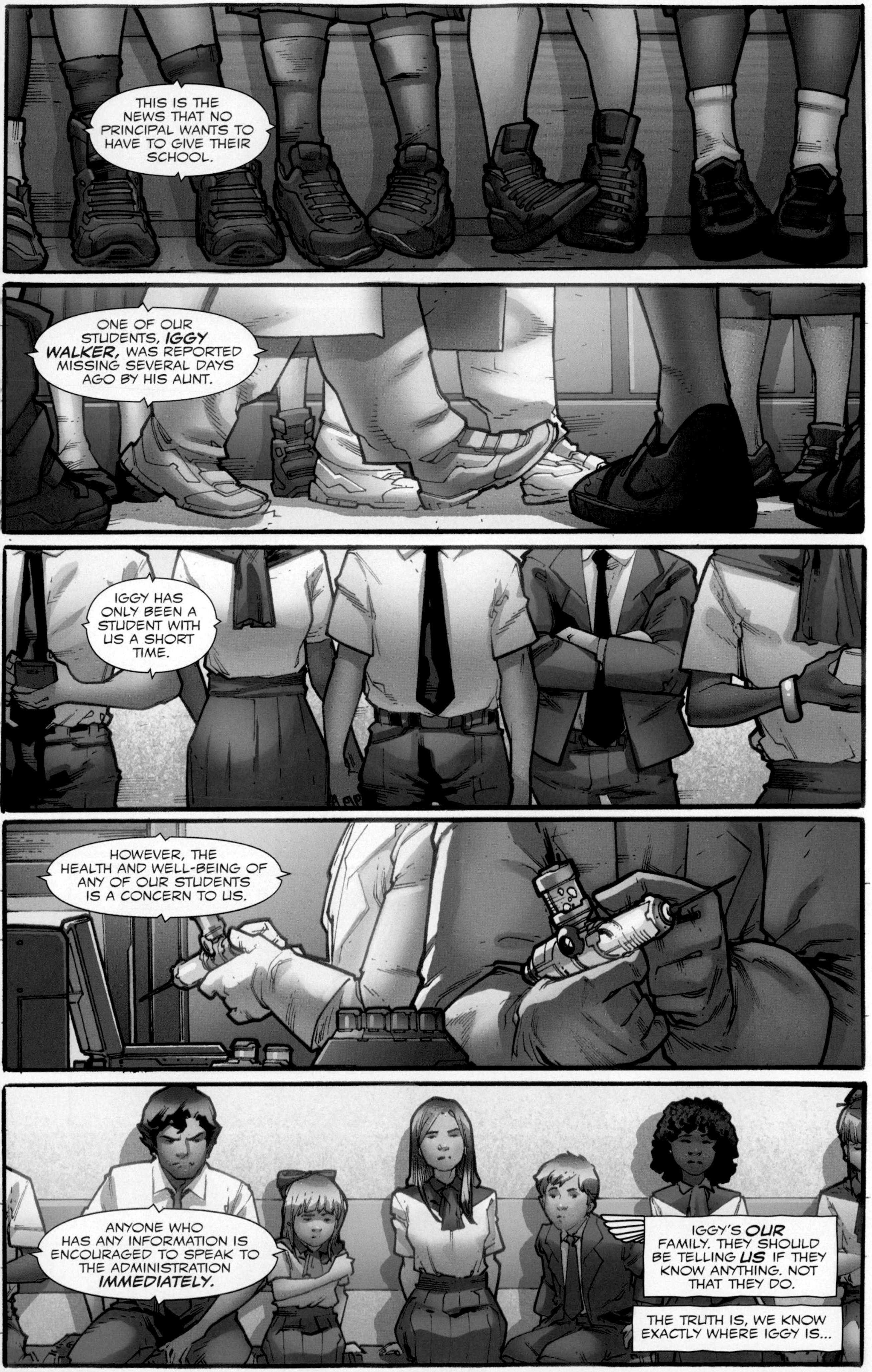
THIS IS THE NEWS THAT NO PRINCIPAL WANTS TO HAVE TO GIVE THEIR SCHOOL.
ONE OF OUR STUDENTS, IGGY WALKER, WAS REPORTED MISSING SEVERAL DAYS AGO BY HIS AUNT.
IGGY HAS ONLY BEEN A STUDENT WITH US A SHORT TIME.
HOWEVER, THE HEALTH AND WELL-BEING OF ANY OF OUR STUDENTS IS A CONCERN TO US.
ANYONE WHO HAS ANY INFORMATION IS ENCOURAGED TO SPEAK TO THE ADMINISTRATION IMMEDIATELY.
IGGY'S OUR FAMILY. THEY SHOULD BE TELLING US IF THEY KNOW ANYTHING. NOT THAT THEY DO.
THE TRUTH IS, WE KNOW EXACTLY WHERE IGGY IS...

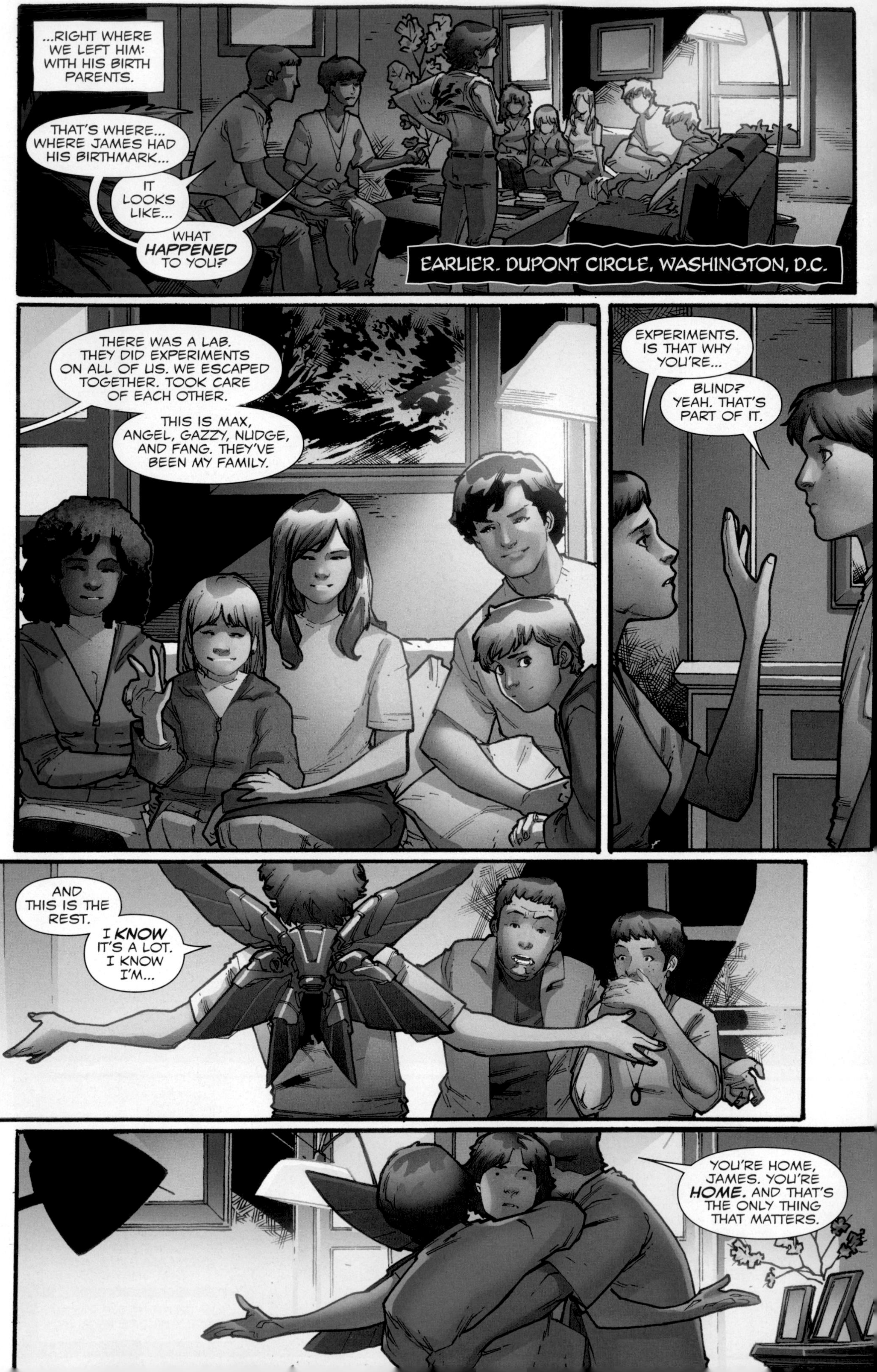
...RIGHT WHERE WE LEFT HIM: WITH HIS BIRTH PARENTS.
THAT'S WHERE... WHERE JAMES HAD HIS BIRTHMARK...
IT LOOKS LIKE...
WHAT *HAPPENED* TO YOU?
EARLIER. DUPONT CIRCLE, WASHINGTON, D.C.
THERE WAS A LAB. THEY DID EXPERIMENTS ON ALL OF US. WE ESCAPED TOGETHER. TOOK CARE OF EACH OTHER.
THIS IS MAX, ANGEL, GAZZY, NUDGE, AND FANG. THEY'VE BEEN MY FAMILY.
EXPERIMENTS. IS THAT WHY YOU'RE...
BLIND? YEAH. THAT'S PART OF IT.
AND THIS IS THE REST.
I *KNOW* IT'S A LOT. I KNOW I'M...
YOU'RE HOME, JAMES. YOU'RE *HOME.* AND THAT'S THE ONLY THING THAT MATTERS.

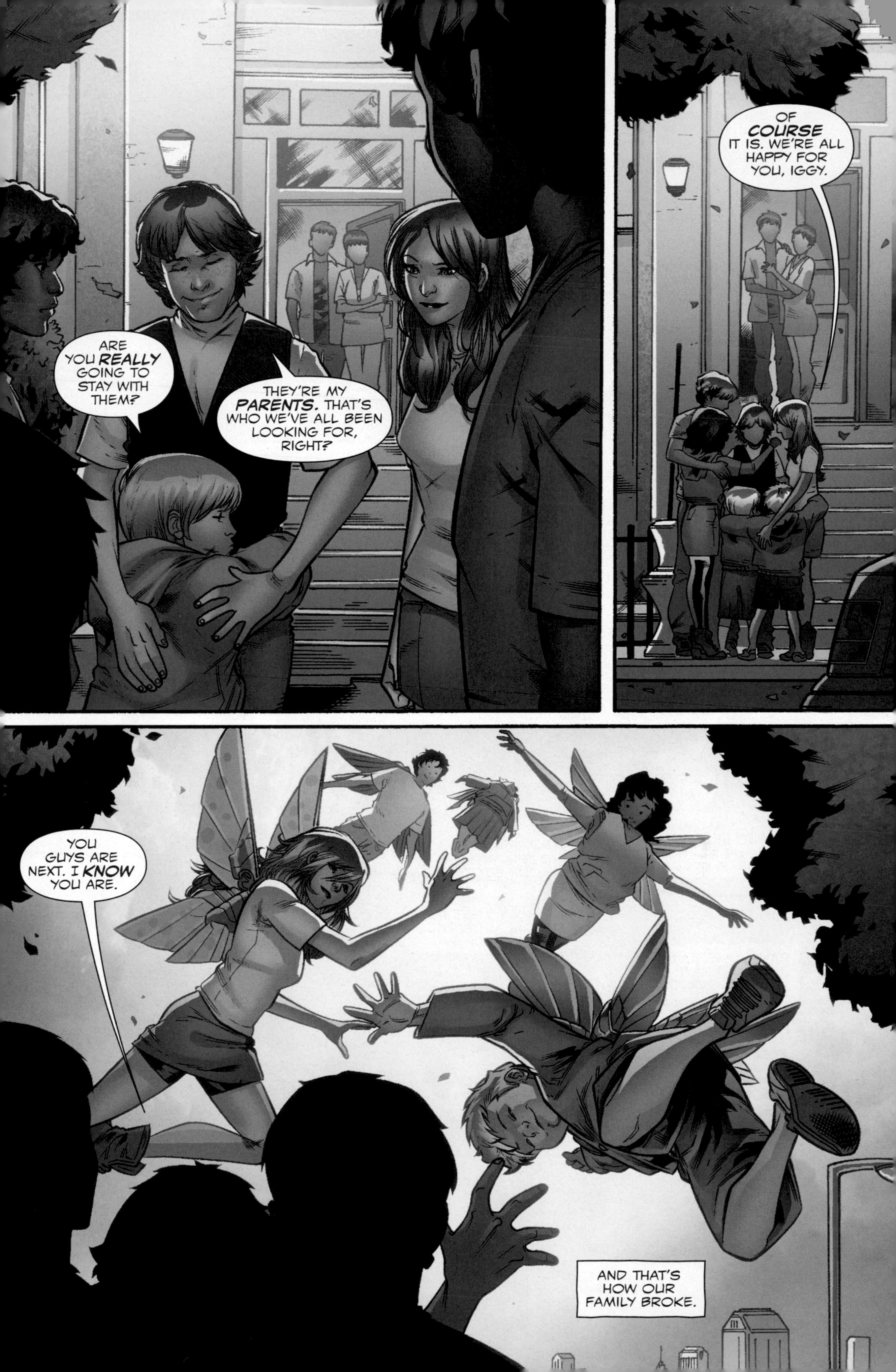
ARE YOU REALLY GOING TO STAY WITH THEM?
THEY'RE MY PARENTS. THAT'S WHO WE'VE ALL BEEN LOOKING FOR, RIGHT?
OF COURSE IT IS. WE'RE ALL HAPPY FOR YOU, IGGY.
YOU GUYS ARE NEXT. I KNOW YOU ARE.
AND THAT'S HOW OUR FAMILY BROKE.

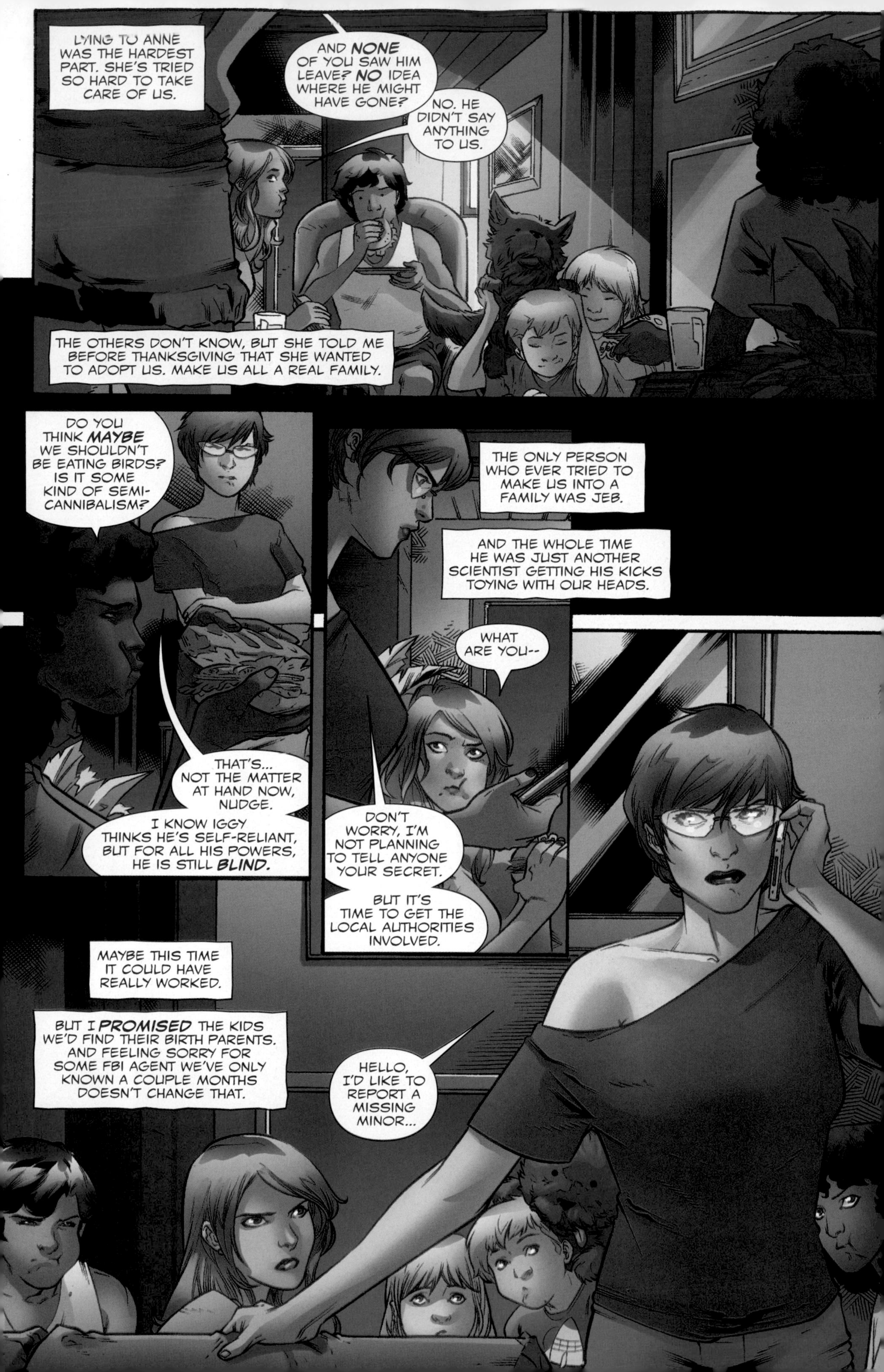
LYING TO ANNE WAS THE HARDEST PART. SHE'S TRIED SO HARD TO TAKE CARE OF US.
AND NONE OF YOU SAW HIM LEAVE? NO IDEA WHERE HE MIGHT HAVE GONE?
NO. HE DIDN'T SAY ANYTHING TO US.
THE OTHERS DON'T KNOW, BUT SHE TOLD ME BEFORE THANKSGIVING THAT SHE WANTED TO ADOPT US. MAKE US ALL A REAL FAMILY.
DO YOU THINK MAYBE WE SHOULDN'T BE EATING BIRDS? IS IT SOME KIND OF SEMI-CANNIBALISM?
THAT'S... NOT THE MATTER AT HAND NOW, NUDGE.
I KNOW IGGY THINKS HE'S SELF-RELIANT, BUT FOR ALL HIS POWERS, HE IS STILL BLIND.
THE ONLY PERSON WHO EVER TRIED TO MAKE US INTO A FAMILY WAS JEB.
AND THE WHOLE TIME HE WAS JUST ANOTHER SCIENTIST GETTING HIS KICKS TOYING WITH OUR HEADS.
WHAT ARE YOU--
DON'T WORRY, I'M NOT PLANNING TO TELL ANYONE YOUR SECRET.
BUT IT'S TIME TO GET THE LOCAL AUTHORITIES INVOLVED.
MAYBE THIS TIME IT COULD HAVE REALLY WORKED.
BUT I PROMISED THE KIDS WE'D FIND THEIR BIRTH PARENTS. AND FEELING SORRY FOR SOME FBI AGENT WE'VE ONLY KNOWN A COUPLE MONTHS DOESN'T CHANGE THAT.
HELLO, I'D LIKE TO REPORT A MISSING MINOR...

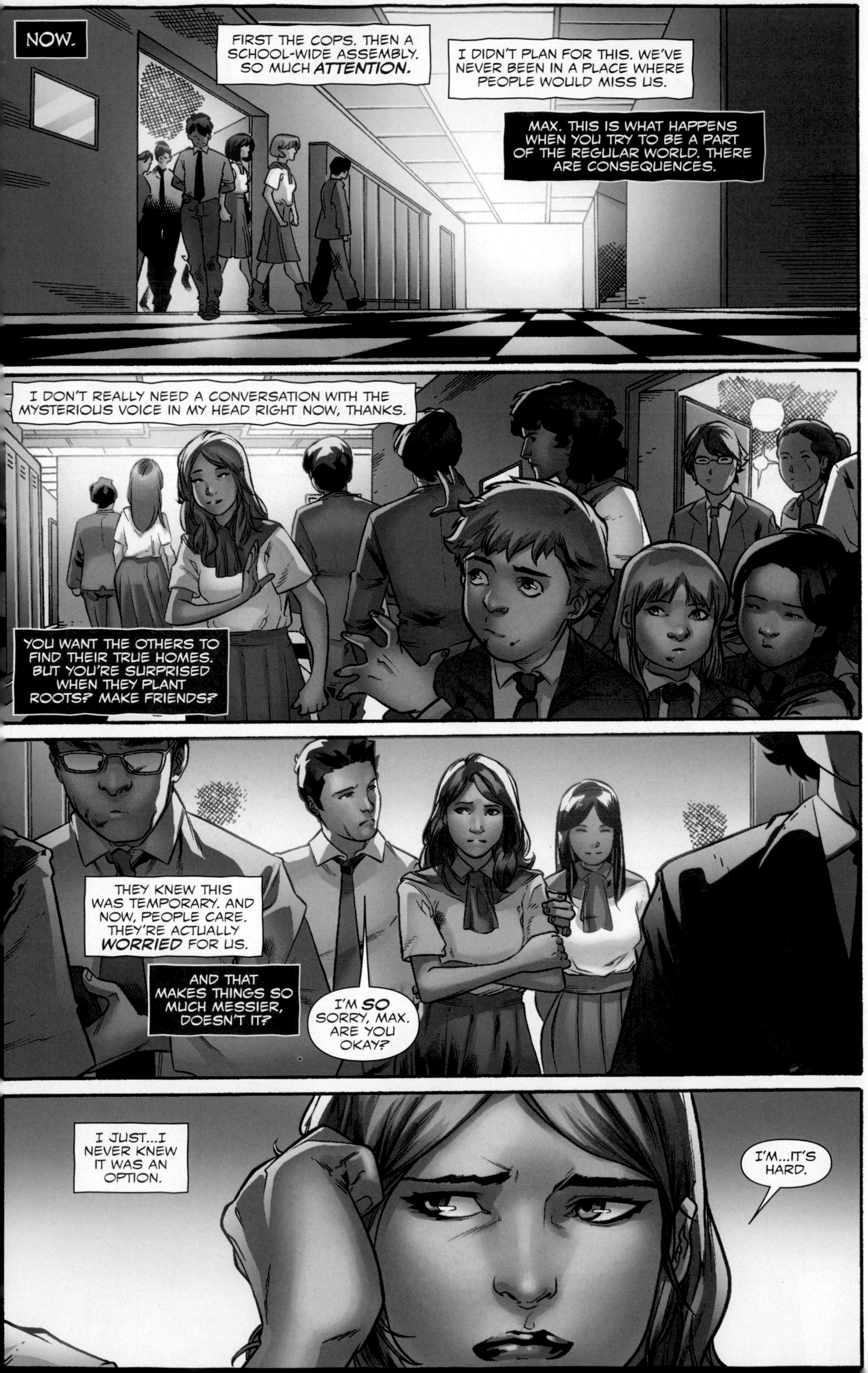
NOW.
FIRST THE COPS. THEN A SCHOOL-WIDE ASSEMBLY. SO MUCH ATTENTION.
I DIDN'T PLAN FOR THIS. WE'VE NEVER BEEN IN A PLACE WHERE PEOPLE WOULD MISS US.
MAX. THIS IS WHAT HAPPENS WHEN YOU TRY TO BE A PART OF THE REGULAR WORLD. THERE ARE CONSEQUENCES.
I DON'T REALLY NEED A CONVERSATION WITH THE MYSTERIOUS VOICE IN MY HEAD RIGHT NOW, THANKS.
YOU WANT THE OTHERS TO FIND THEIR TRUE HOMES. BUT YOU'RE SURPRISED WHEN THEY PLANT ROOTS? MAKE FRIENDS?
THEY KNEW THIS WAS TEMPORARY. AND NOW, PEOPLE CARE. THEY'RE ACTUALLY WORRIED FOR US.
AND THAT MAKES THINGS SO MUCH MESSIER, DOESN'T IT?
I'M SO SORRY, MAX. ARE YOU OKAY?
I JUST...I NEVER KNEW IT WAS AN OPTION.
I'M...IT'S HARD.

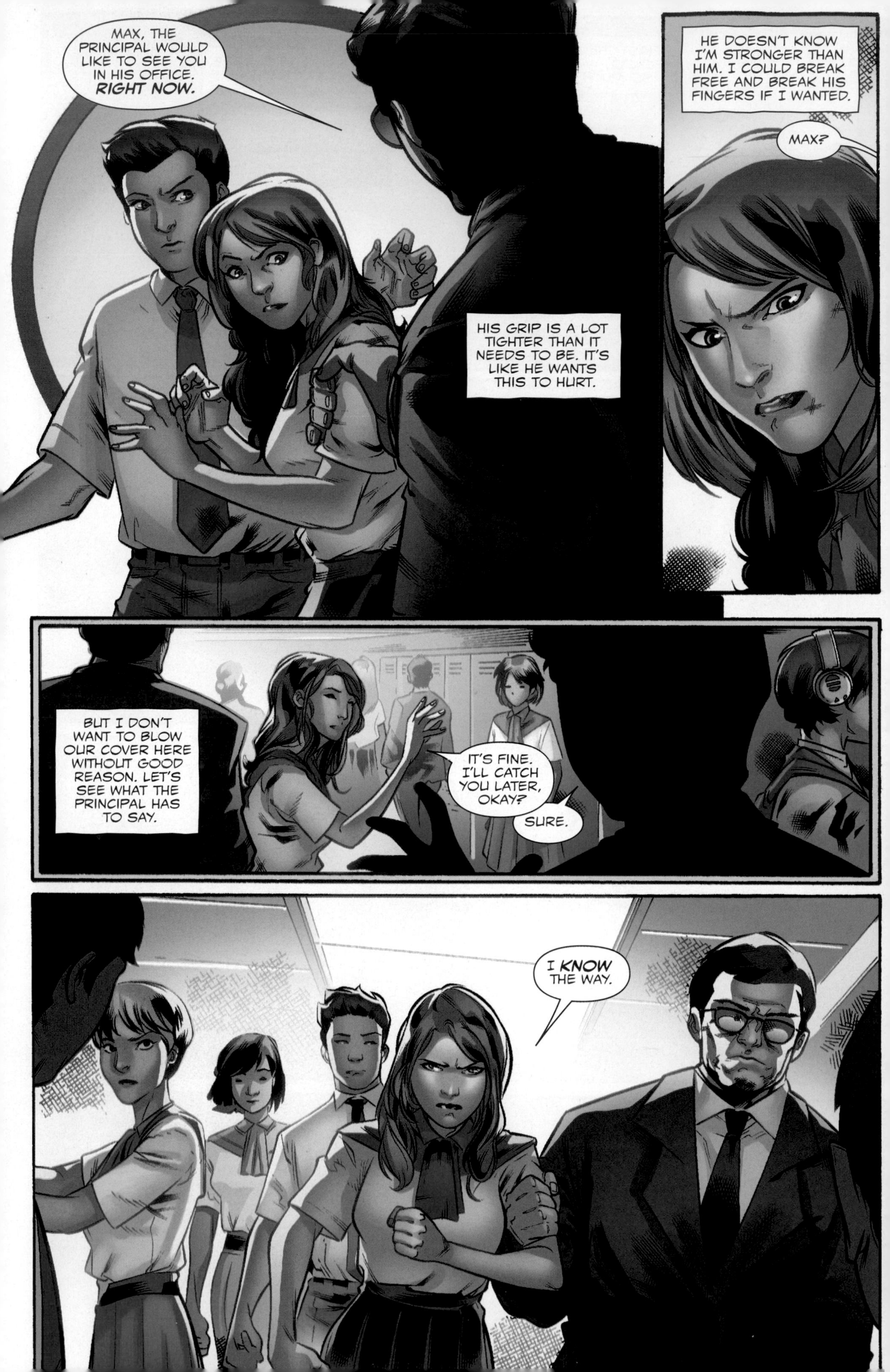
MAX, THE PRINCIPAL WOULD LIKE TO SEE YOU IN HIS OFFICE. ***RIGHT NOW.***
HIS GRIP IS A LOT TIGHTER THAN IT NEEDS TO BE. IT'S LIKE HE WANTS THIS TO HURT.
HE DOESN'T KNOW I'M STRONGER THAN HIM. I COULD BREAK FREE AND BREAK HIS FINGERS IF I WANTED.
MAX?
BUT I DON'T WANT TO BLOW OUR COVER HERE WITHOUT GOOD REASON. LET'S SEE WHAT THE PRINCIPAL HAS TO SAY.
IT'S FINE. I'LL CATCH YOU LATER, OKAY?
SURE.
I ***KNOW*** THE WAY.

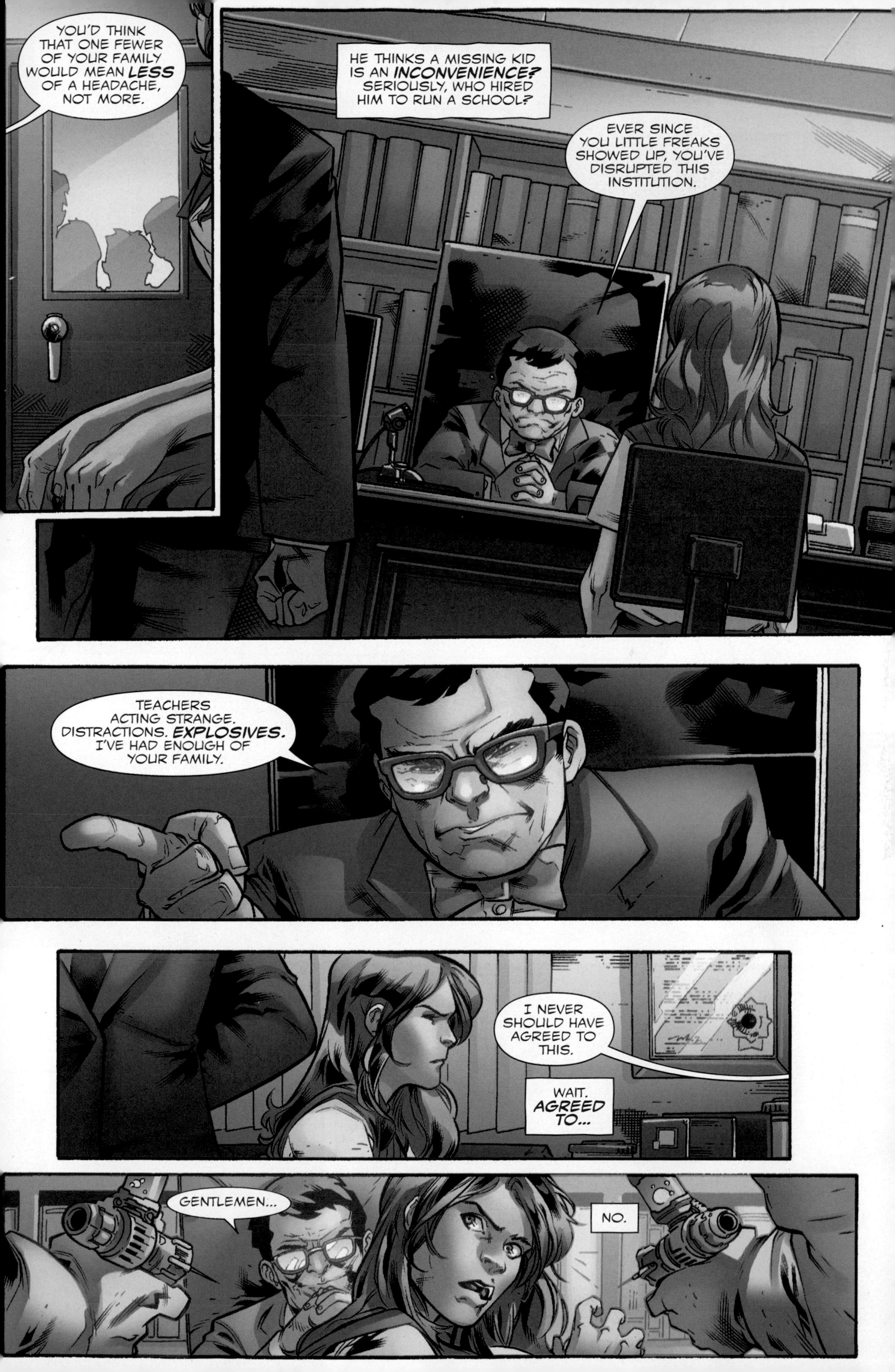
YOU'D THINK THAT ONE FEWER OF YOUR FAMILY WOULD MEAN LESS OF A HEADACHE, NOT MORE.
HE THINKS A MISSING KID IS AN INCONVENIENCE? SERIOUSLY, WHO HIRED HIM TO RUN A SCHOOL?
EVER SINCE YOU LITTLE FREAKS SHOWED UP, YOU'VE DISRUPTED THIS INSTITUTION.
TEACHERS ACTING STRANGE. DISTRACTIONS. EXPLOSIVES. I'VE HAD ENOUGH OF YOUR FAMILY.
I NEVER SHOULD HAVE AGREED TO THIS.
WAIT. AGREED TO...
GENTLEMEN...
NO.

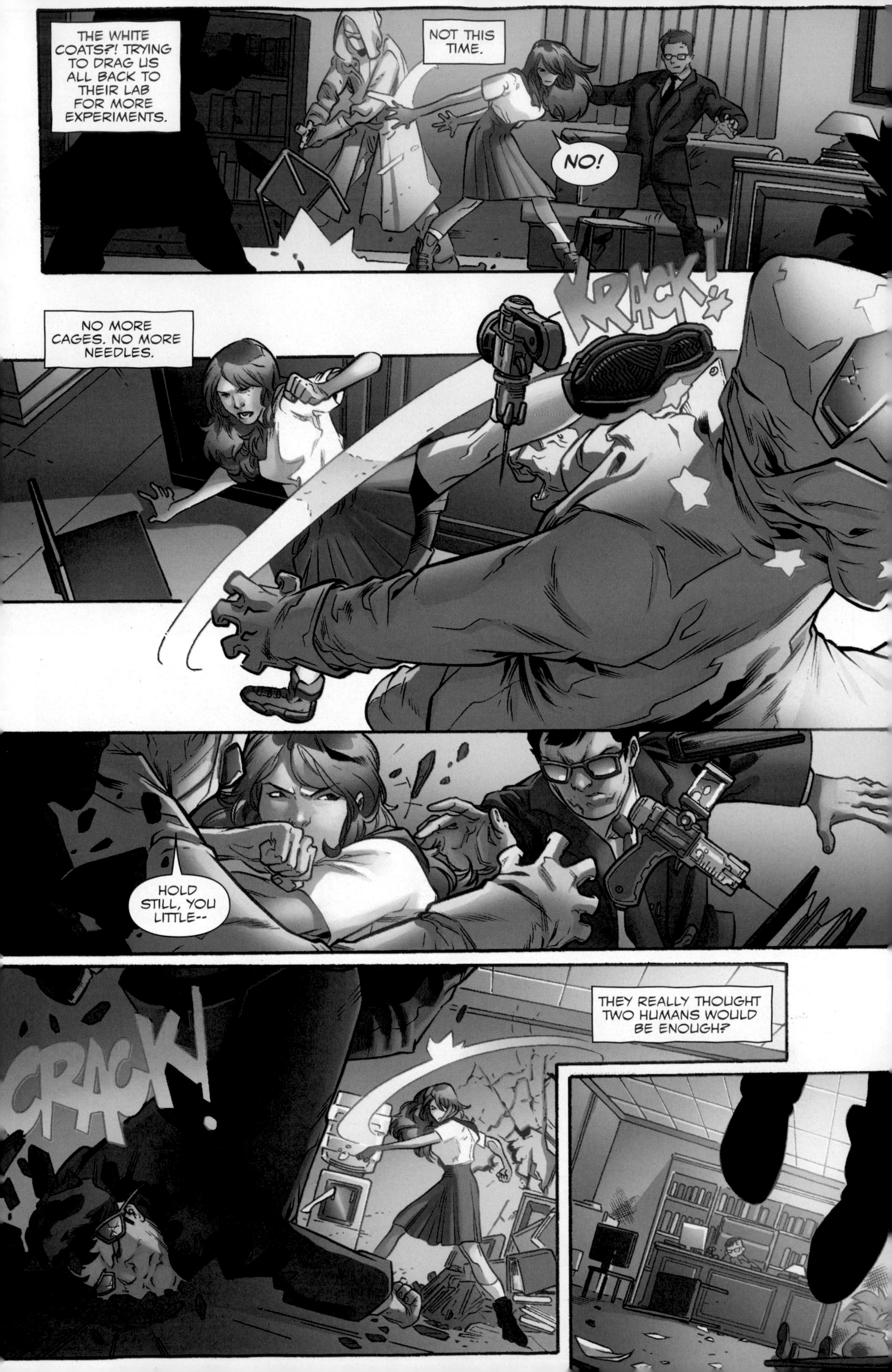
THE WHITE COATS?! TRYING TO DRAG US ALL BACK TO THEIR LAB FOR MORE EXPERIMENTS.
NOT THIS TIME.
NO!
KRACK!
NO MORE CAGES. NO MORE NEEDLES.
HOLD STILL, YOU LITTLE--
CRACK!
THEY REALLY THOUGHT TWO HUMANS WOULD BE ENOUGH?

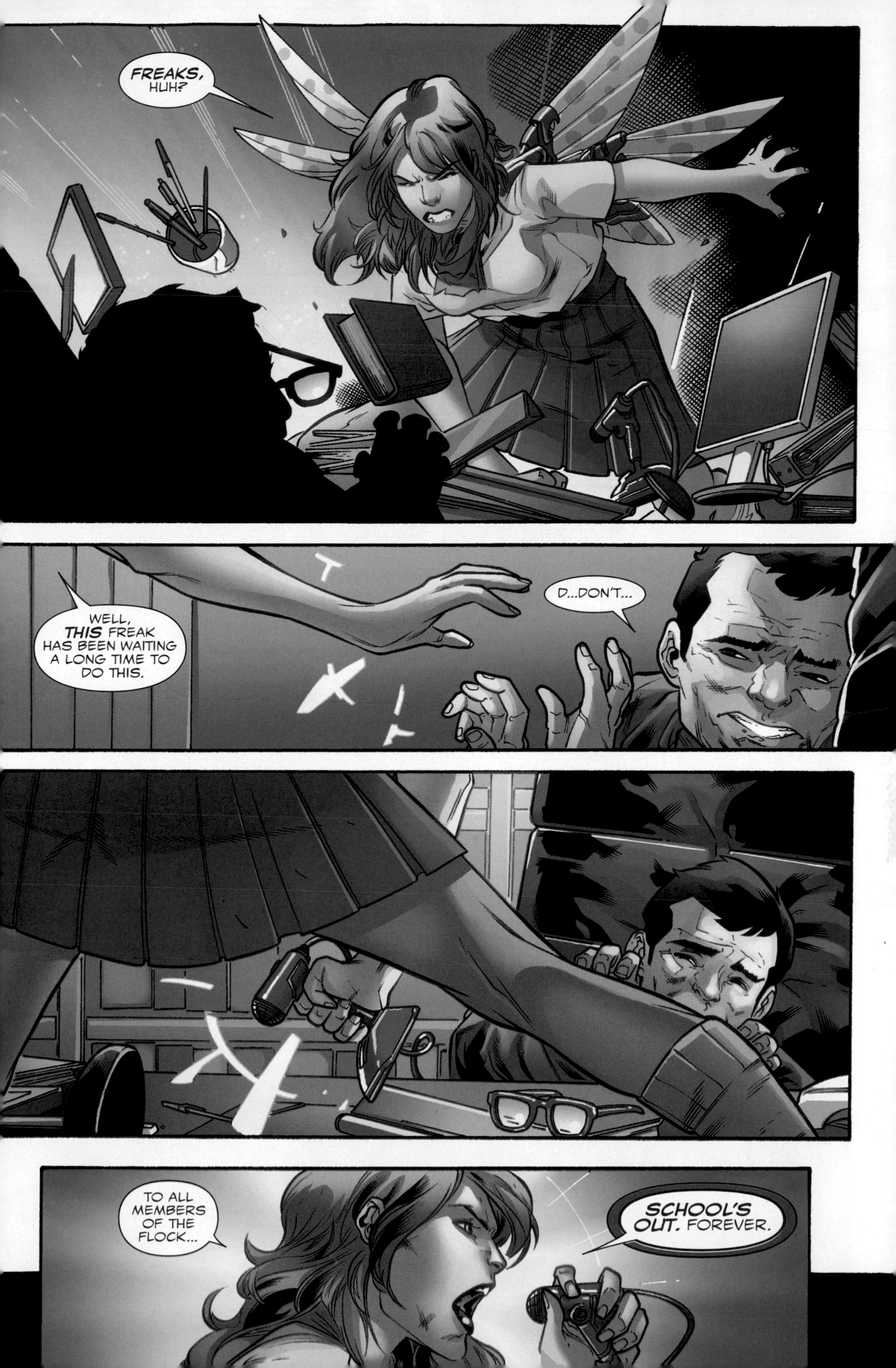
FREAKS, HUH?
WELL, THIS FREAK HAS BEEN WAITING A LONG TIME TO DO THIS.
D...DON'T...
TO ALL MEMBERS OF THE FLOCK...
SCHOOL'S OUT. FOREVER.

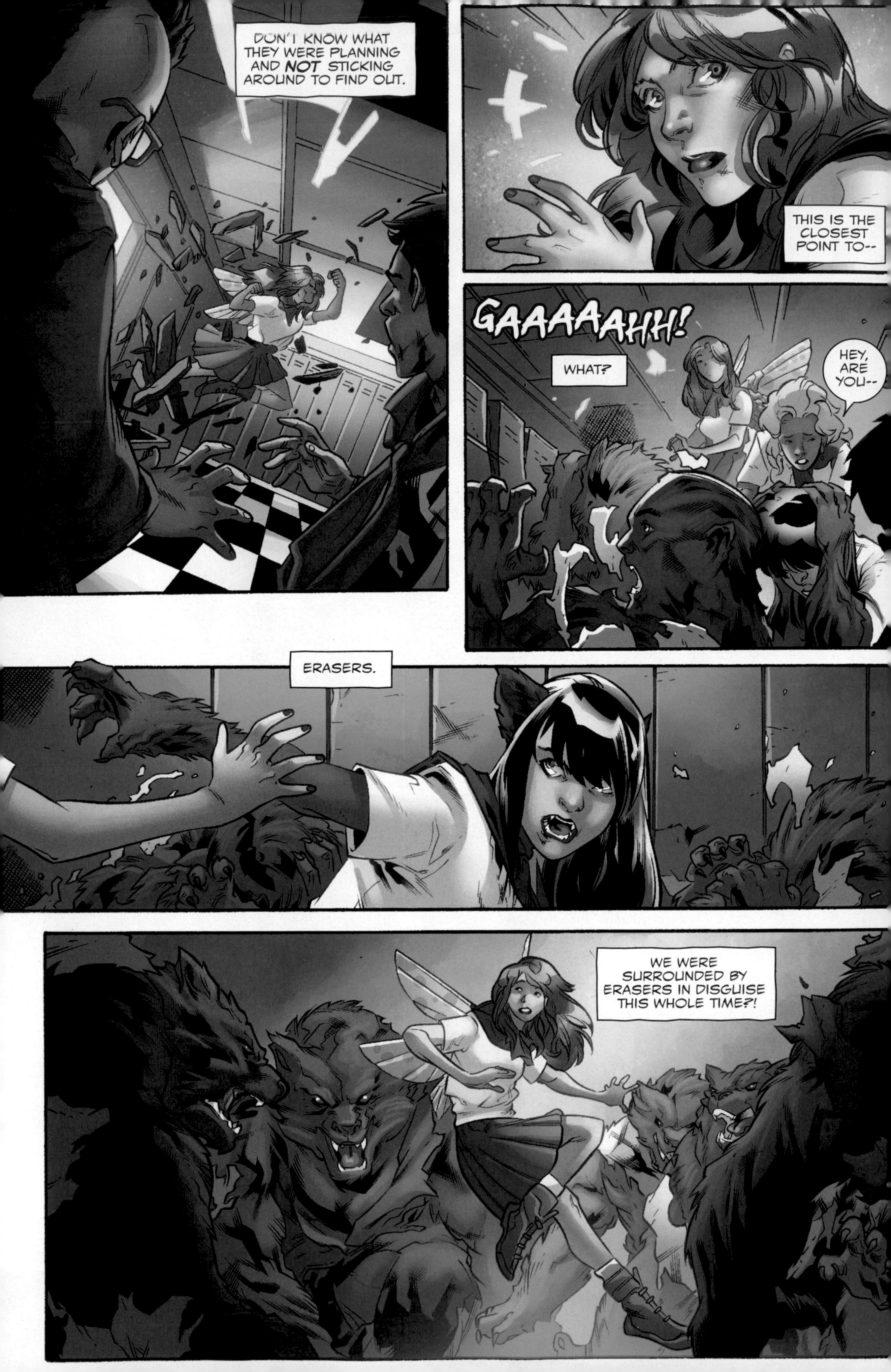
DON'T KNOW WHAT THEY WERE PLANNING AND NOT STICKING AROUND TO FIND OUT.
THIS IS THE CLOSEST POINT TO--
GAAAAAHH!
WHAT?
HEY, ARE YOU--
ERASERS.
WE WERE SURROUNDED BY ERASERS IN DISGUISE THIS WHOLE TIME?!

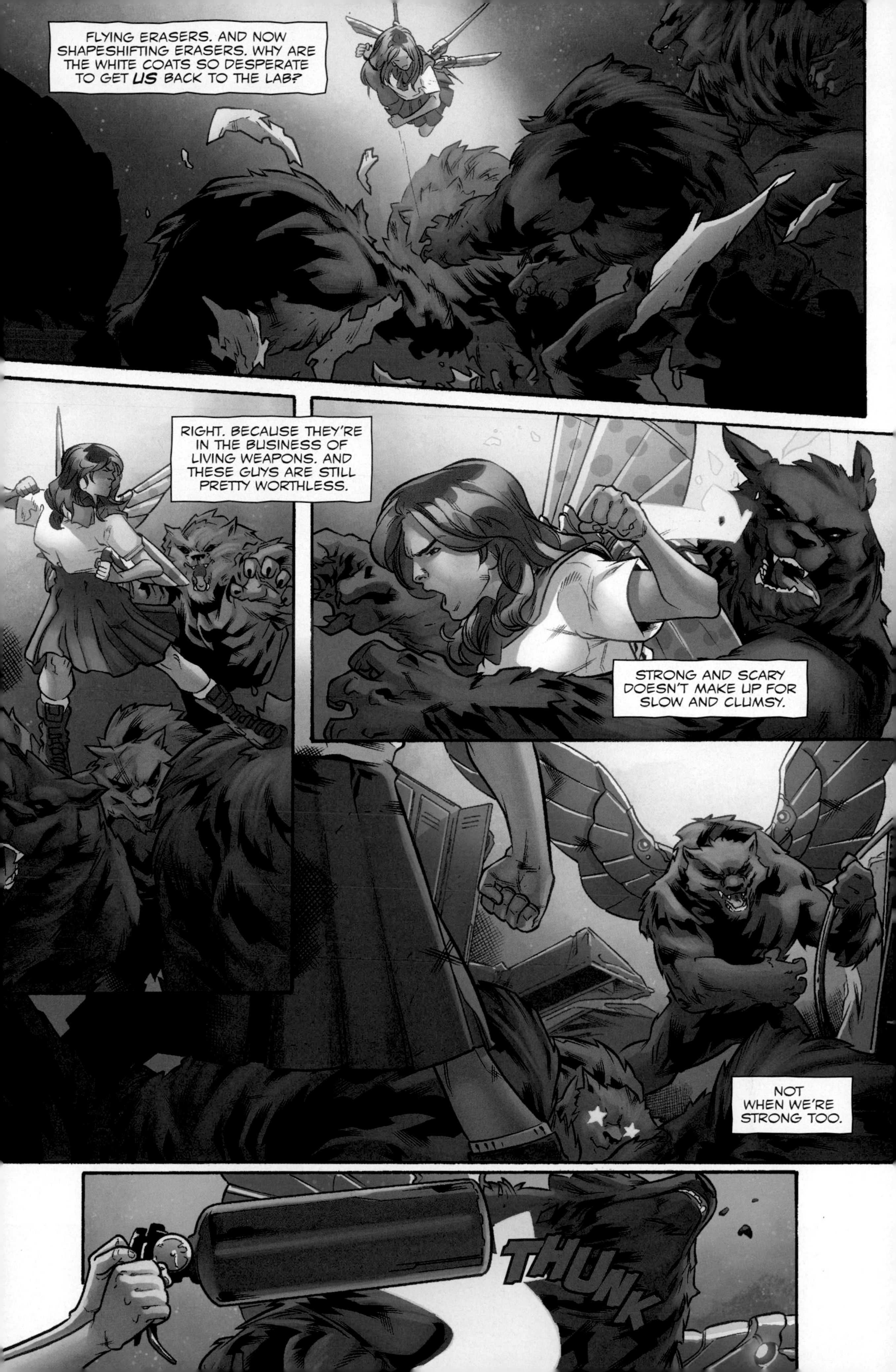
FLYING ERASERS. AND NOW SHAPESHIFTING ERASERS. WHY ARE THE WHITE COATS SO DESPERATE TO GET US BACK TO THE LAB?
RIGHT. BECAUSE THEY'RE IN THE BUSINESS OF LIVING WEAPONS. AND THESE GUYS ARE STILL PRETTY WORTHLESS.
STRONG AND SCARY DOESN'T MAKE UP FOR SLOW AND CLUMSY.
NOT WHEN WE'RE STRONG TOO.
THUNK

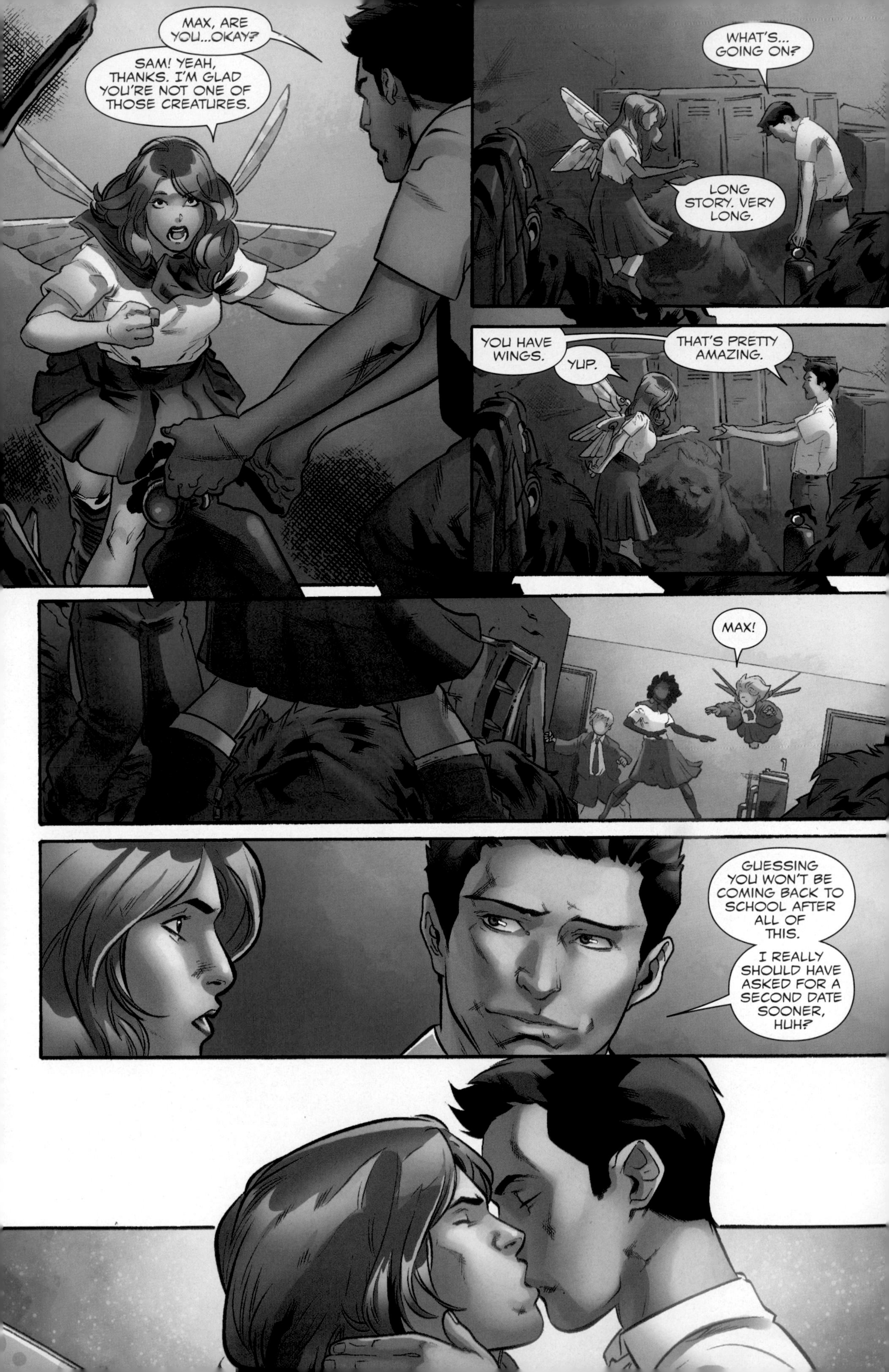
MAX, ARE YOU...OKAY?
SAM! YEAH, THANKS. I'M GLAD YOU'RE NOT ONE OF THOSE CREATURES.
WHAT'S... GOING ON?
LONG STORY. VERY LONG.
YOU HAVE WINGS.
YUP.
THAT'S PRETTY AMAZING.
MAX!
GUESSING YOU WON'T BE COMING BACK TO SCHOOL AFTER ALL OF THIS.
I REALLY SHOULD HAVE ASKED FOR A SECOND DATE SOONER, HUH?

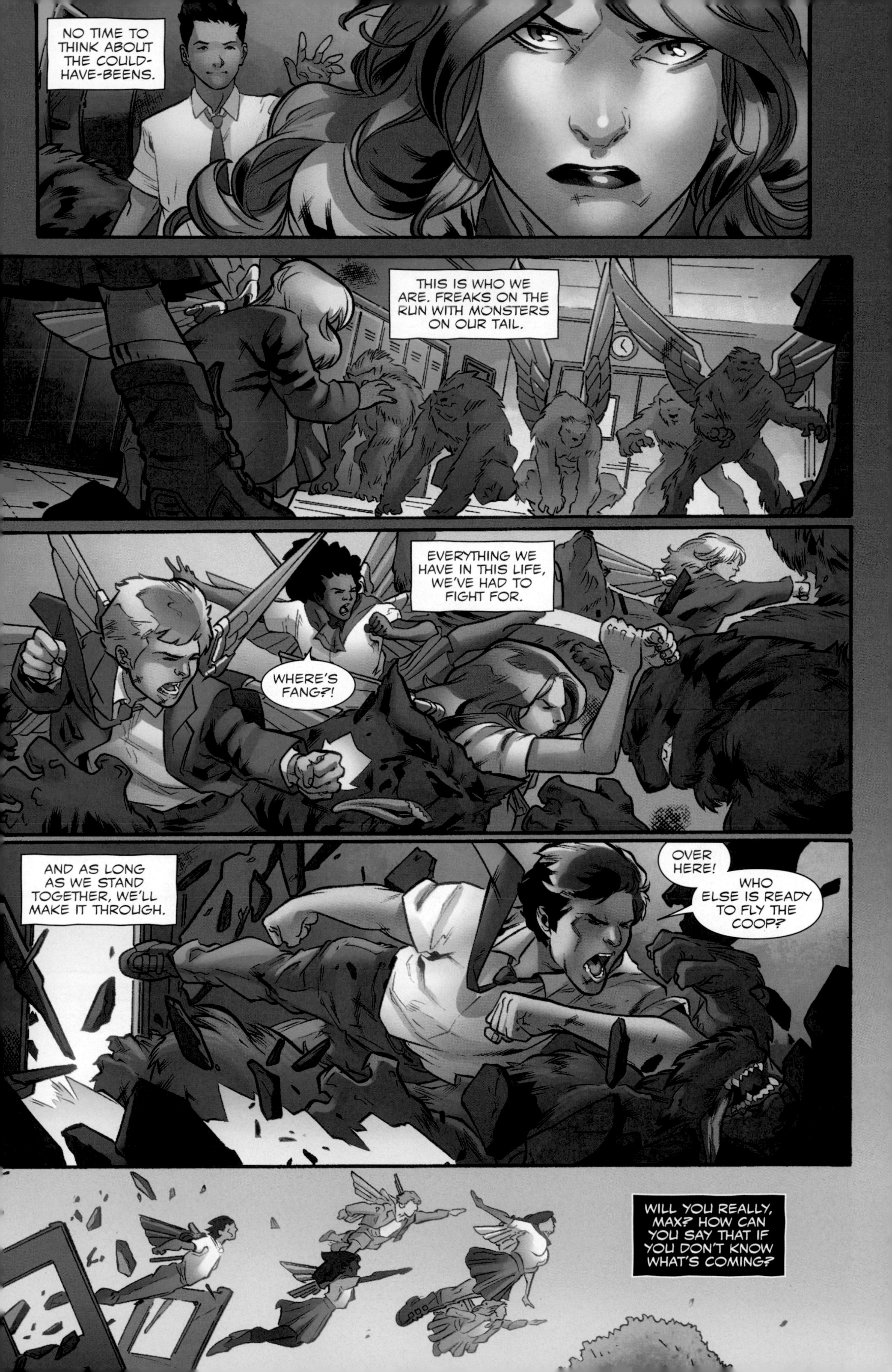
NO TIME TO THINK ABOUT THE COULD-HAVE-BEENS.
THIS IS WHO WE ARE. FREAKS ON THE RUN WITH MONSTERS ON OUR TAIL.
EVERYTHING WE HAVE IN THIS LIFE, WE'VE HAD TO FIGHT FOR.
WHERE'S FANG?!
AND AS LONG AS WE STAND TOGETHER, WE'LL MAKE IT THROUGH.
OVER HERE!
WHO ELSE IS READY TO FLY THE COOP?
WILL YOU REALLY, MAX? HOW CAN YOU SAY THAT IF YOU DON'T KNOW WHAT'S COMING?

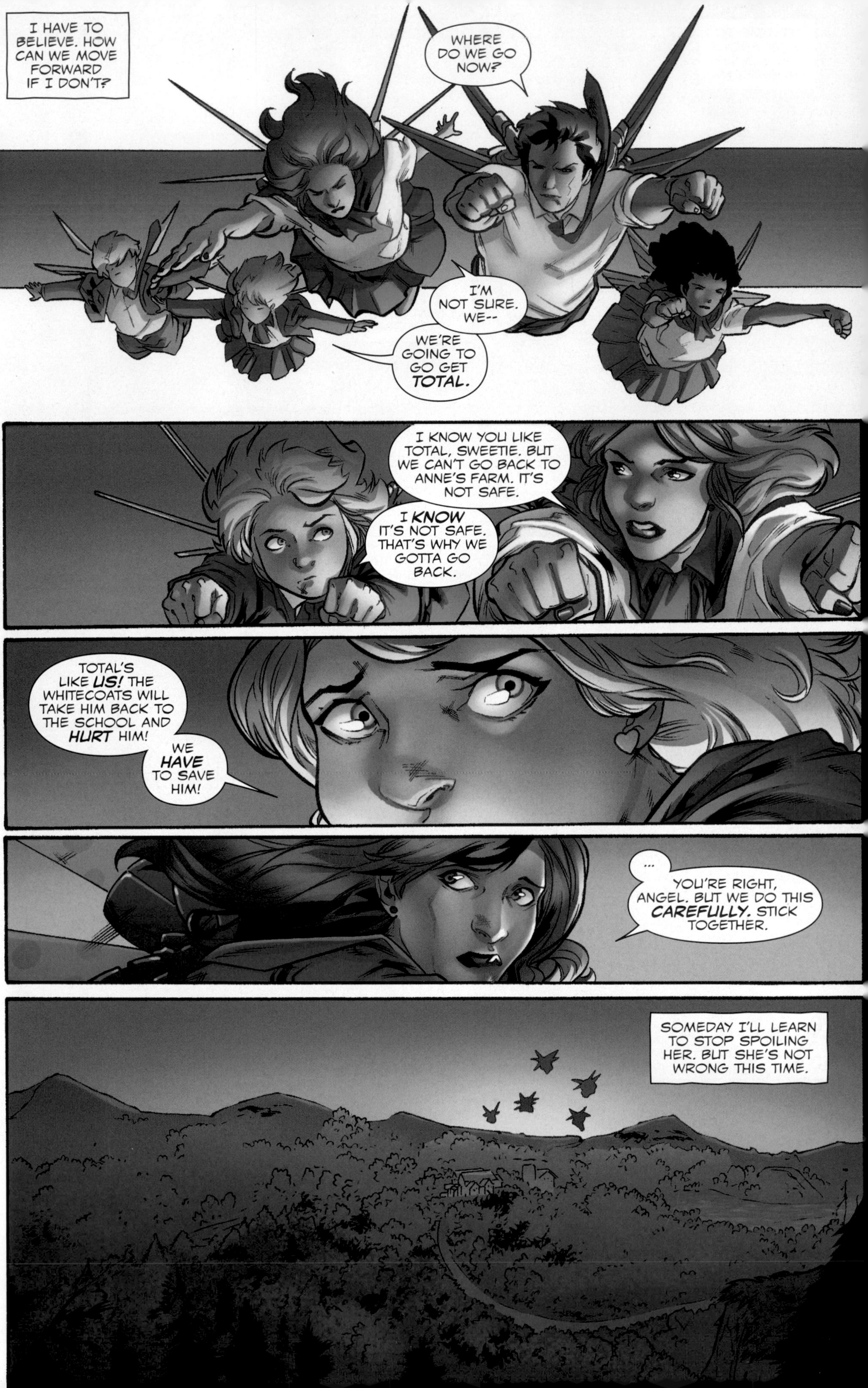

I HAVE TO BELIEVE. HOW CAN WE MOVE FORWARD IF I DON'T?
WHERE DO WE GO NOW?
I'M NOT SURE. WE--
WE'RE GOING TO GO GET TOTAL.
I KNOW YOU LIKE TOTAL, SWEETIE. BUT WE CAN'T GO BACK TO ANNE'S FARM. IT'S NOT SAFE.
I KNOW IT'S NOT SAFE. THAT'S WHY WE GOTTA GO BACK.
TOTAL'S LIKE US! THE WHITECOATS WILL TAKE HIM BACK TO THE SCHOOL AND HURT HIM!
WE HAVE TO SAVE HIM!
... YOU'RE RIGHT, ANGEL. BUT WE DO THIS CAREFULLY. STICK TOGETHER.
SOMEDAY I'LL LEARN TO STOP SPOILING HER. BUT SHE'S NOT WRONG THIS TIME.

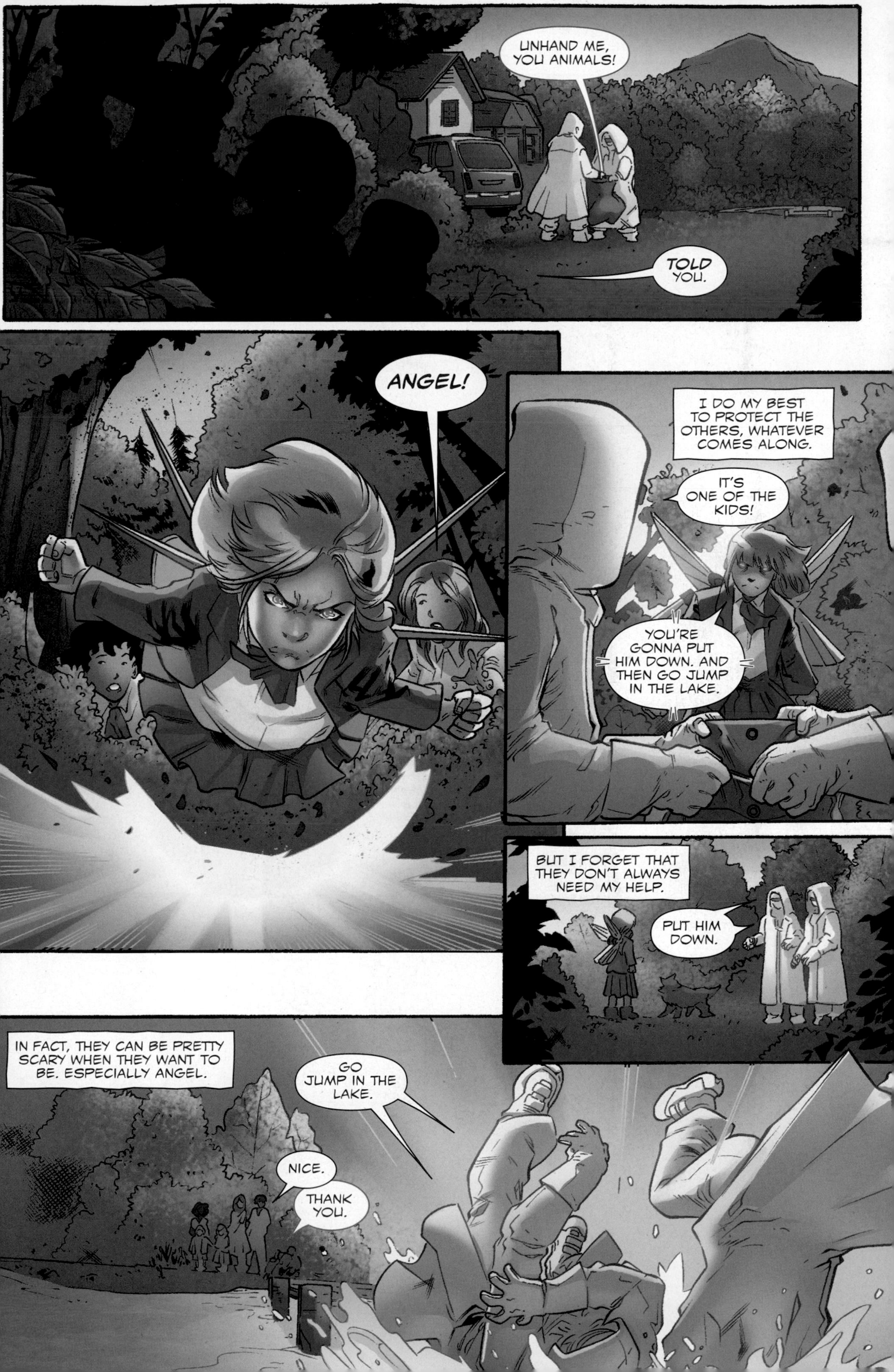

UNHAND ME, YOU ANIMALS!
TOLD YOU.
ANGEL!
I DO MY BEST TO PROTECT THE OTHERS, WHATEVER COMES ALONG.
IT'S ONE OF THE KIDS!
YOU'RE GONNA PUT HIM DOWN. AND THEN GO JUMP IN THE LAKE.
BUT I FORGET THAT THEY DON'T ALWAYS NEED MY HELP.
PUT HIM DOWN.
IN FACT, THEY CAN BE PRETTY SCARY WHEN THEY WANT TO BE. ESPECIALLY ANGEL.
GO JUMP IN THE LAKE.
NICE.
THANK YOU.

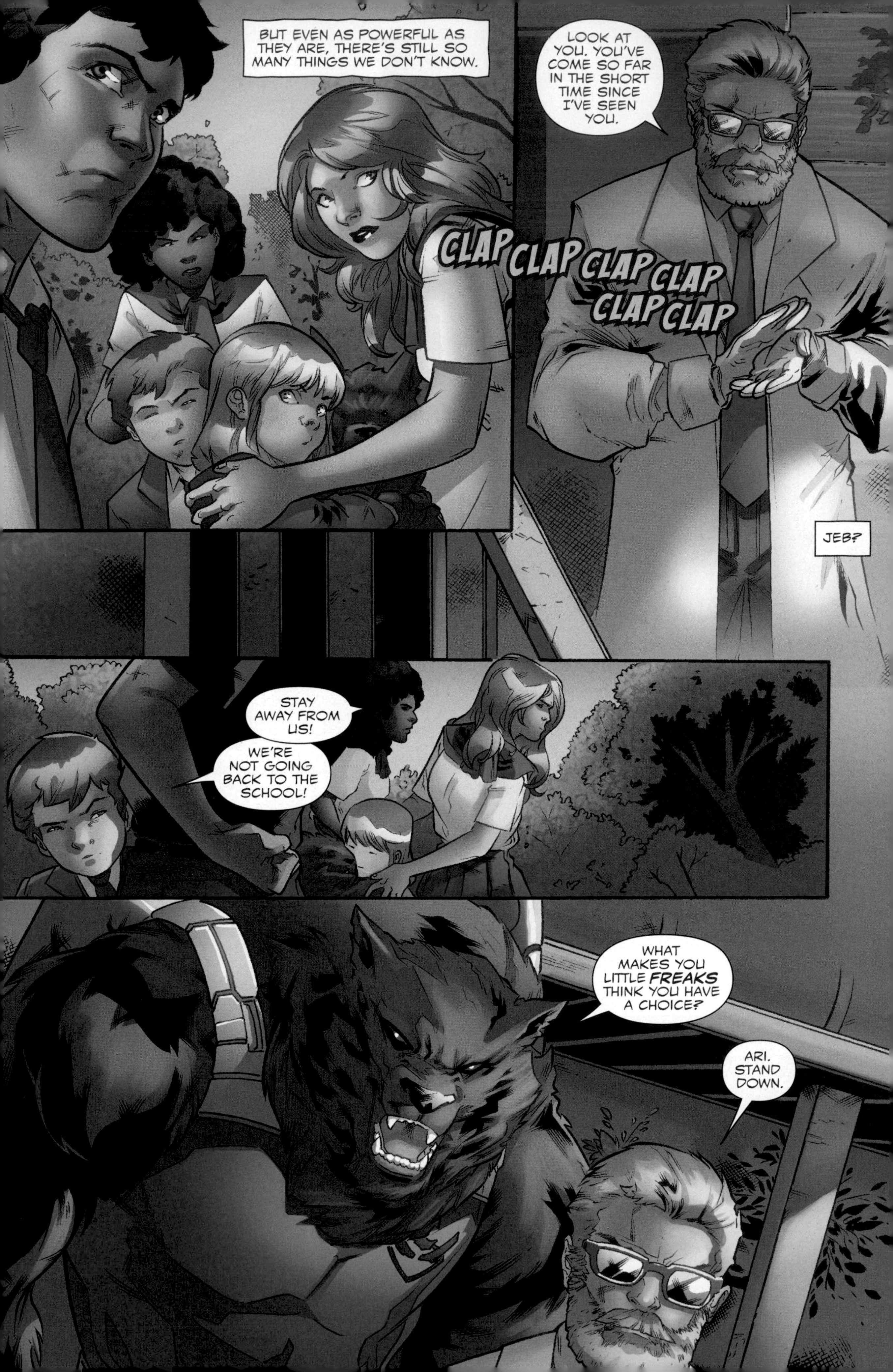
BUT EVEN AS POWERFUL AS THEY ARE, THERE'S STILL SO MANY THINGS WE DON'T KNOW.
LOOK AT YOU. YOU'VE COME SO FAR IN THE SHORT TIME SINCE I'VE SEEN YOU.
CLAP CLAP CLAP CLAP CLAP CLAP
JEB?
STAY AWAY FROM US!
WE'RE NOT GOING BACK TO THE SCHOOL!
WHAT MAKES YOU LITTLE **FREAKS** THINK YOU HAVE A CHOICE?
ARI. STAND DOWN.

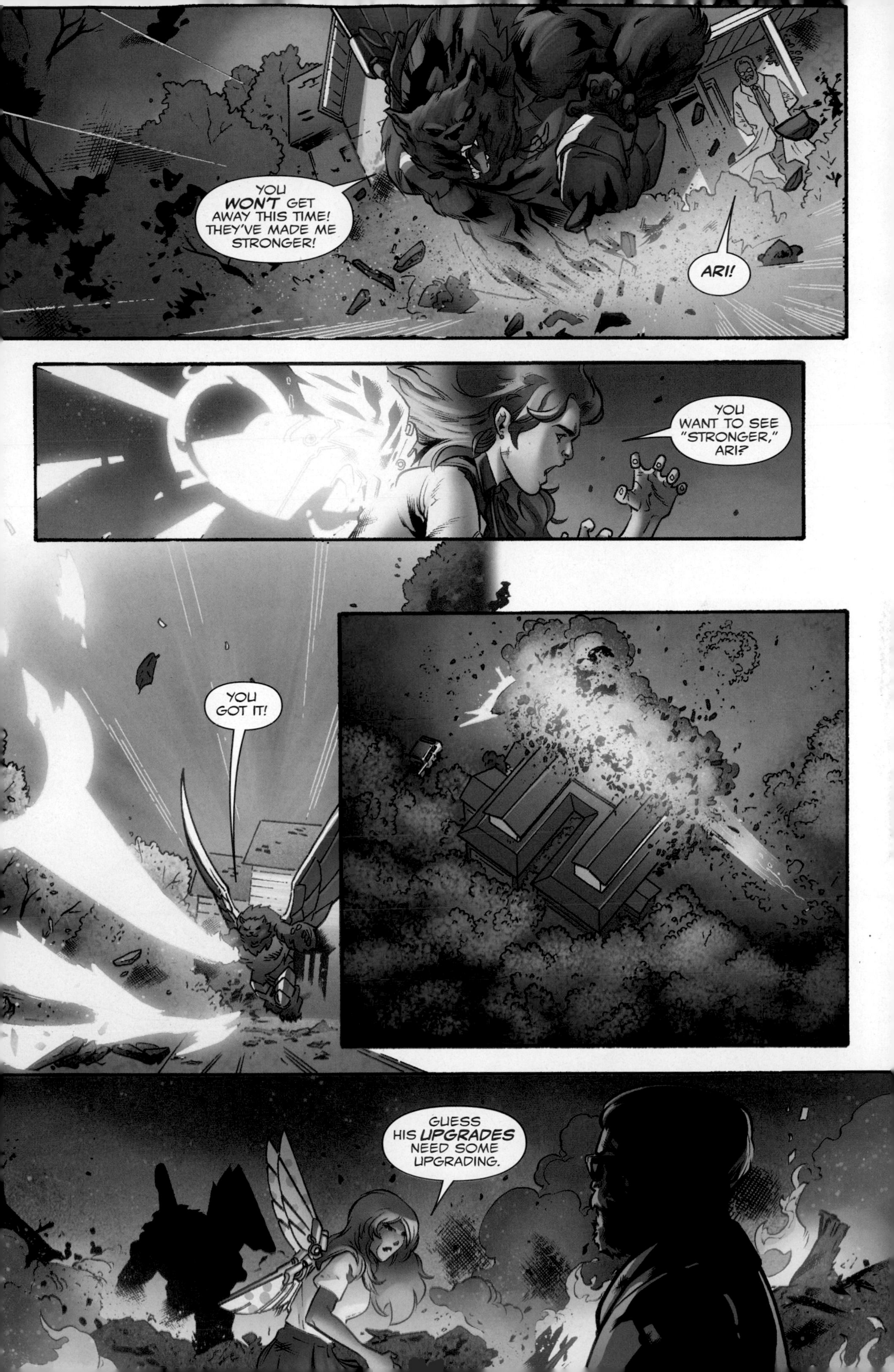

YOU WON'T GET AWAY THIS TIME! THEY'VE MADE ME STRONGER!
ARI!
YOU WANT TO SEE "STRONGER," ARI?
YOU GOT IT!
GUESS HIS UPGRADES NEED SOME UPGRADING.

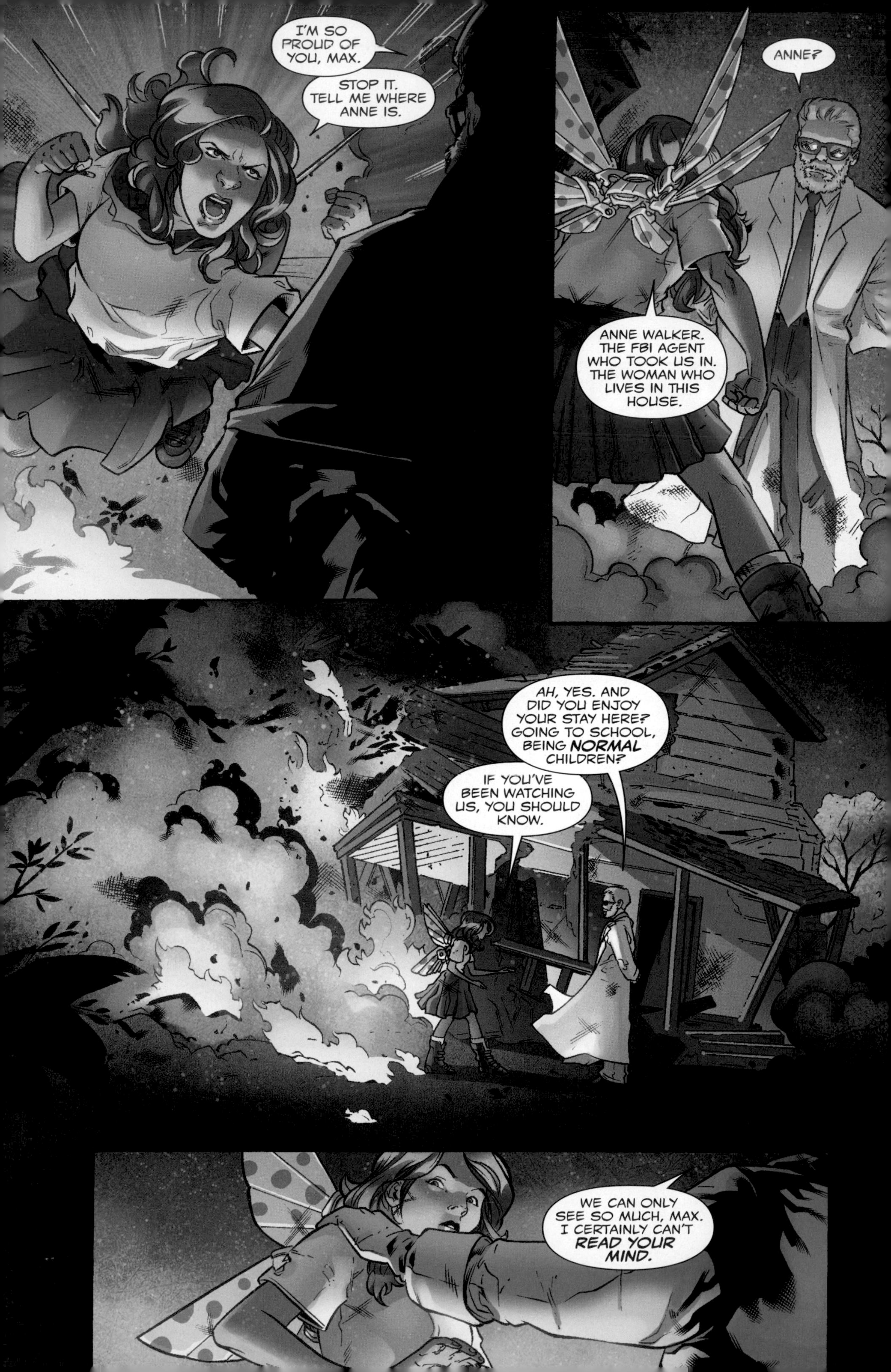

I'M SO PROUD OF YOU, MAX.
STOP IT. TELL ME WHERE ANNE IS.
ANNE?
ANNE WALKER. THE FBI AGENT WHO TOOK US IN. THE WOMAN WHO LIVES IN THIS HOUSE.
AH, YES. AND DID YOU ENJOY YOUR STAY HERE? GOING TO SCHOOL, BEING NORMAL CHILDREN?
IF YOU'VE BEEN WATCHING US, YOU SHOULD KNOW.
WE CAN ONLY SEE SO MUCH, MAX. I CERTAINLY CAN'T READ YOUR MIND.

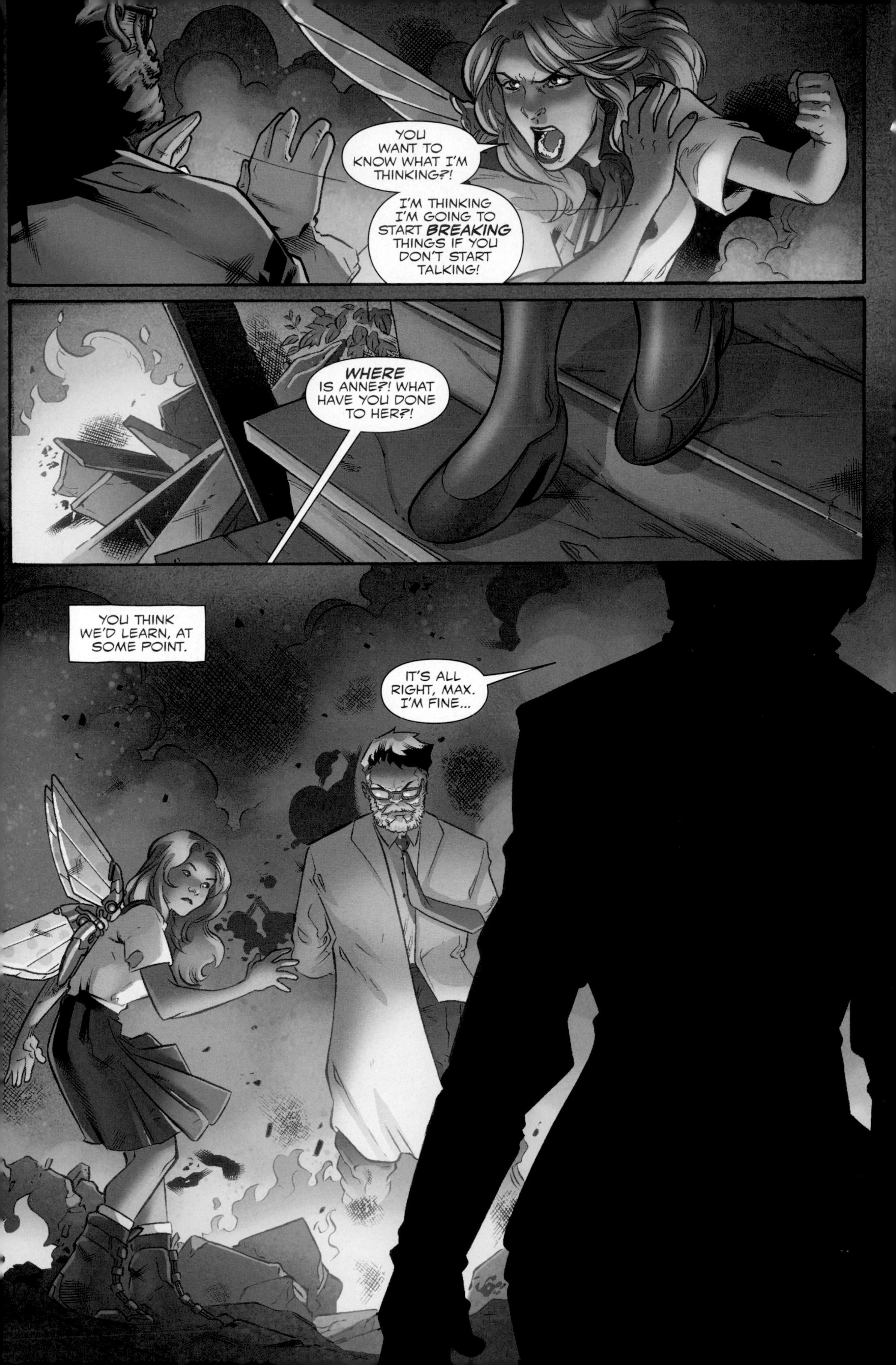
YOU WANT TO KNOW WHAT I'M THINKING?!
I'M THINKING I'M GOING TO START **BREAKING** THINGS IF YOU DON'T START TALKING!
WHERE IS ANNE?! WHAT HAVE YOU DONE TO HER?!
YOU THINK WE'D LEARN, AT SOME POINT.
IT'S ALL RIGHT, MAX. I'M FINE...

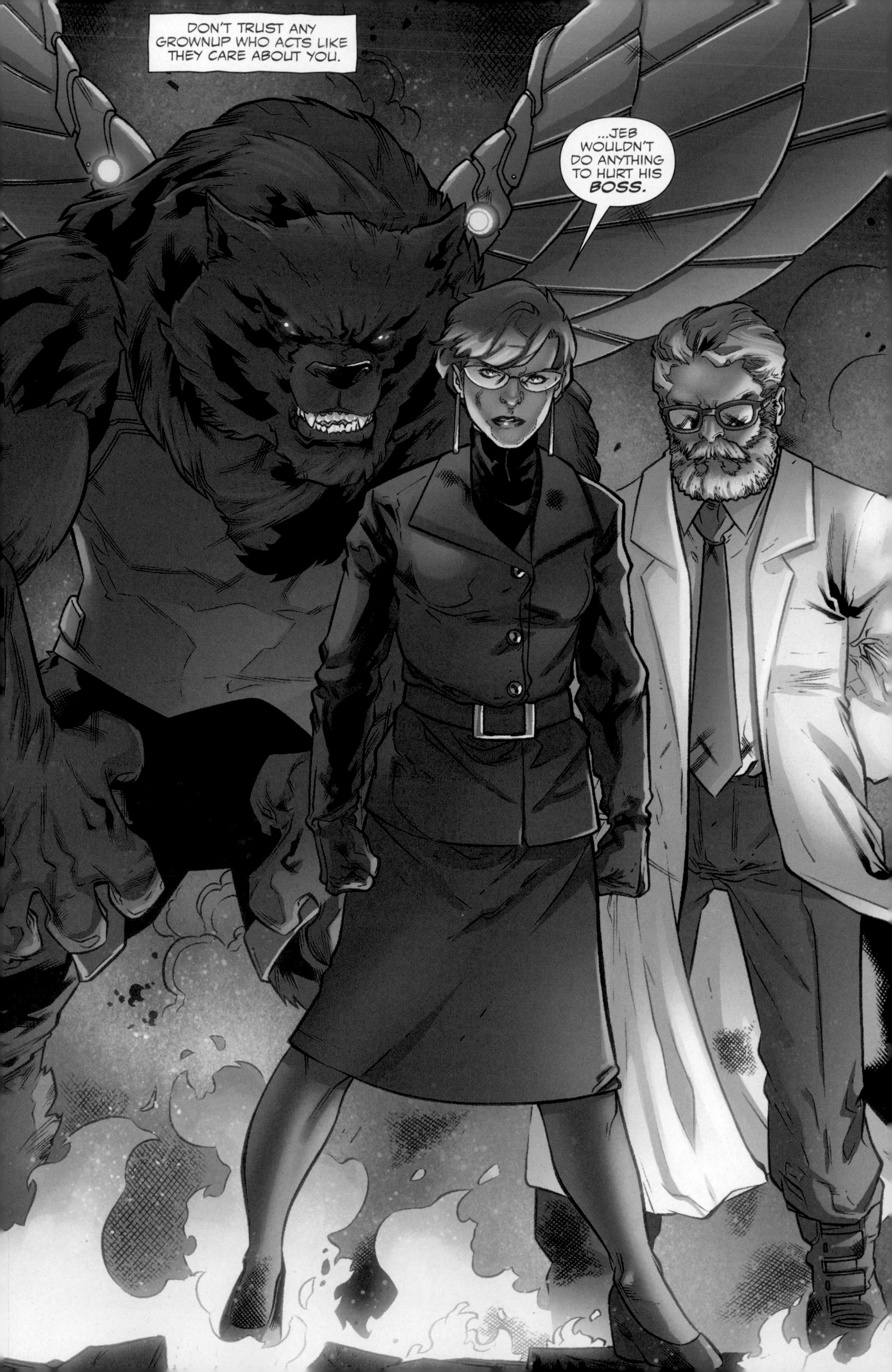
DON'T TRUST ANY GROWNUP WHO ACTS LIKE THEY CARE ABOUT YOU.
...JEB WOULDN'T DO ANYTHING TO HURT HIS BOSS.

CHAPTER 4

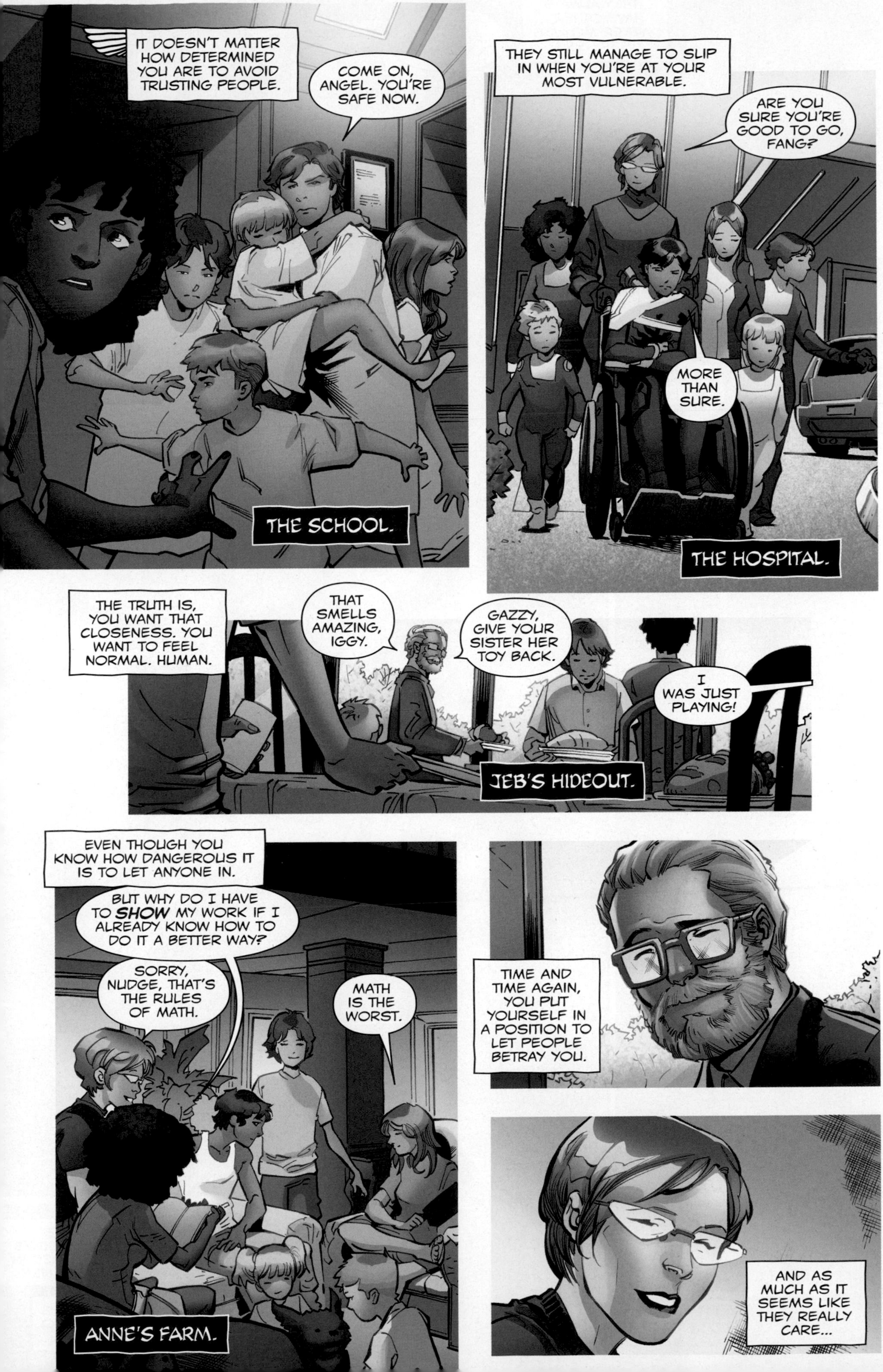
IT DOESN'T MATTER HOW DETERMINED YOU ARE TO AVOID TRUSTING PEOPLE.
COME ON, ANGEL. YOU'RE SAFE NOW.
THE SCHOOL.
THEY STILL MANAGE TO SLIP IN WHEN YOU'RE AT YOUR MOST VULNERABLE.
ARE YOU SURE YOU'RE GOOD TO GO, FANG?
MORE THAN SURE.
THE HOSPITAL.
THE TRUTH IS, YOU WANT THAT CLOSENESS. YOU WANT TO FEEL NORMAL. HUMAN.
THAT SMELLS AMAZING, IGGY.
GAZZY, GIVE YOUR SISTER HER TOY BACK.
I WAS JUST PLAYING!
JEB'S HIDEOUT.
EVEN THOUGH YOU KNOW HOW DANGEROUS IT IS TO LET ANYONE IN.
BUT WHY DO I HAVE TO SHOW MY WORK IF I ALREADY KNOW HOW TO DO IT A BETTER WAY?
SORRY, NUDGE, THAT'S THE RULES OF MATH.
MATH IS THE WORST.
ANNE'S FARM.
TIME AND TIME AGAIN, YOU PUT YOURSELF IN A POSITION TO LET PEOPLE BETRAY YOU.
AND AS MUCH AS IT SEEMS LIKE THEY REALLY CARE...

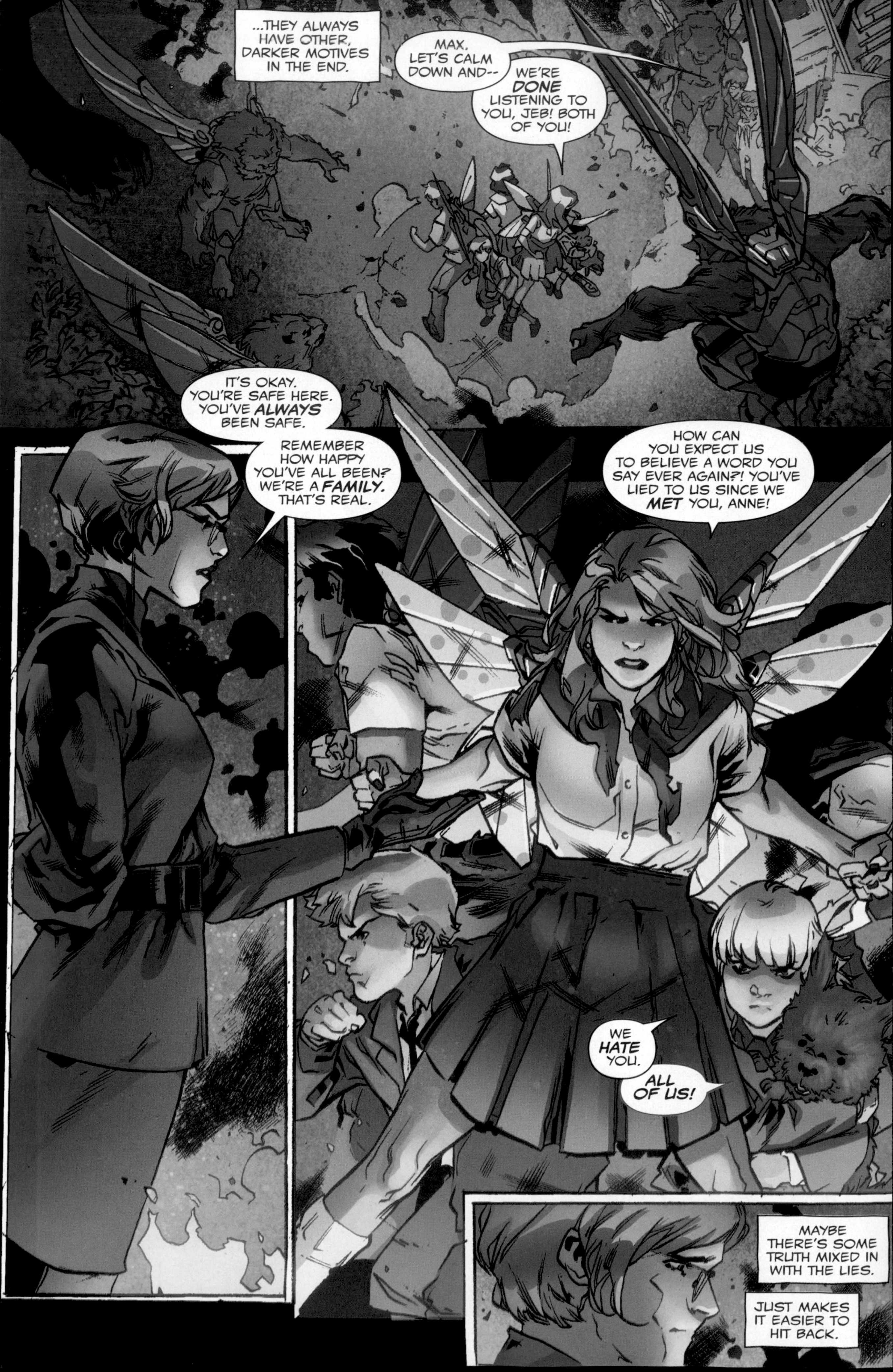
...THEY ALWAYS HAVE OTHER, DARKER MOTIVES IN THE END.
MAX. LET'S CALM DOWN AND--
WE'RE DONE LISTENING TO YOU, JEB! BOTH OF YOU!
IT'S OKAY. YOU'RE SAFE HERE. YOU'VE ALWAYS BEEN SAFE.
REMEMBER HOW HAPPY YOU'VE ALL BEEN? WE'RE A FAMILY. THAT'S REAL.
HOW CAN YOU EXPECT US TO BELIEVE A WORD YOU SAY EVER AGAIN?! YOU'VE LIED TO US SINCE WE MET YOU, ANNE!
WE HATE YOU.
ALL OF US!
MAYBE THERE'S SOME TRUTH MIXED IN WITH THE LIES.
JUST MAKES IT EASIER TO HIT BACK.

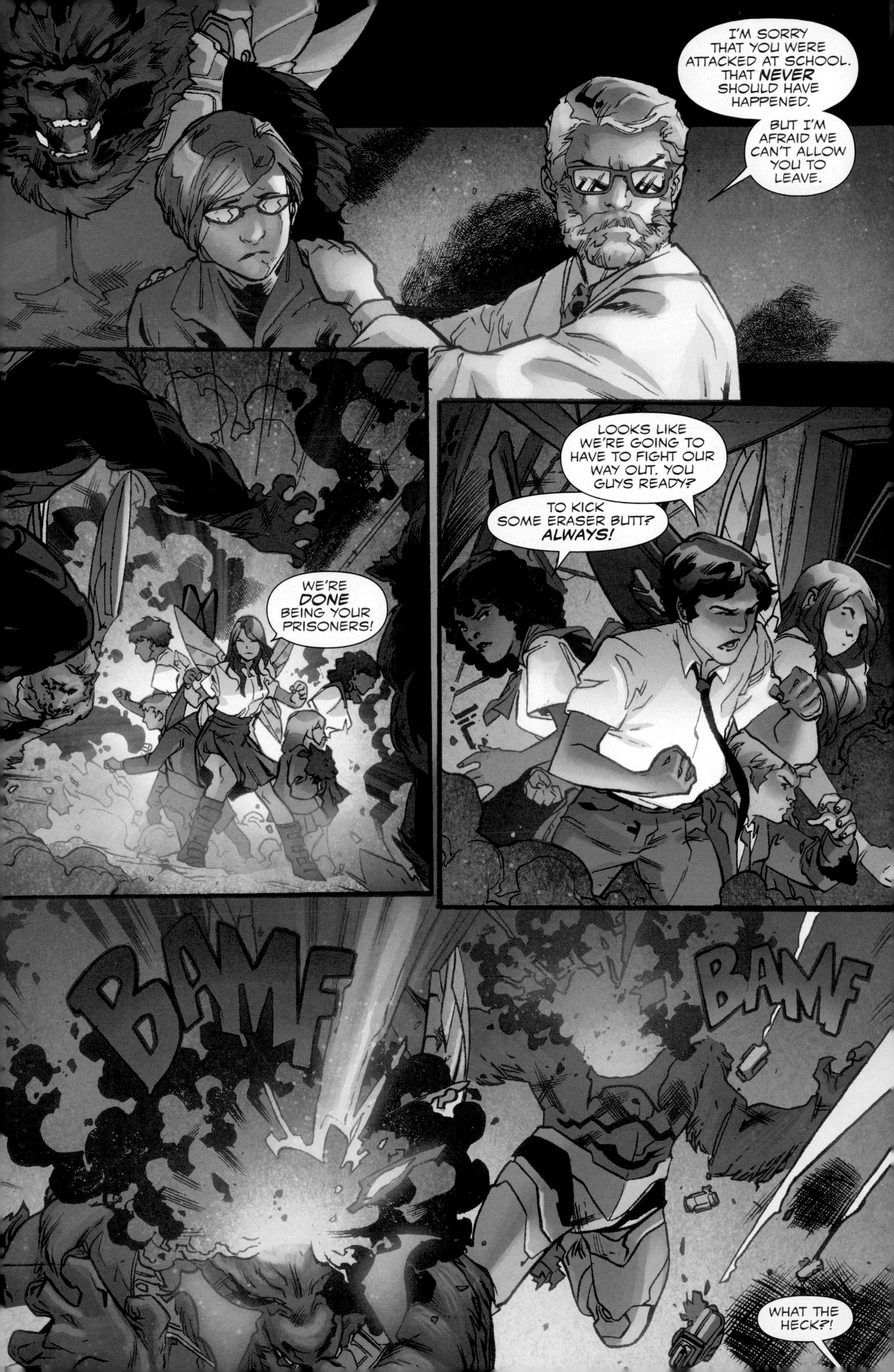
I'M SORRY THAT YOU WERE ATTACKED AT SCHOOL. THAT NEVER SHOULD HAVE HAPPENED.
BUT I'M AFRAID WE CAN'T ALLOW YOU TO LEAVE.
WE'RE DONE BEING YOUR PRISONERS!
LOOKS LIKE WE'RE GOING TO HAVE TO FIGHT OUR WAY OUT. YOU GUYS READY?
TO KICK SOME ERASER BUTT? ALWAYS!
BAMF
BAMF
WHAT THE HECK?!

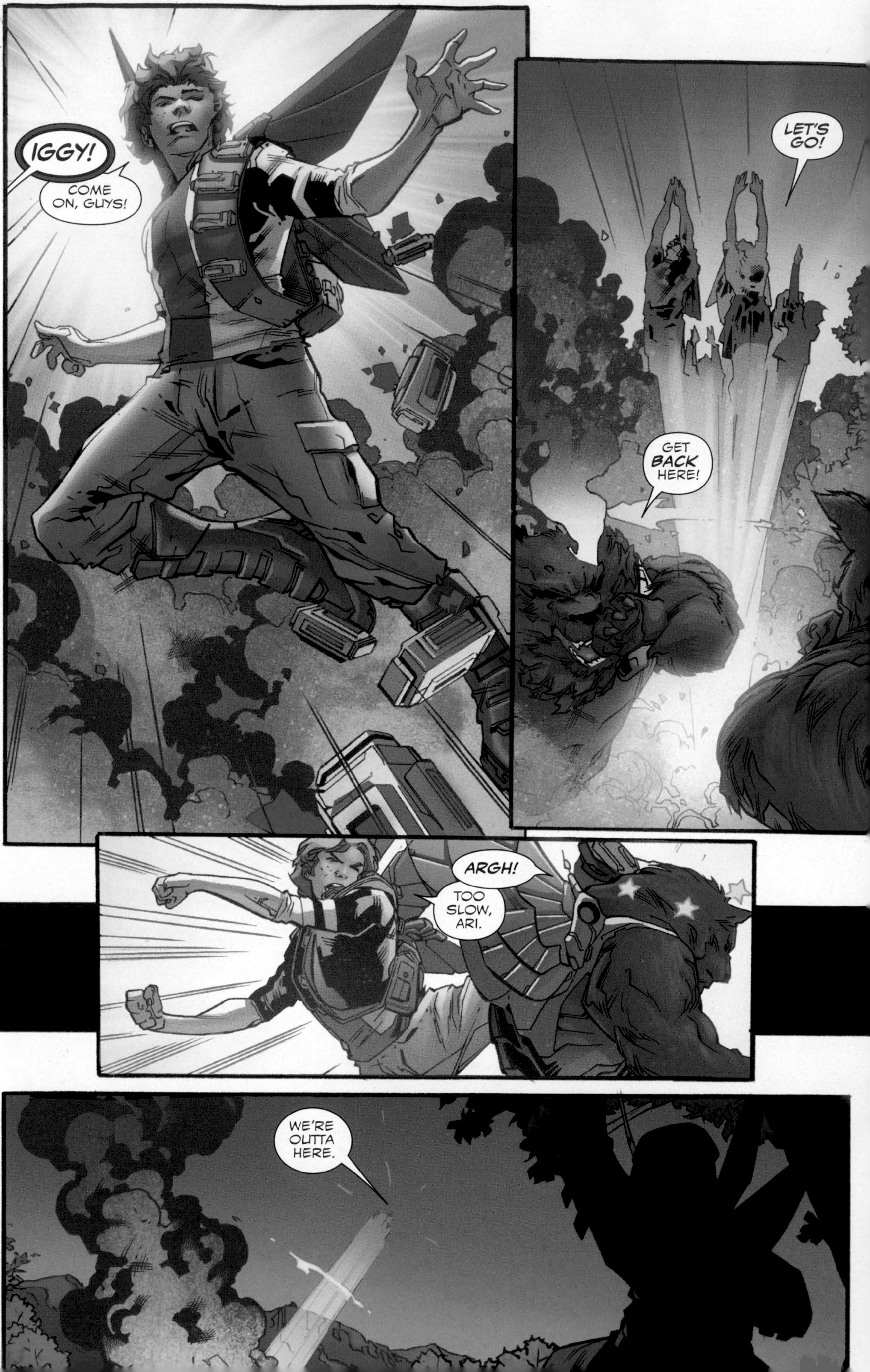
IGGY!
COME ON, GUYS!
LET'S GO!
GET BACK HERE!
ARGH!
TOO SLOW, ARI.
WE'RE OUTTA HERE.

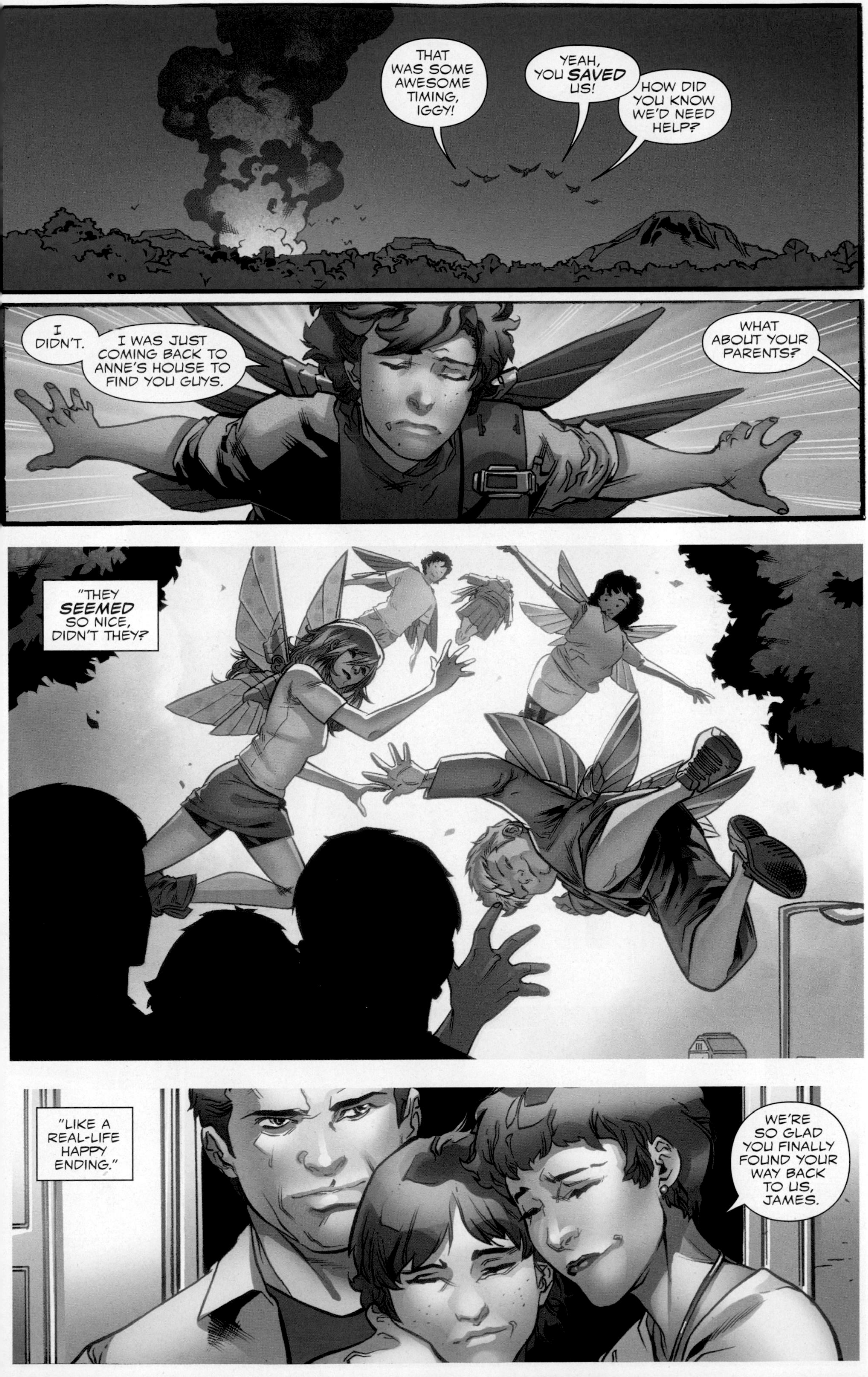
THAT WAS SOME AWESOME TIMING, IGGY!
YEAH, YOU SAVED US!
HOW DID YOU KNOW WE'D NEED HELP?
I DIDN'T.
I WAS JUST COMING BACK TO ANNE'S HOUSE TO FIND YOU GUYS.
WHAT ABOUT YOUR PARENTS?
"THEY SEEMED SO NICE, DIDN'T THEY?
"LIKE A REAL-LIFE HAPPY ENDING."
WE'RE SO GLAD YOU FINALLY FOUND YOUR WAY BACK TO US, JAMES.

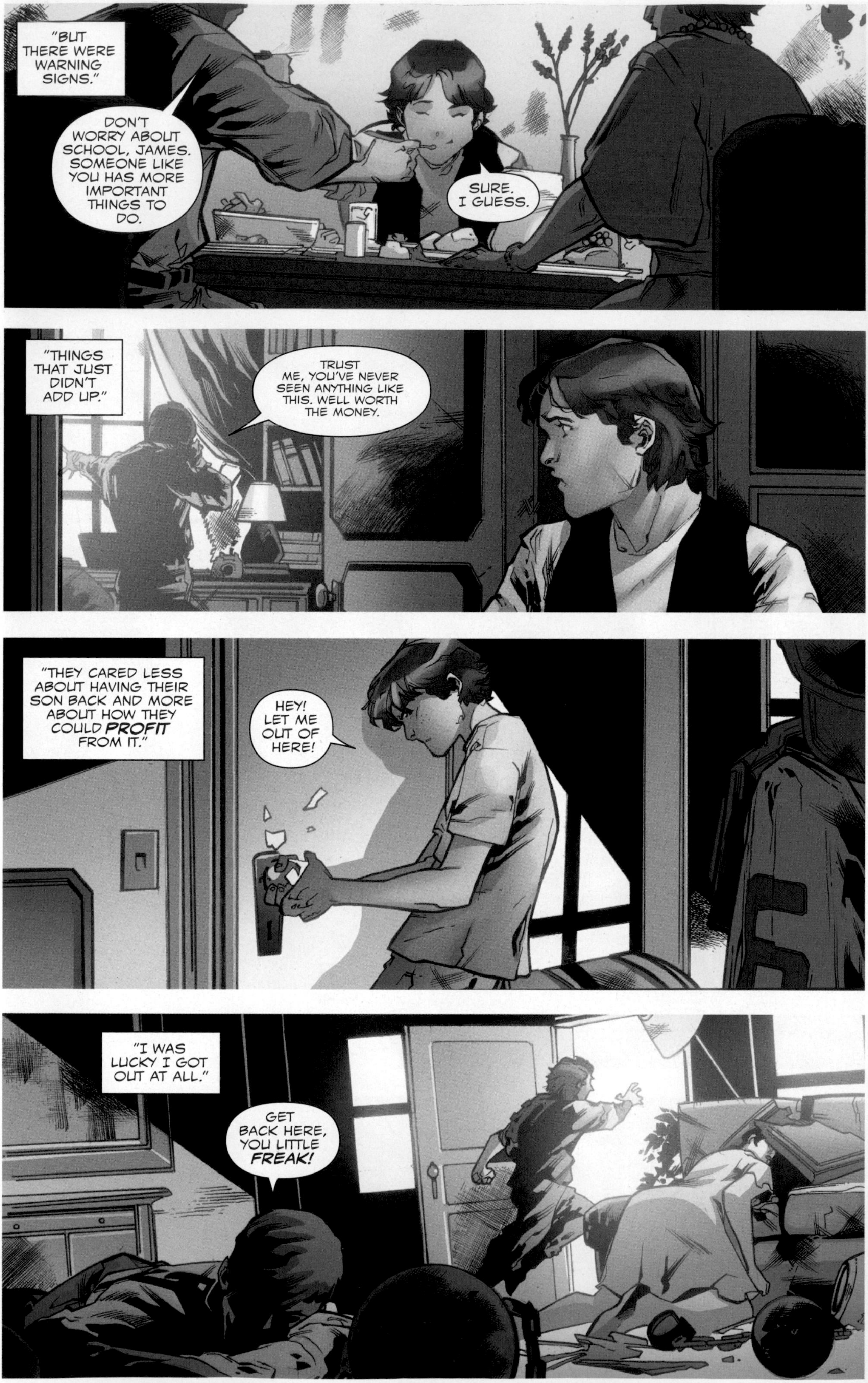
"BUT THERE WERE WARNING SIGNS."
DON'T WORRY ABOUT SCHOOL, JAMES. SOMEONE LIKE YOU HAS MORE IMPORTANT THINGS TO DO.
SURE. I GUESS.
"THINGS THAT JUST DIDN'T ADD UP."
TRUST ME, YOU'VE NEVER SEEN ANYTHING LIKE THIS. WELL WORTH THE MONEY.
"THEY CARED LESS ABOUT HAVING THEIR SON BACK AND MORE ABOUT HOW THEY COULD **PROFIT** FROM IT."
HEY! LET ME OUT OF HERE!
"I WAS LUCKY I GOT OUT AT ALL."
GET BACK HERE, YOU LITTLE **FREAK!**

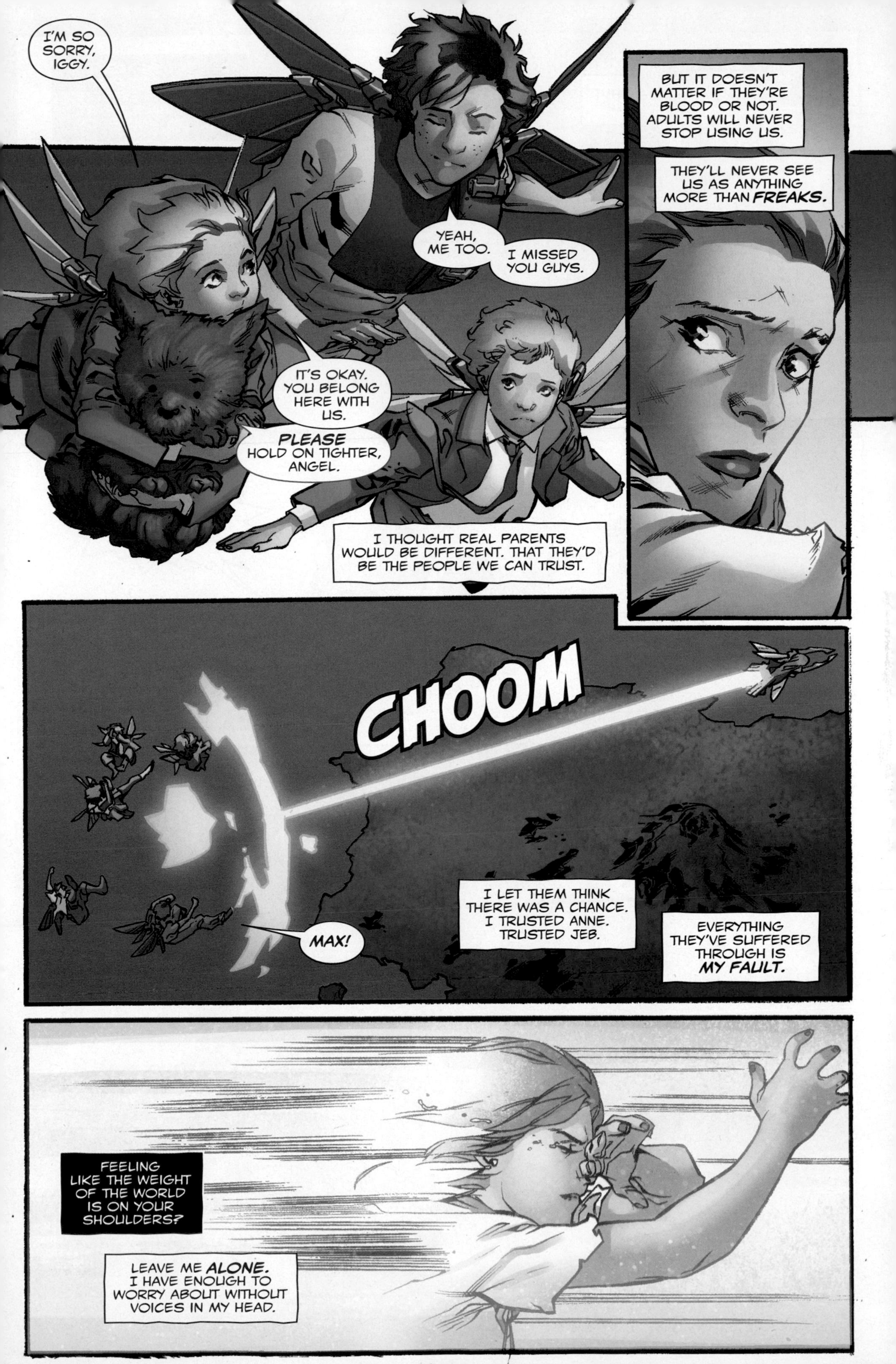
I'M SO SORRY, IGGY.
YEAH, ME TOO.
I MISSED YOU GUYS.
BUT IT DOESN'T MATTER IF THEY'RE BLOOD OR NOT. ADULTS WILL NEVER STOP USING US.
THEY'LL NEVER SEE US AS ANYTHING MORE THAN FREAKS.
IT'S OKAY. YOU BELONG HERE WITH US.
PLEASE HOLD ON TIGHTER, ANGEL.
I THOUGHT REAL PARENTS WOULD BE DIFFERENT. THAT THEY'D BE THE PEOPLE WE CAN TRUST.
CHOOM
I LET THEM THINK THERE WAS A CHANCE. I TRUSTED ANNE. TRUSTED JEB.
MAX!
EVERYTHING THEY'VE SUFFERED THROUGH IS MY FAULT.
FEELING LIKE THE WEIGHT OF THE WORLD IS ON YOUR SHOULDERS?
LEAVE ME ALONE. I HAVE ENOUGH TO WORRY ABOUT WITHOUT VOICES IN MY HEAD.

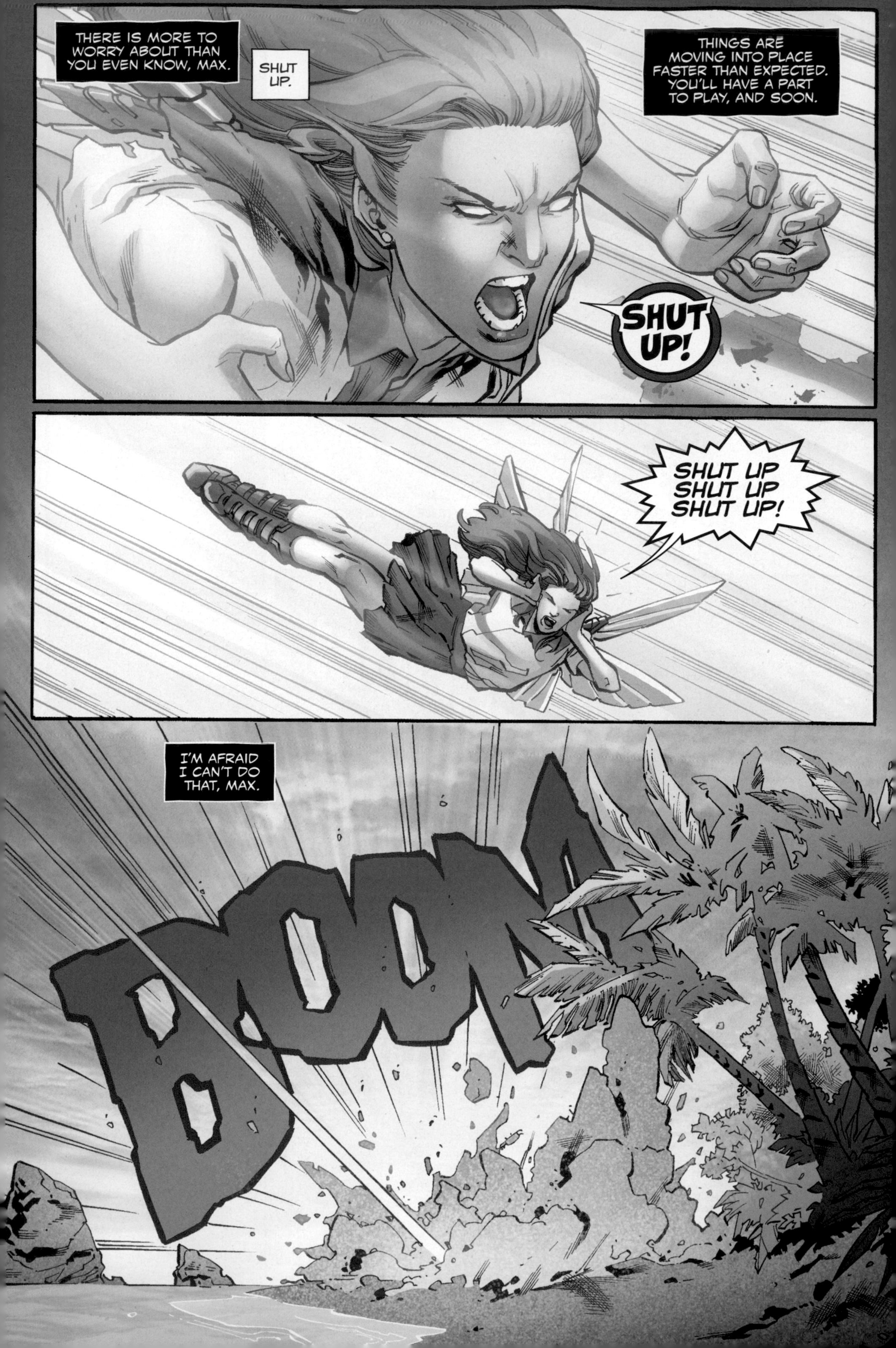
THERE IS MORE TO WORRY ABOUT THAN YOU EVEN KNOW, MAX.
SHUT UP.
THINGS ARE MOVING INTO PLACE FASTER THAN EXPECTED. YOU'LL HAVE A PART TO PLAY, AND SOON.
SHUT UP!
SHUT UP SHUT UP SHUT UP!
I'M AFRAID I CAN'T DO THAT, MAX.
BOOM

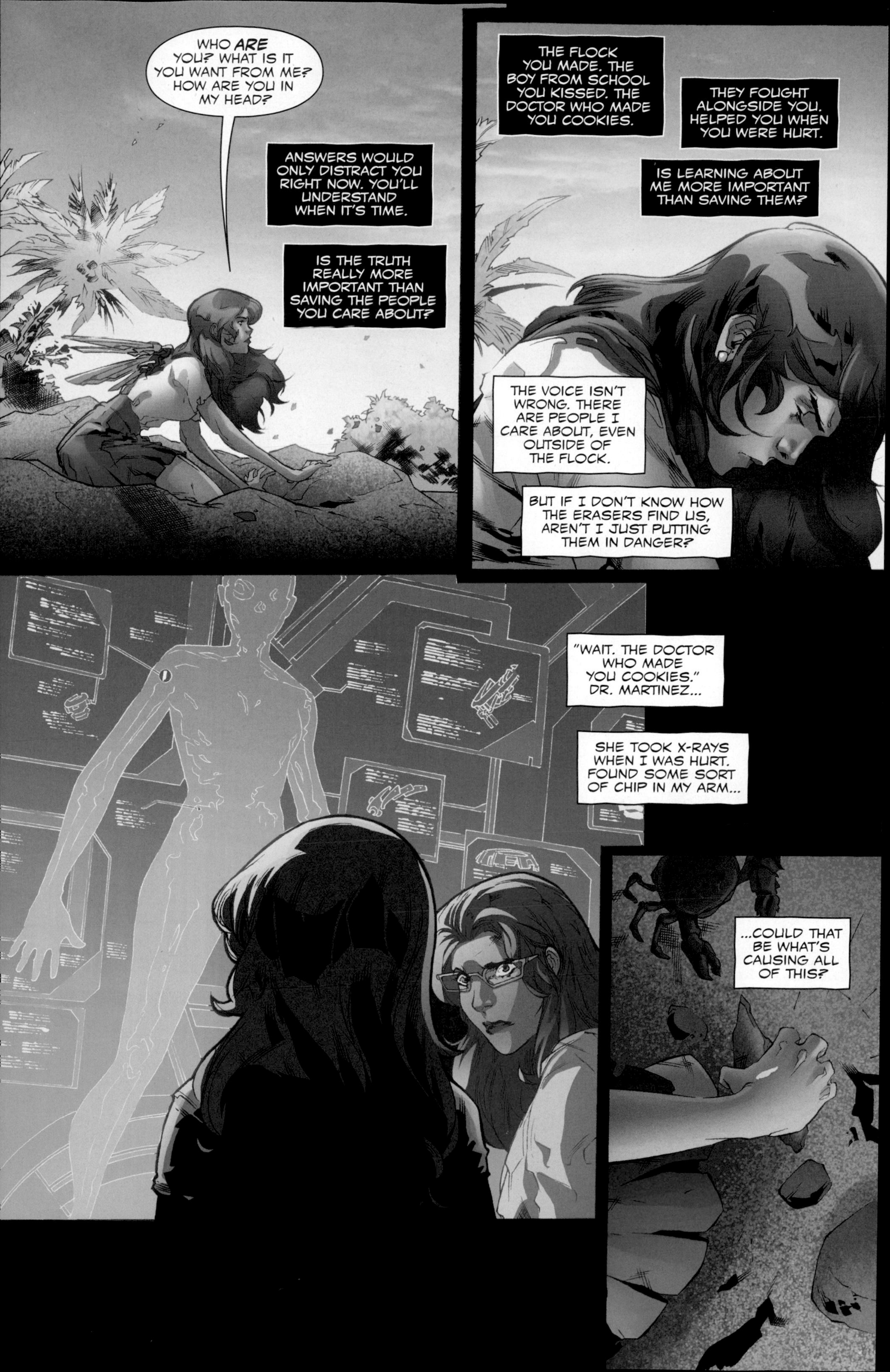

WHO ARE YOU? WHAT IS IT YOU WANT FROM ME? HOW ARE YOU IN MY HEAD?
ANSWERS WOULD ONLY DISTRACT YOU RIGHT NOW. YOU'LL UNDERSTAND WHEN IT'S TIME.
IS THE TRUTH REALLY MORE IMPORTANT THAN SAVING THE PEOPLE YOU CARE ABOUT?
THE FLOCK YOU MADE. THE BOY FROM SCHOOL YOU KISSED. THE DOCTOR WHO MADE YOU COOKIES.
THEY FOUGHT ALONGSIDE YOU. HELPED YOU WHEN YOU WERE HURT.
IS LEARNING ABOUT ME MORE IMPORTANT THAN SAVING THEM?
THE VOICE ISN'T WRONG. THERE ARE PEOPLE I CARE ABOUT, EVEN OUTSIDE OF THE FLOCK.
BUT IF I DON'T KNOW HOW THE ERASERS FIND US, AREN'T I JUST PUTTING THEM IN DANGER?
"WAIT. THE DOCTOR WHO MADE YOU COOKIES." DR. MARTINEZ...
SHE TOOK X-RAYS WHEN I WAS HURT. FOUND SOME SORT OF CHIP IN MY ARM...
...COULD THAT BE WHAT'S CAUSING ALL OF THIS?

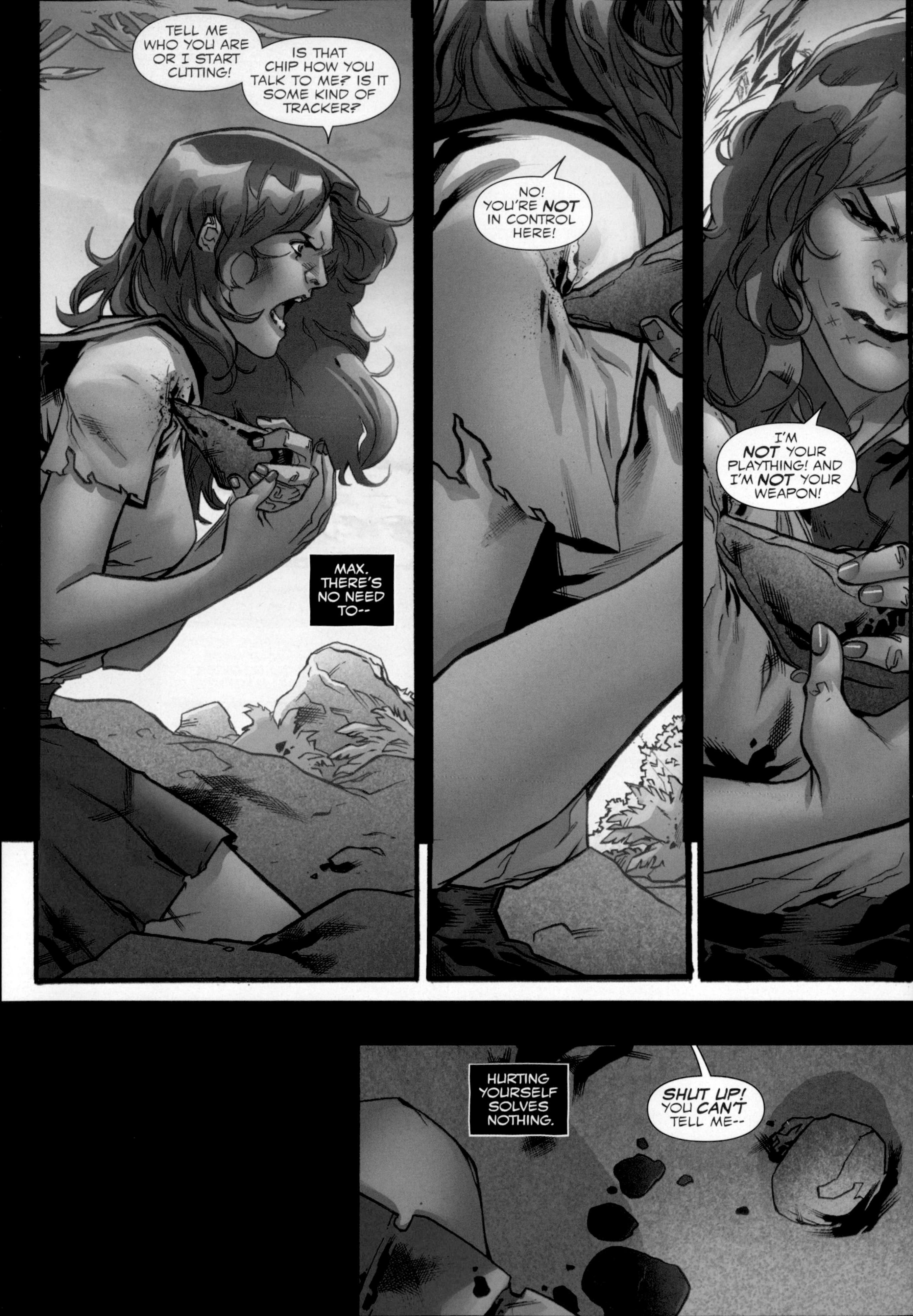
TELL ME WHO YOU ARE OR I START CUTTING!
IS THAT CHIP HOW YOU TALK TO ME? IS IT SOME KIND OF TRACKER?
MAX. THERE'S NO NEED TO--
NO! YOU'RE NOT IN CONTROL HERE!
I'M NOT YOUR PLAYTHING! AND I'M NOT YOUR WEAPON!
HURTING YOURSELF SOLVES NOTHING.
SHUT UP! YOU CAN'T TELL ME--

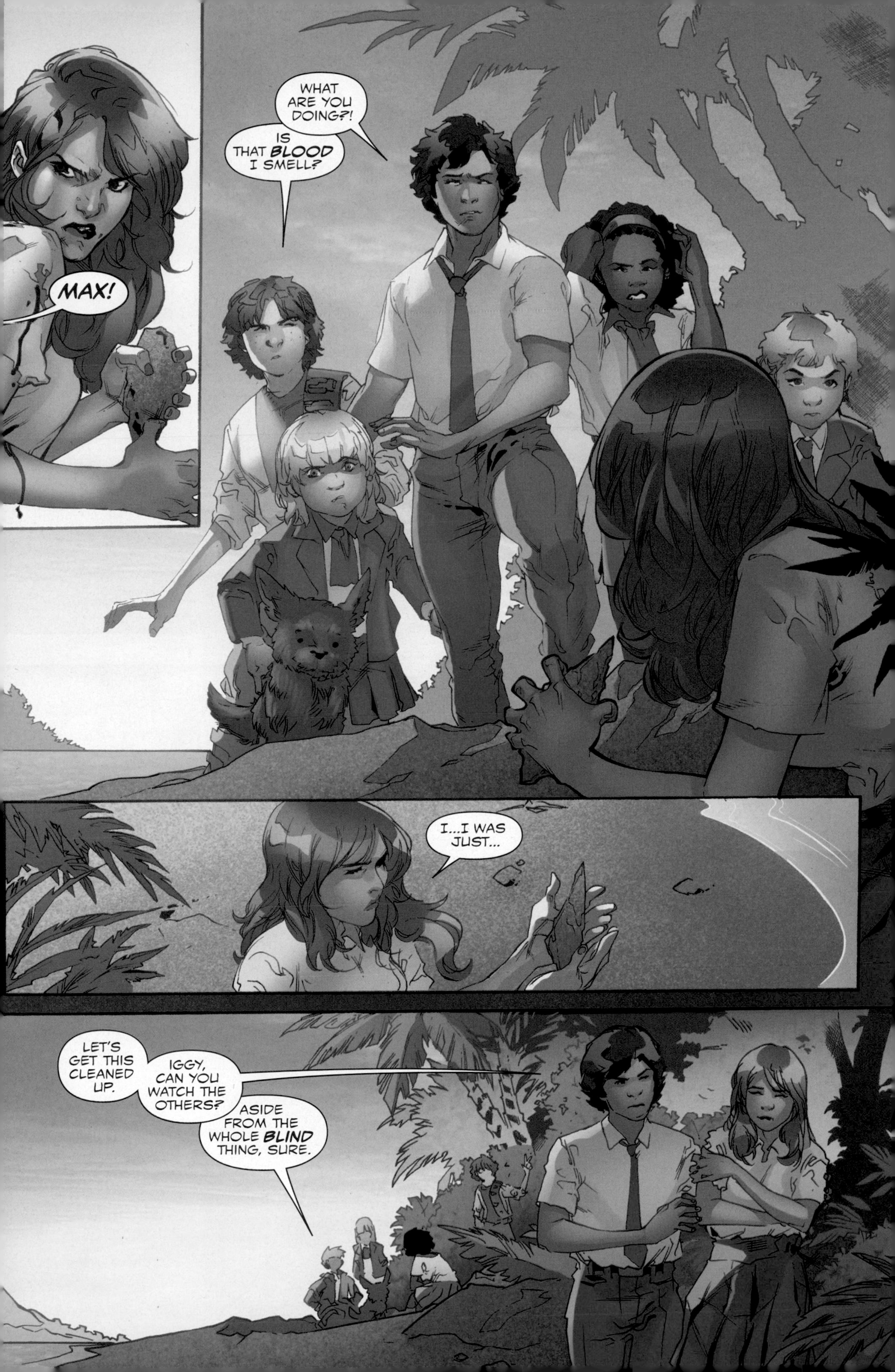
MAX!
WHAT ARE YOU DOING?!
IS THAT BLOOD I SMELL?
I...I WAS JUST...
LET'S GET THIS CLEANED UP.
IGGY, CAN YOU WATCH THE OTHERS?
ASIDE FROM THE WHOLE BLIND THING, SURE.

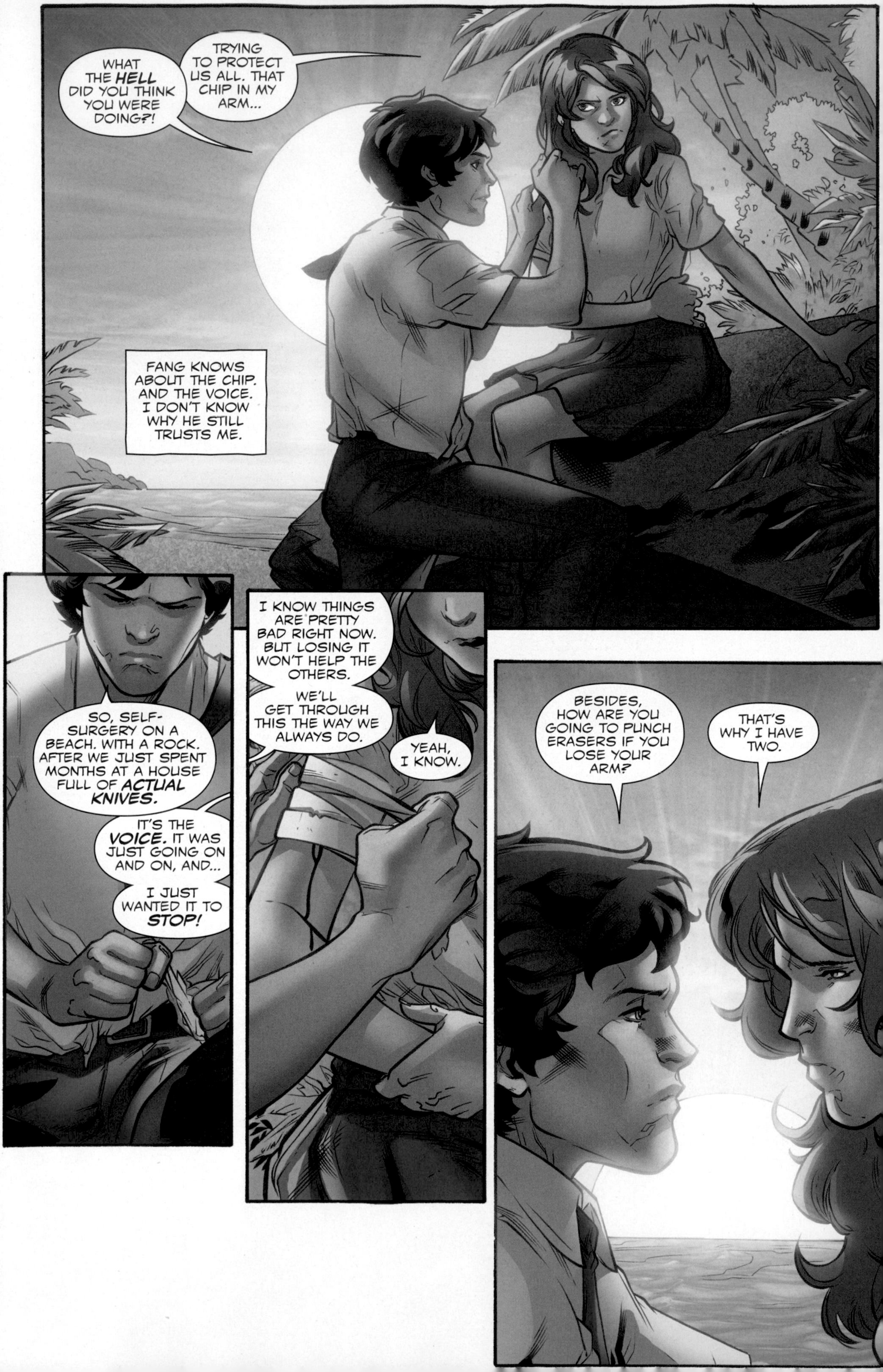
WHAT THE HELL DID YOU THINK YOU WERE DOING?!
TRYING TO PROTECT US ALL. THAT CHIP IN MY ARM...
FANG KNOWS ABOUT THE CHIP. AND THE VOICE. I DON'T KNOW WHY HE STILL TRUSTS ME.
SO, SELF-SURGERY ON A BEACH. WITH A ROCK. AFTER WE JUST SPENT MONTHS AT A HOUSE FULL OF ACTUAL KNIVES.
IT'S THE VOICE. IT WAS JUST GOING ON AND ON, AND...
I JUST WANTED IT TO STOP!
I KNOW THINGS ARE PRETTY BAD RIGHT NOW. BUT LOSING IT WON'T HELP THE OTHERS.
WE'LL GET THROUGH THIS THE WAY WE ALWAYS DO.
YEAH, I KNOW.
BESIDES, HOW ARE YOU GOING TO PUNCH ERASERS IF YOU LOSE YOUR ARM?
THAT'S WHY I HAVE TWO.

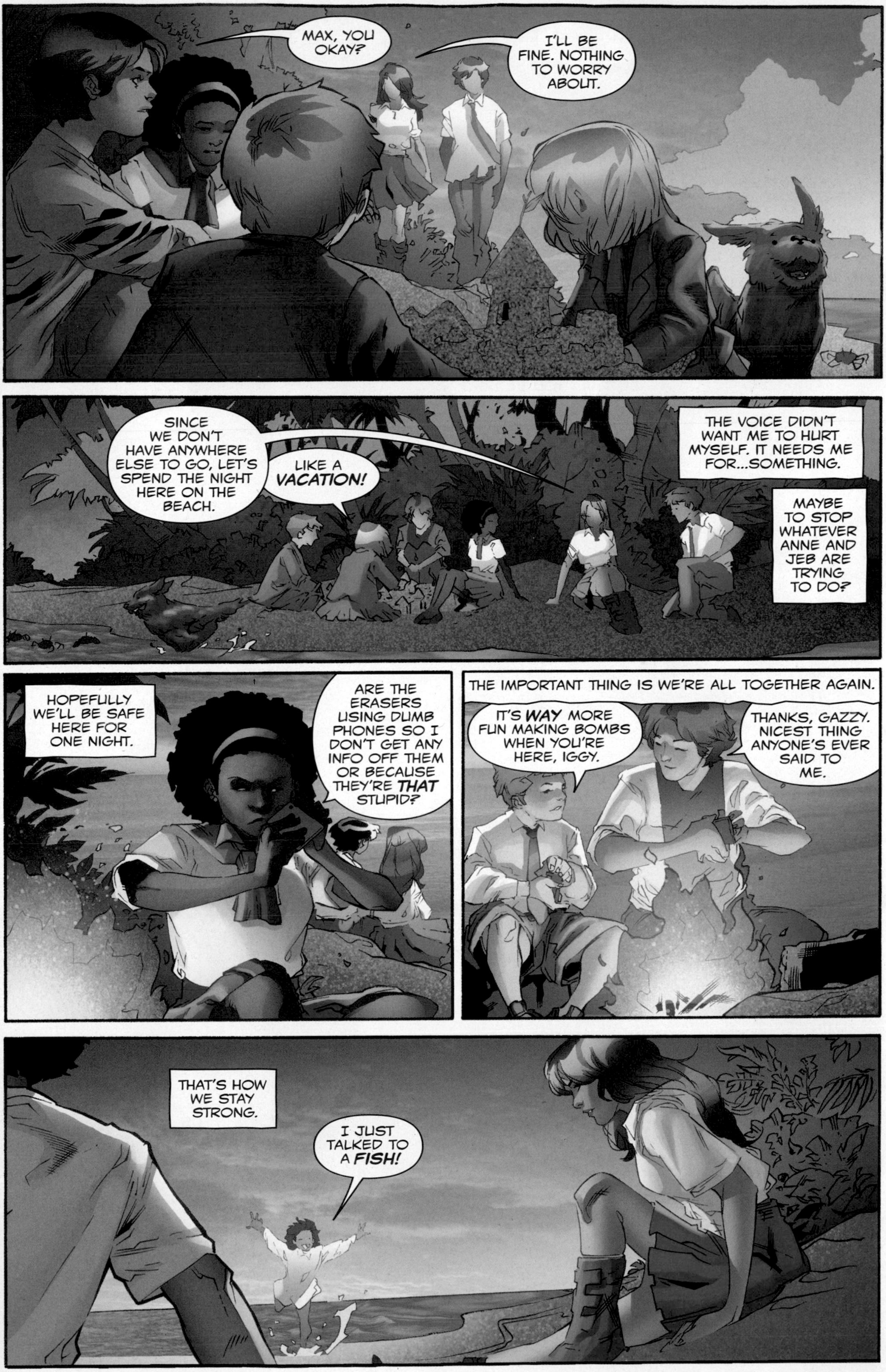
MAX, YOU OKAY?
I'LL BE FINE. NOTHING TO WORRY ABOUT.
SINCE WE DON'T HAVE ANYWHERE ELSE TO GO, LET'S SPEND THE NIGHT HERE ON THE BEACH.
LIKE A *VACATION!*
THE VOICE DIDN'T WANT ME TO HURT MYSELF. IT NEEDS ME FOR...SOMETHING.
MAYBE TO STOP WHATEVER ANNE AND JEB ARE TRYING TO DO?
HOPEFULLY WE'LL BE SAFE HERE FOR ONE NIGHT.
ARE THE ERASERS USING DUMB PHONES SO I DON'T GET ANY INFO OFF THEM OR BECAUSE THEY'RE *THAT* STUPID?
THE IMPORTANT THING IS WE'RE ALL TOGETHER AGAIN.
IT'S *WAY* MORE FUN MAKING BOMBS WHEN YOU'RE HERE, IGGY.
THANKS, GAZZY. NICEST THING ANYONE'S EVER SAID TO ME.
THAT'S HOW WE STAY STRONG.
I JUST TALKED TO A *FISH!*

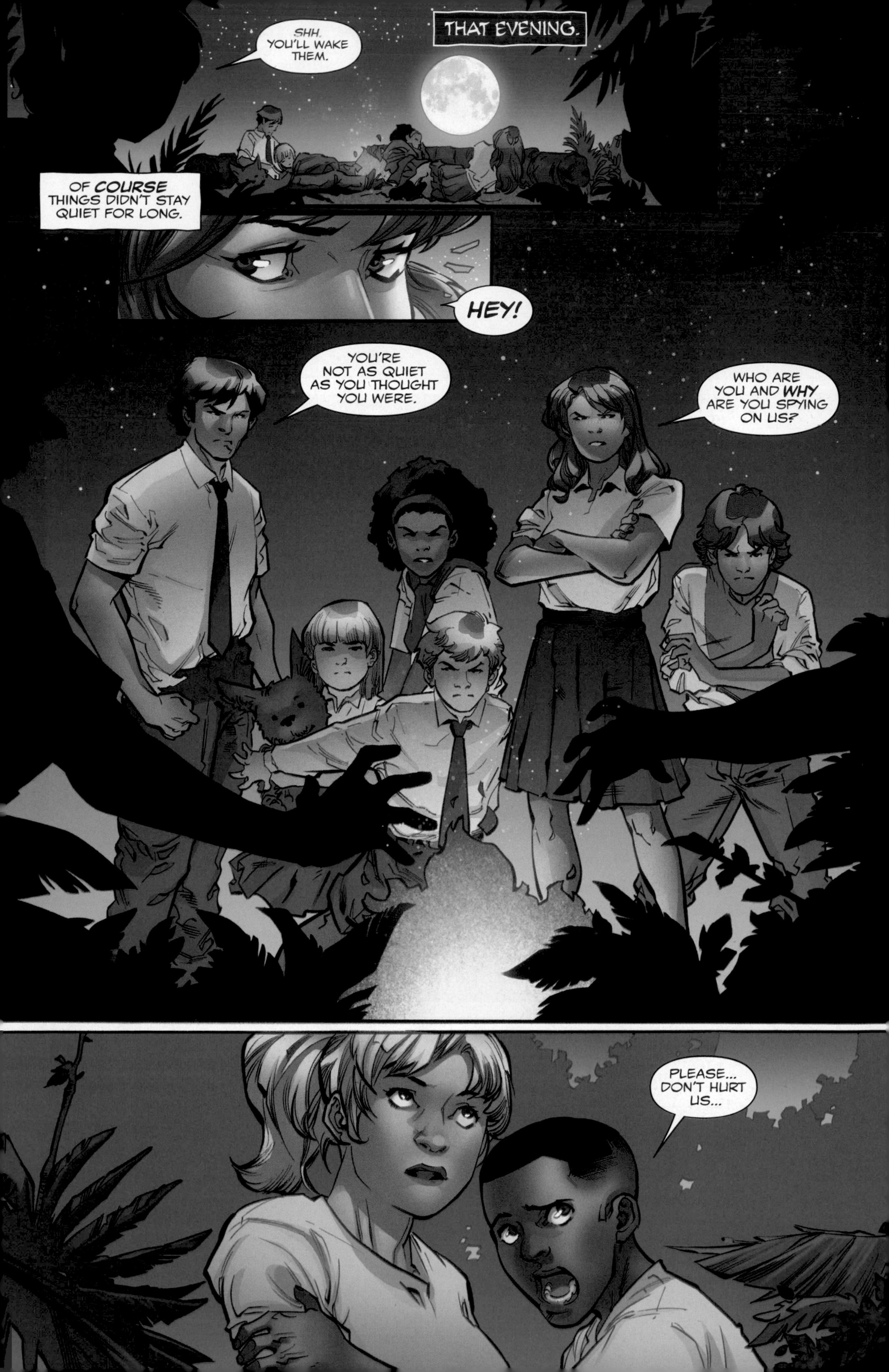
THAT EVENING.
SHH. YOU'LL WAKE THEM.
OF COURSE THINGS DIDN'T STAY QUIET FOR LONG.
HEY!
YOU'RE NOT AS QUIET AS YOU THOUGHT YOU WERE.
WHO ARE YOU AND WHY ARE YOU SPYING ON US?
PLEASE... DON'T HURT US...

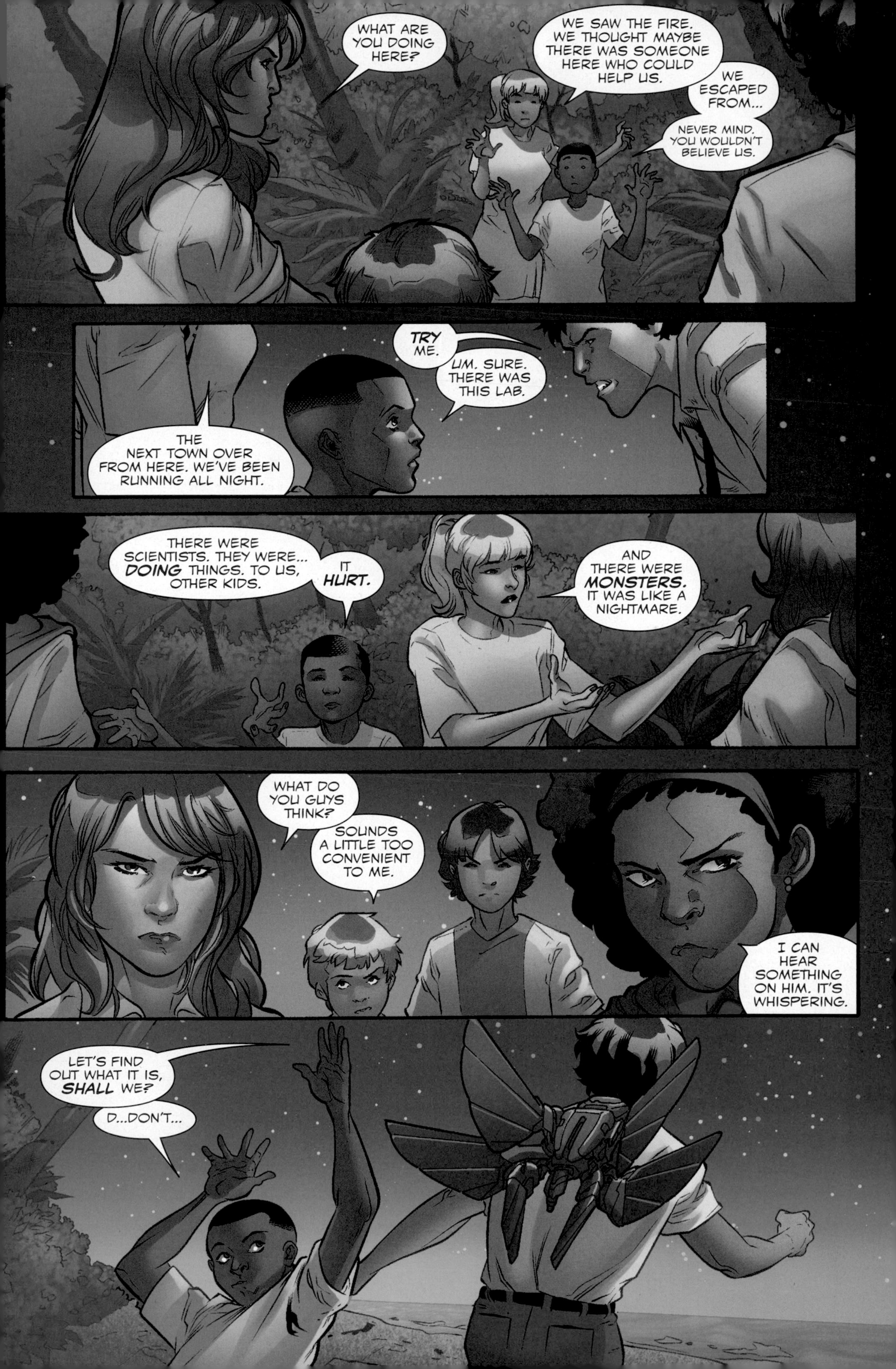
WHAT ARE YOU DOING HERE?
WE SAW THE FIRE. WE THOUGHT MAYBE THERE WAS SOMEONE HERE WHO COULD HELP US.
WE ESCAPED FROM...
NEVER MIND. YOU WOULDN'T BELIEVE US.
TRY ME.
UM. SURE. THERE WAS THIS LAB.
THE NEXT TOWN OVER FROM HERE. WE'VE BEEN RUNNING ALL NIGHT.
THERE WERE SCIENTISTS. THEY WERE... DOING THINGS. TO US, OTHER KIDS.
IT HURT.
AND THERE WERE MONSTERS. IT WAS LIKE A NIGHTMARE.
WHAT DO YOU GUYS THINK?
SOUNDS A LITTLE TOO CONVENIENT TO ME.
I CAN HEAR SOMETHING ON HIM. IT'S WHISPERING.
LET'S FIND OUT WHAT IT IS, SHALL WE?
D...DON'T...

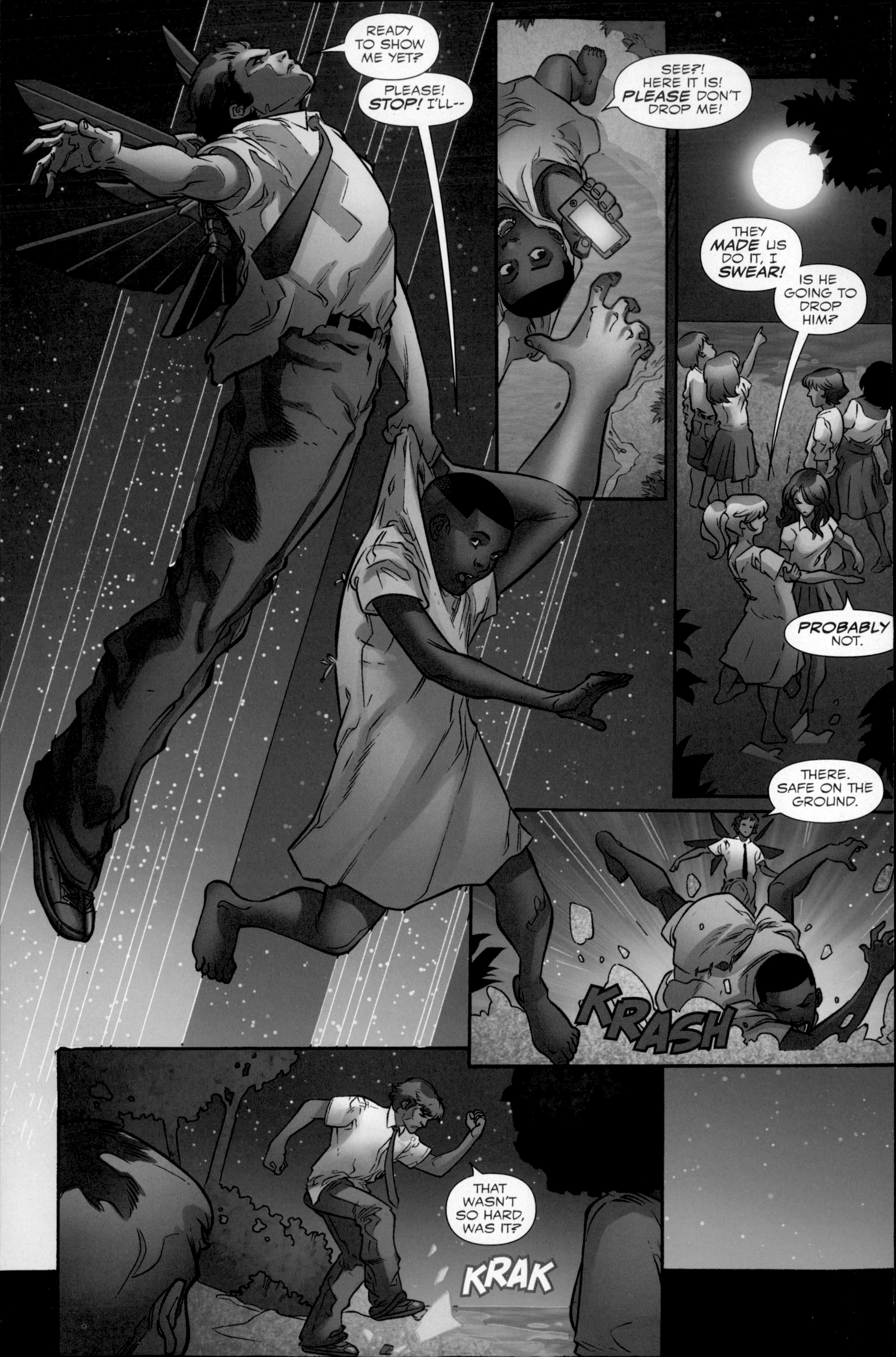

READY TO SHOW ME YET?
PLEASE! STOP! I'LL--
SEE?! HERE IT IS! PLEASE DON'T DROP ME!
THEY MADE US DO IT, I SWEAR!
IS HE GOING TO DROP HIM?
PROBABLY NOT.
THERE. SAFE ON THE GROUND.
KRASH
THAT WASN'T SO HARD, WAS IT?
KRAK

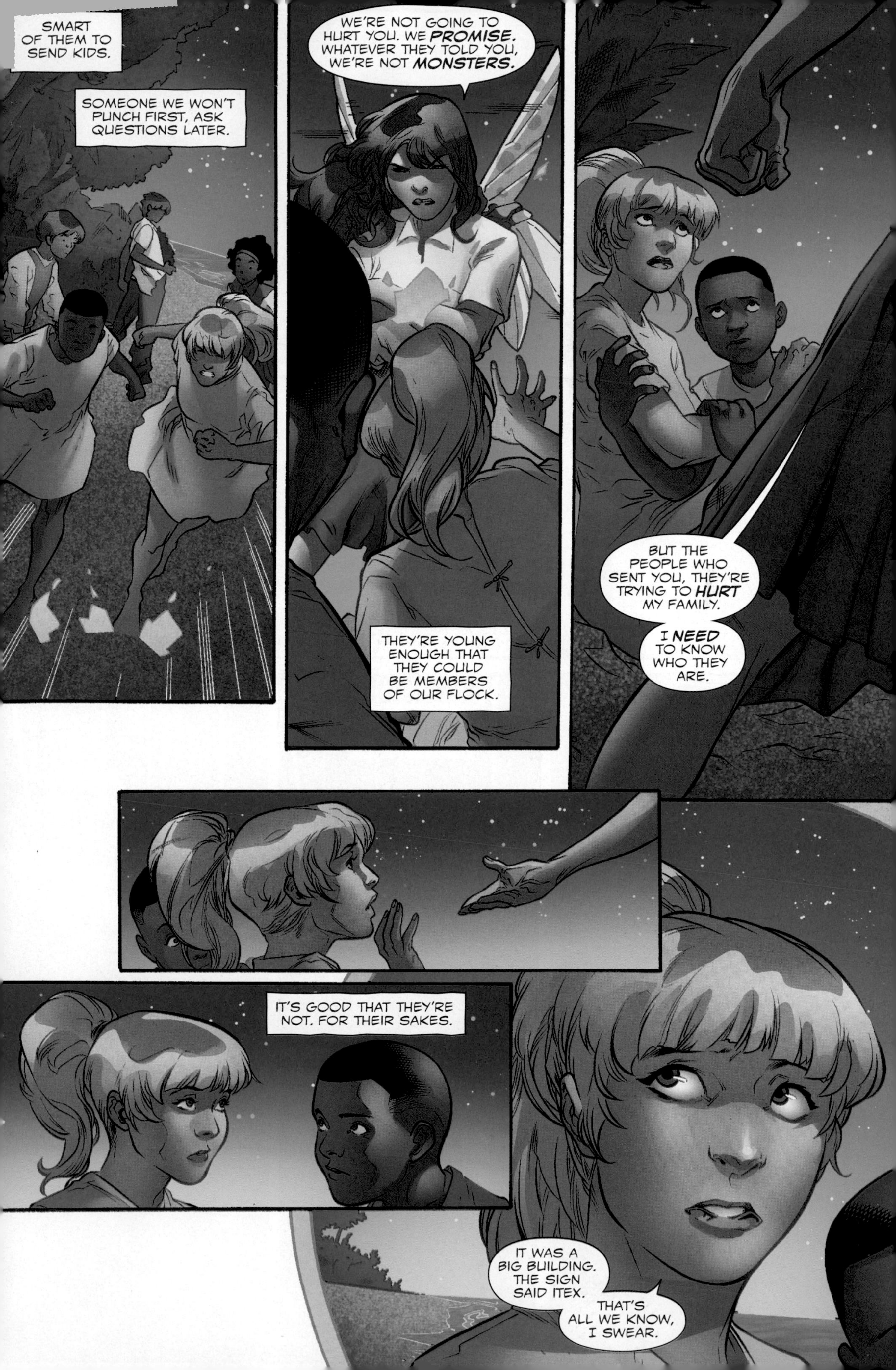

SMART OF THEM TO SEND KIDS.
SOMEONE WE WON'T PUNCH FIRST, ASK QUESTIONS LATER.
WE'RE NOT GOING TO HURT YOU. WE PROMISE. WHATEVER THEY TOLD YOU, WE'RE NOT MONSTERS.
THEY'RE YOUNG ENOUGH THAT THEY COULD BE MEMBERS OF OUR FLOCK.
BUT THE PEOPLE WHO SENT YOU, THEY'RE TRYING TO HURT MY FAMILY.
I NEED TO KNOW WHO THEY ARE.
IT'S GOOD THAT THEY'RE NOT. FOR THEIR SAKES.
IT WAS A BIG BUILDING. THE SIGN SAID ITEX.
THAT'S ALL WE KNOW, I SWEAR.

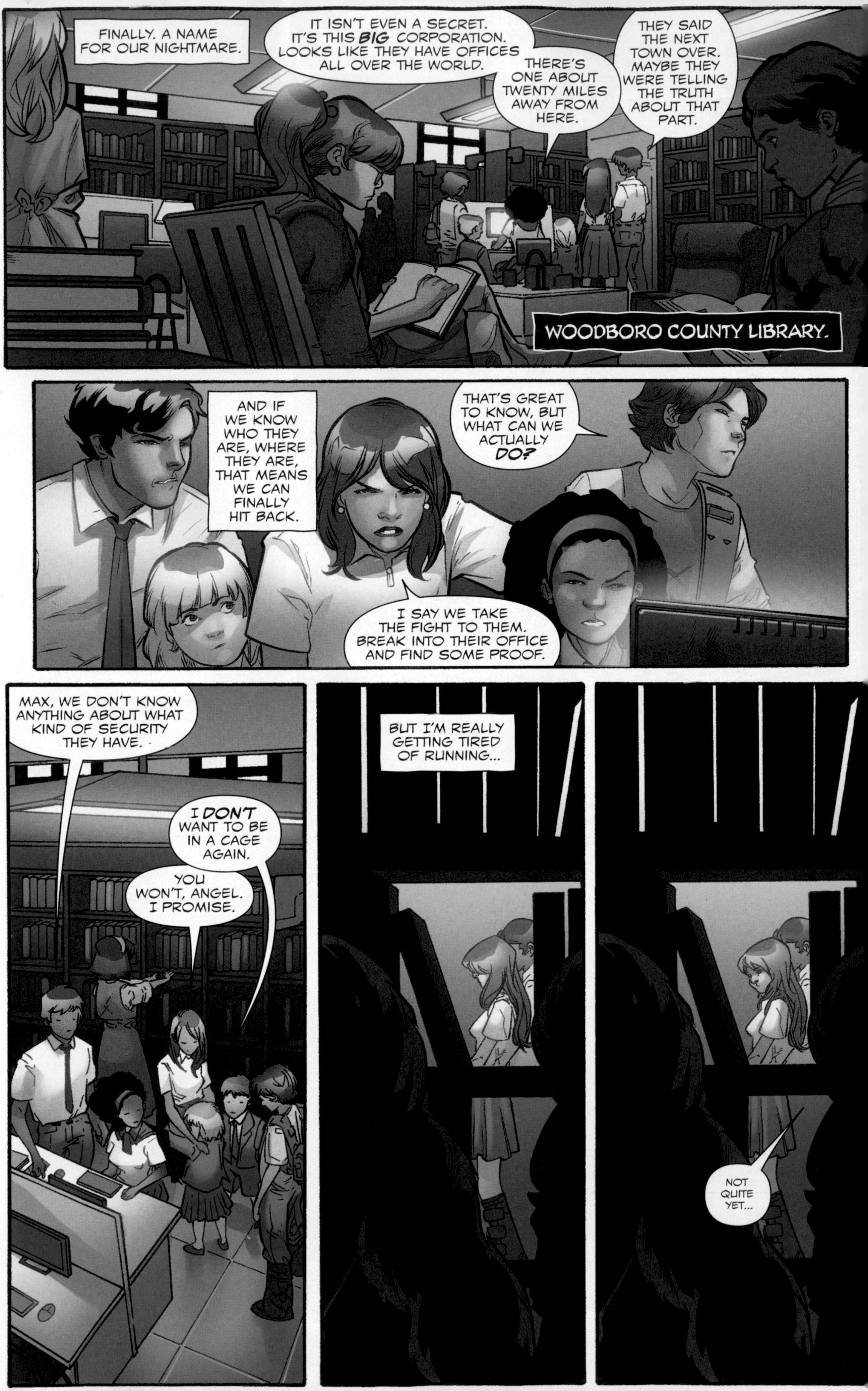
FINALLY. A NAME FOR OUR NIGHTMARE.
IT ISN'T EVEN A SECRET. IT'S THIS BIG CORPORATION. LOOKS LIKE THEY HAVE OFFICES ALL OVER THE WORLD.
THERE'S ONE ABOUT TWENTY MILES AWAY FROM HERE.
THEY SAID THE NEXT TOWN OVER. MAYBE THEY WERE TELLING THE TRUTH ABOUT THAT PART.
WOODBORO COUNTY LIBRARY.
AND IF WE KNOW WHO THEY ARE, WHERE THEY ARE, THAT MEANS WE CAN FINALLY HIT BACK.
THAT'S GREAT TO KNOW, BUT WHAT CAN WE ACTUALLY DO?
I SAY WE TAKE THE FIGHT TO THEM. BREAK INTO THEIR OFFICE AND FIND SOME PROOF.
MAX, WE DON'T KNOW ANYTHING ABOUT WHAT KIND OF SECURITY THEY HAVE.
I DON'T WANT TO BE IN A CAGE AGAIN.
YOU WON'T, ANGEL. I PROMISE.
BUT I'M REALLY GETTING TIRED OF RUNNING...
NOT QUITE YET...

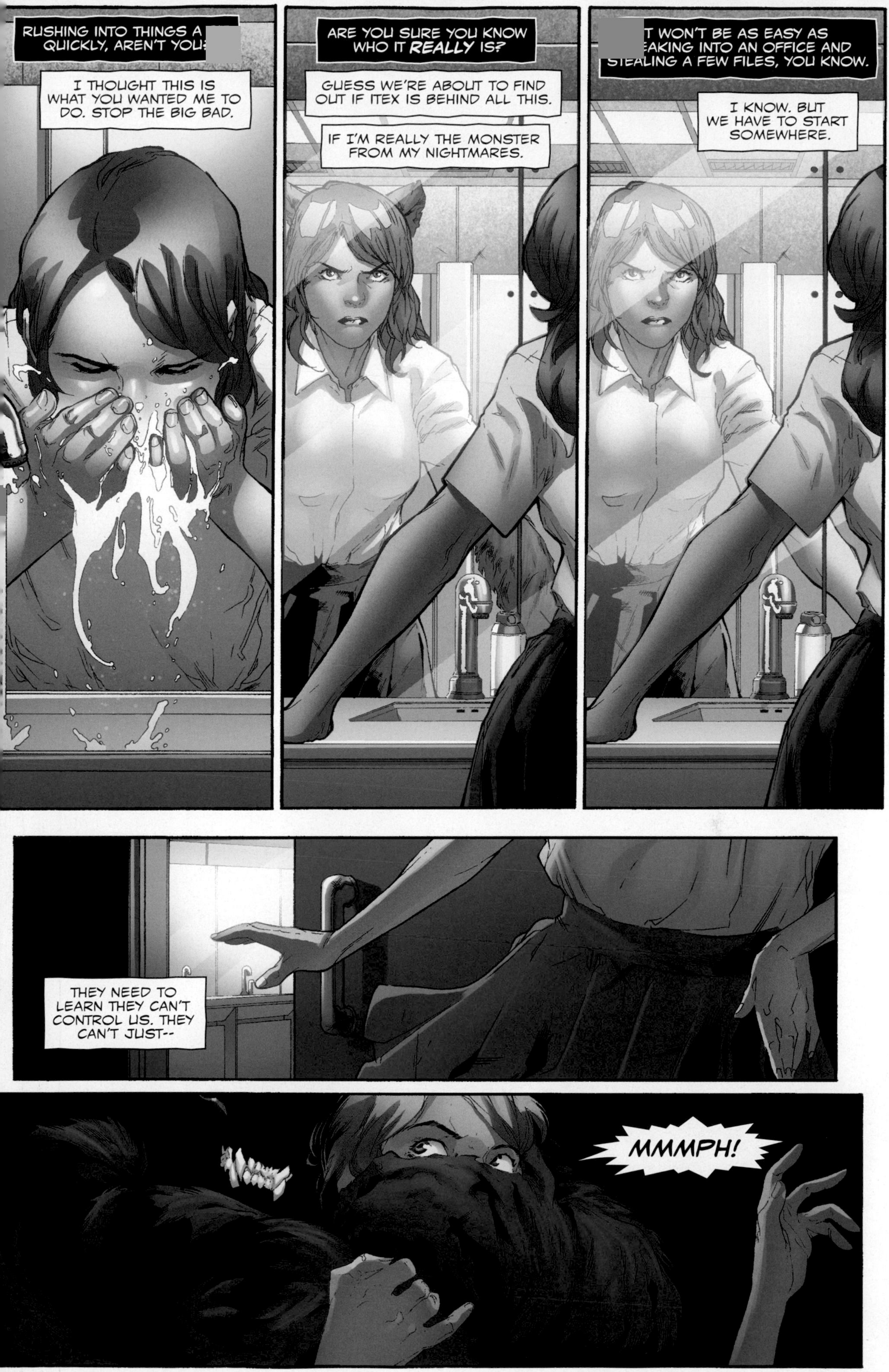
RUSHING INTO THINGS A [redacted] QUICKLY, AREN'T YOU[redacted]
I THOUGHT THIS IS WHAT YOU WANTED ME TO DO. STOP THE BIG BAD.
ARE YOU SURE YOU KNOW WHO IT *REALLY* IS?
GUESS WE'RE ABOUT TO FIND OUT IF ITEX IS BEHIND ALL THIS.
IF I'M REALLY THE MONSTER FROM MY NIGHTMARES.
[redacted]T WON'T BE AS EASY AS [redacted]EAKING INTO AN OFFICE AND STEALING A FEW FILES, YOU KNOW.
I KNOW. BUT WE HAVE TO START SOMEWHERE.
THEY NEED TO LEARN THEY CAN'T CONTROL US. THEY CAN'T JUST--
MMMPH!

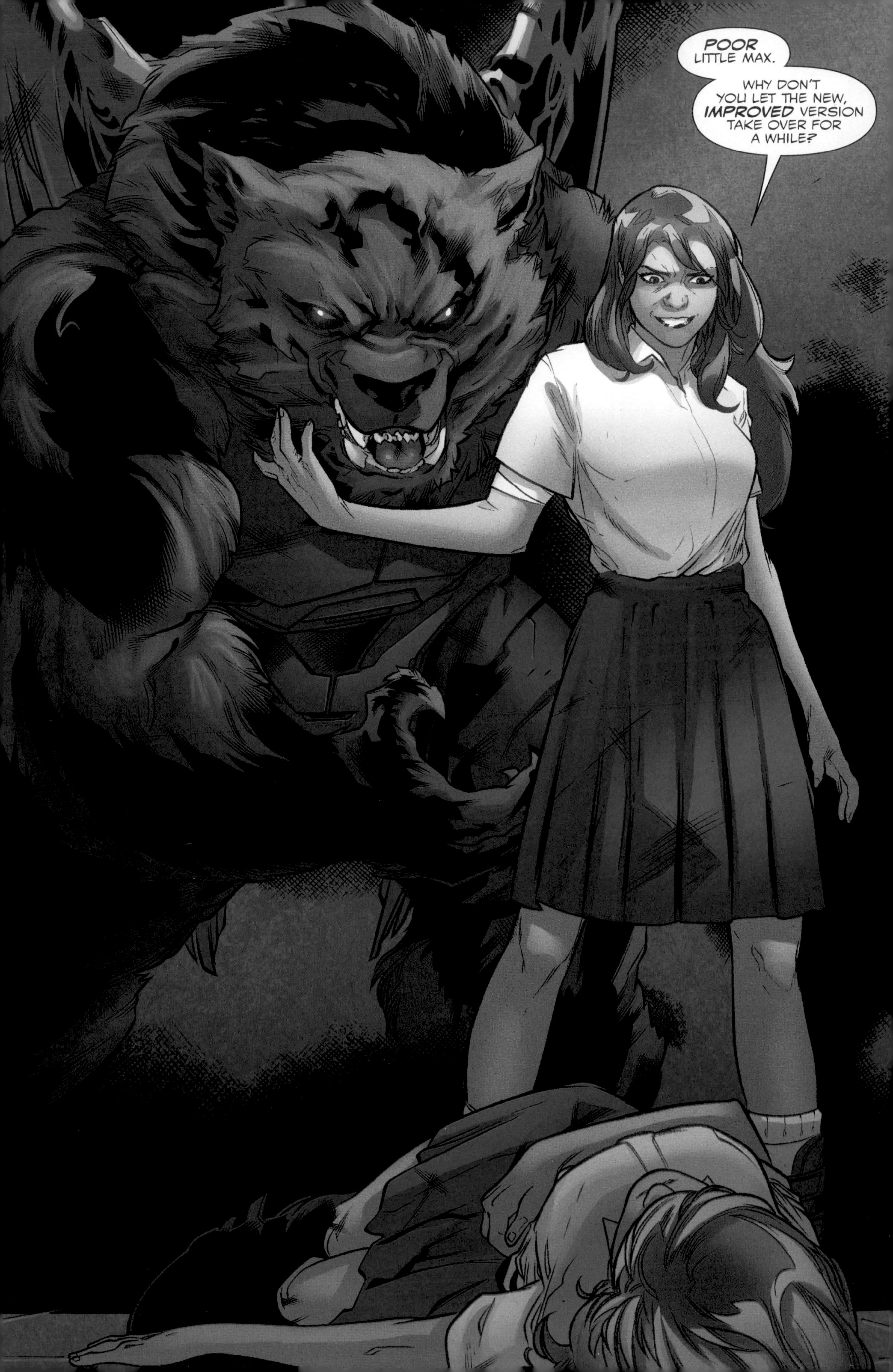
POOR LITTLE MAX.
WHY DON'T YOU LET THE NEW, IMPROVED VERSION TAKE OVER FOR A WHILE?

CHAPTER 5

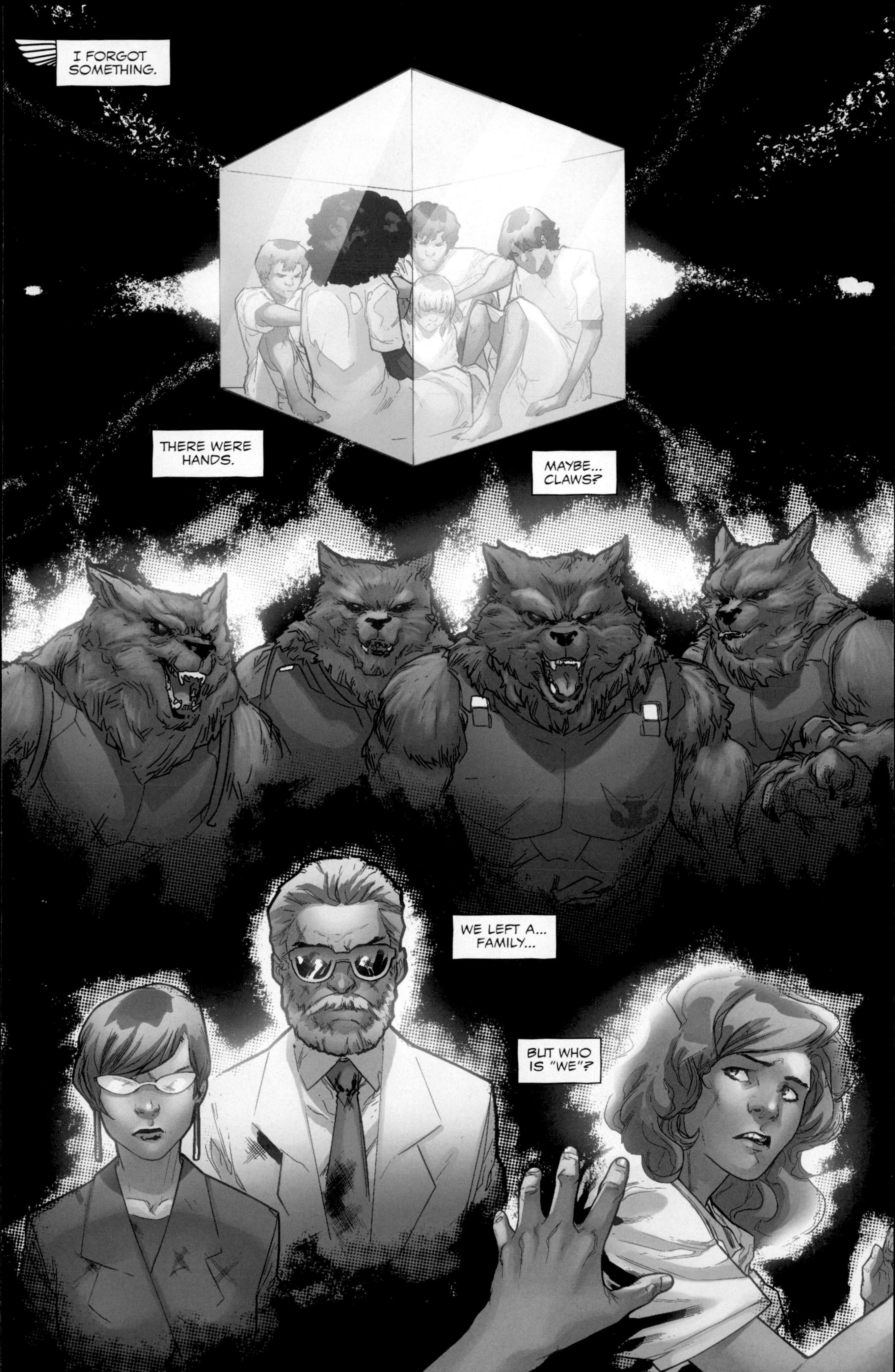
I FORGOT SOMETHING.
THERE WERE HANDS.
MAYBE... CLAWS?
WE LEFT A... FAMILY...
BUT WHO IS "WE"?

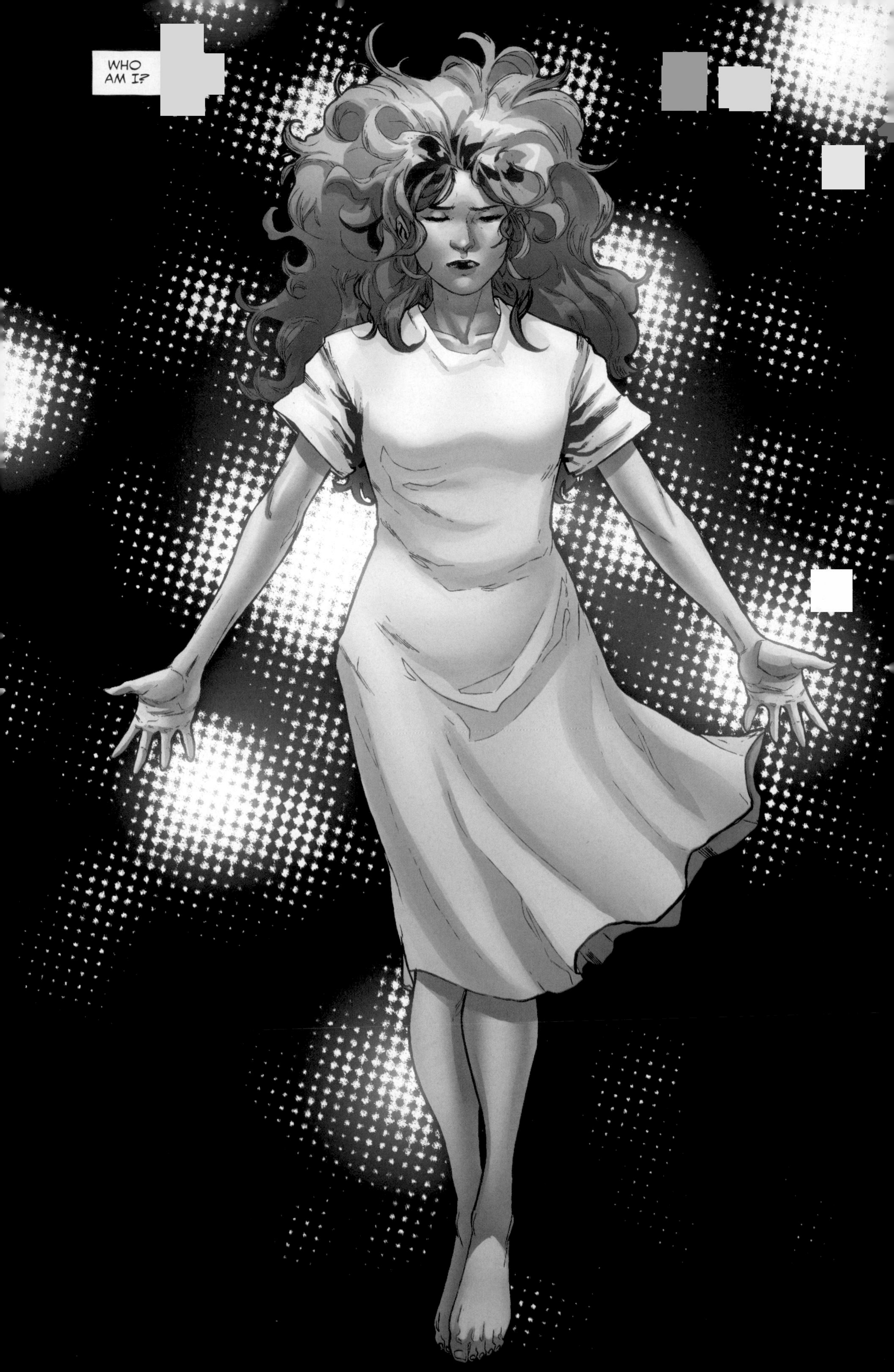
WHO AM I?

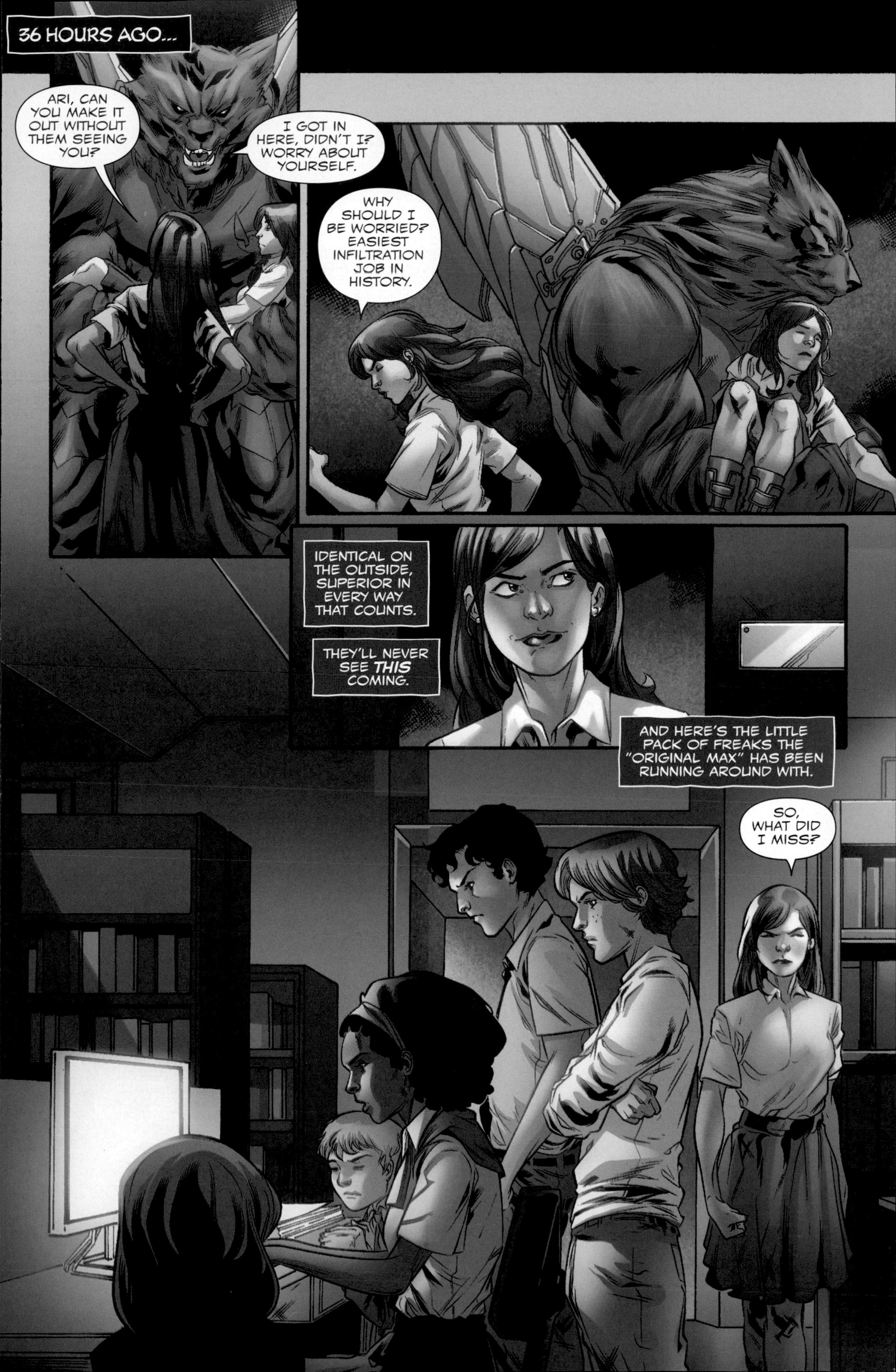
36 HOURS AGO...
ARI, CAN YOU MAKE IT OUT WITHOUT THEM SEEING YOU?
I GOT IN HERE, DIDN'T I? WORRY ABOUT YOURSELF.
WHY SHOULD I BE WORRIED? EASIEST INFILTRATION JOB IN HISTORY.
IDENTICAL ON THE OUTSIDE, SUPERIOR IN EVERY WAY THAT COUNTS.
THEY'LL NEVER SEE THIS COMING.
AND HERE'S THE LITTLE PACK OF FREAKS THE "ORIGINAL MAX" HAS BEEN RUNNING AROUND WITH.
SO, WHAT DID I MISS?

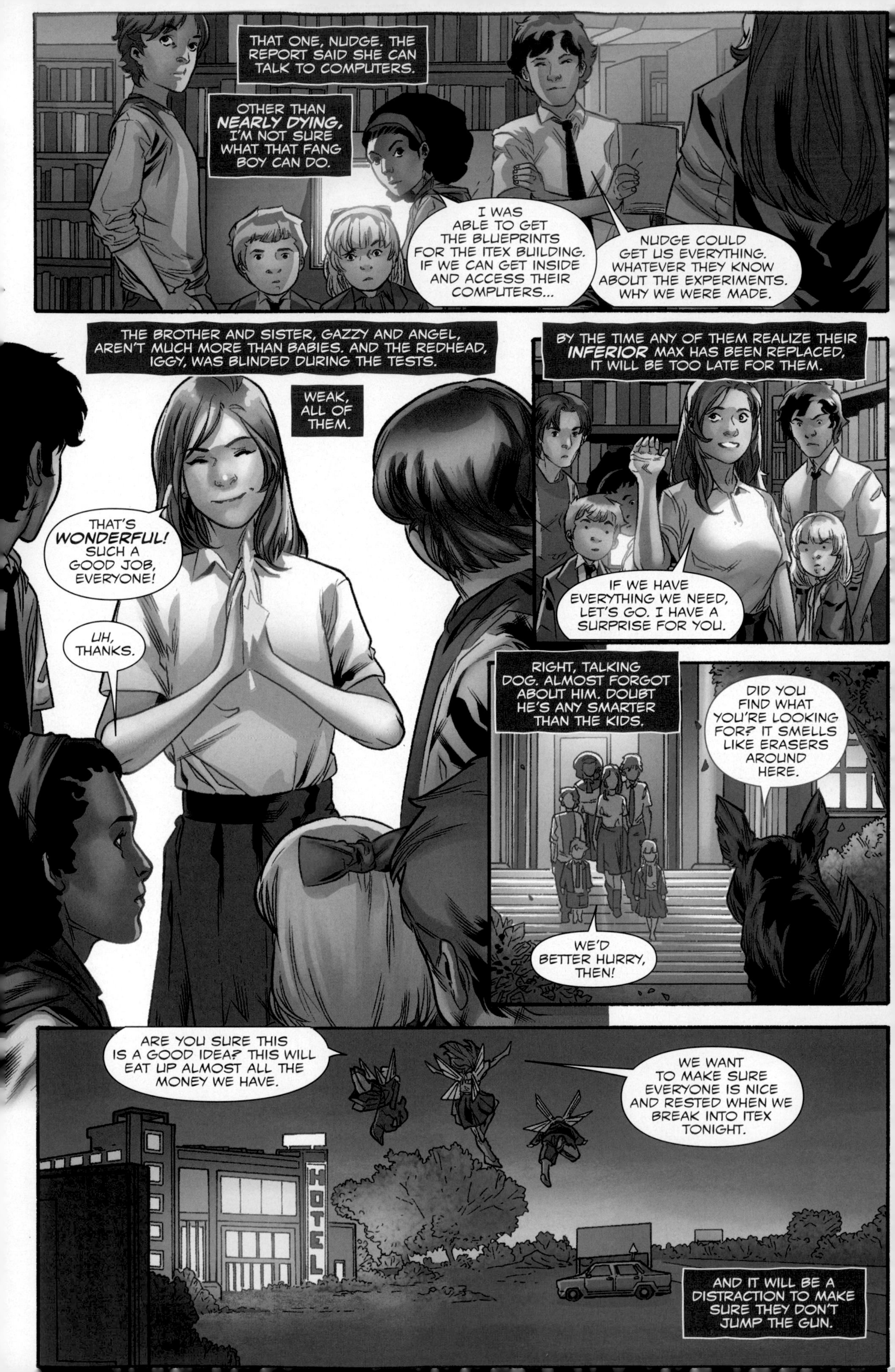
THAT ONE, NUDGE. THE REPORT SAID SHE CAN TALK TO COMPUTERS.
OTHER THAN NEARLY DYING, I'M NOT SURE WHAT THAT FANG BOY CAN DO.
I WAS ABLE TO GET THE BLUEPRINTS FOR THE ITEX BUILDING. IF WE CAN GET INSIDE AND ACCESS THEIR COMPUTERS...
NUDGE COULD GET US EVERYTHING. WHATEVER THEY KNOW ABOUT THE EXPERIMENTS. WHY WE WERE MADE.
THE BROTHER AND SISTER, GAZZY AND ANGEL, AREN'T MUCH MORE THAN BABIES. AND THE REDHEAD, IGGY, WAS BLINDED DURING THE TESTS.
WEAK, ALL OF THEM.
THAT'S WONDERFUL! SUCH A GOOD JOB, EVERYONE!
UH, THANKS.
BY THE TIME ANY OF THEM REALIZE THEIR INFERIOR MAX HAS BEEN REPLACED, IT WILL BE TOO LATE FOR THEM.
IF WE HAVE EVERYTHING WE NEED, LET'S GO. I HAVE A SURPRISE FOR YOU.
RIGHT, TALKING DOG. ALMOST FORGOT ABOUT HIM. DOUBT HE'S ANY SMARTER THAN THE KIDS.
DID YOU FIND WHAT YOU'RE LOOKING FOR? IT SMELLS LIKE ERASERS AROUND HERE.
WE'D BETTER HURRY, THEN!
ARE YOU SURE THIS IS A GOOD IDEA? THIS WILL EAT UP ALMOST ALL THE MONEY WE HAVE.
WE WANT TO MAKE SURE EVERYONE IS NICE AND RESTED WHEN WE BREAK INTO ITEX TONIGHT.
HOTEL
AND IT WILL BE A DISTRACTION TO MAKE SURE THEY DON'T JUMP THE GUN.

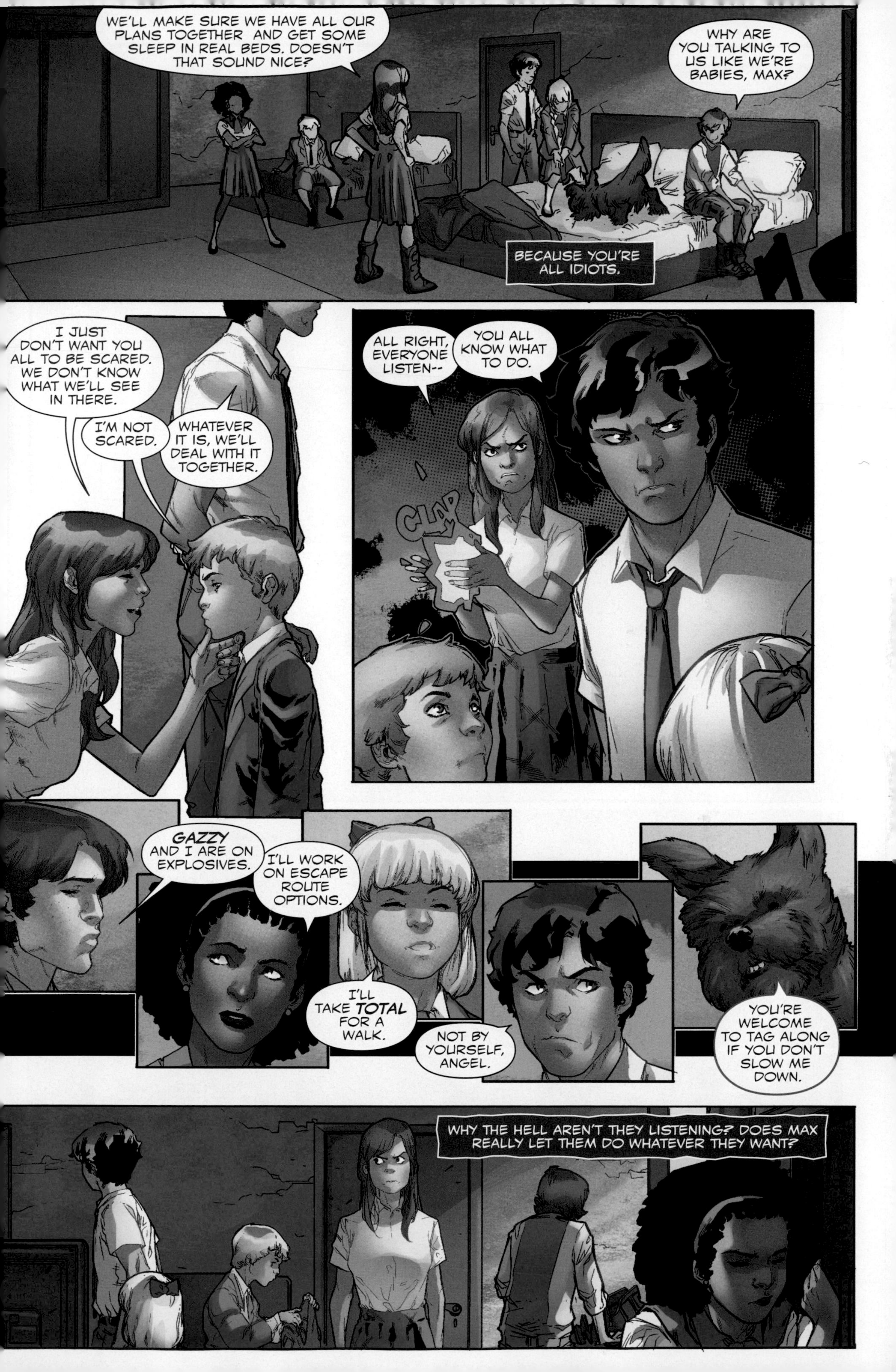
WE'LL MAKE SURE WE HAVE ALL OUR PLANS TOGETHER AND GET SOME SLEEP IN REAL BEDS. DOESN'T THAT SOUND NICE?
WHY ARE YOU TALKING TO US LIKE WE'RE BABIES, MAX?
BECAUSE YOU'RE ALL IDIOTS.
I JUST DON'T WANT YOU ALL TO BE SCARED. WE DON'T KNOW WHAT WE'LL SEE IN THERE.
I'M NOT SCARED.
WHATEVER IT IS, WE'LL DEAL WITH IT TOGETHER.
ALL RIGHT, EVERYONE LISTEN--
CLAP
YOU ALL KNOW WHAT TO DO.
GAZZY AND I ARE ON EXPLOSIVES.
I'LL WORK ON ESCAPE ROUTE OPTIONS.
I'LL TAKE TOTAL FOR A WALK.
NOT BY YOURSELF, ANGEL.
YOU'RE WELCOME TO TAG ALONG IF YOU DON'T SLOW ME DOWN.
WHY THE HELL AREN'T THEY LISTENING? DOES MAX REALLY LET THEM DO WHATEVER THEY WANT?

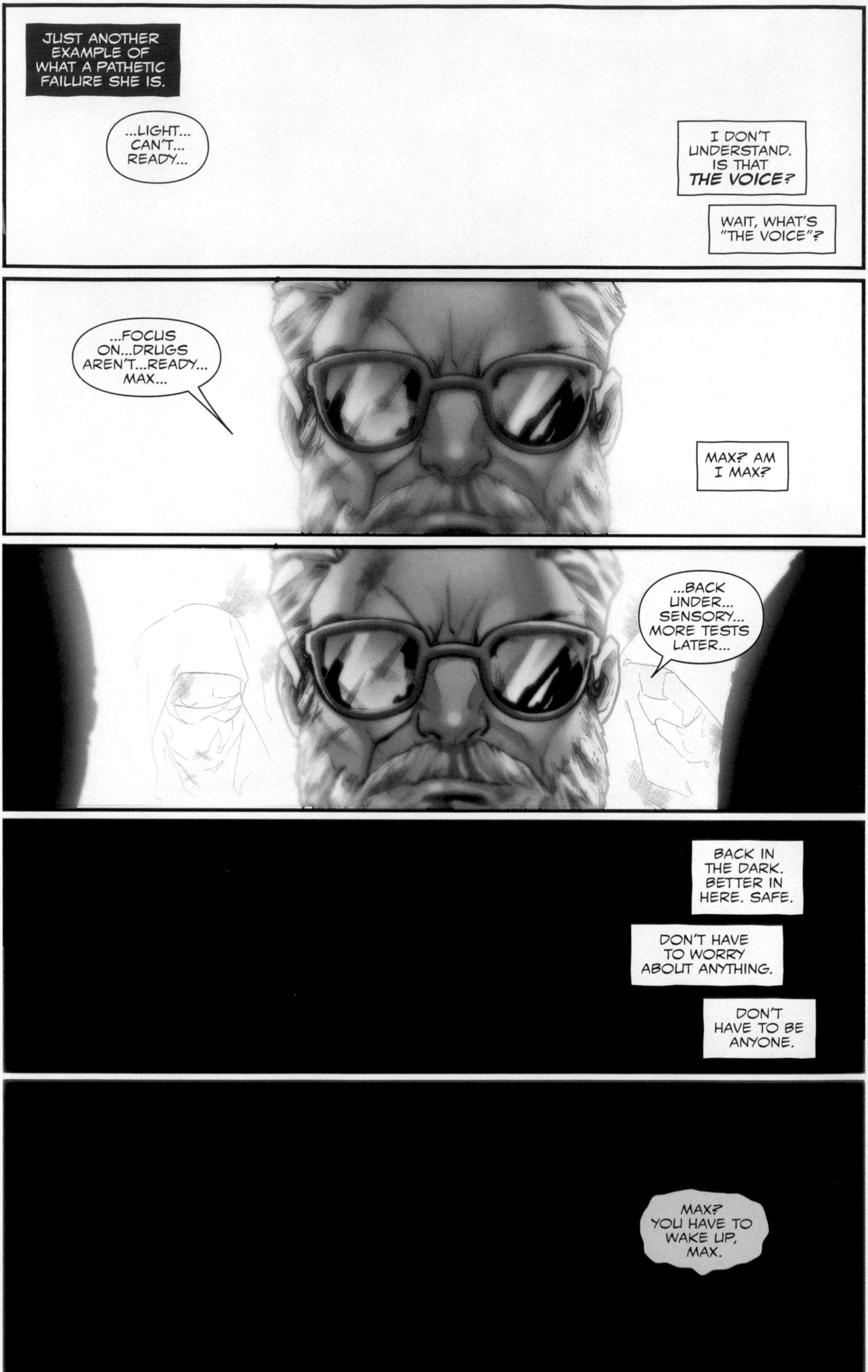
JUST ANOTHER EXAMPLE OF WHAT A PATHETIC FAILURE SHE IS.
...LIGHT... CAN'T... READY...
I DON'T UNDERSTAND. IS THAT THE VOICE?
WAIT, WHAT'S "THE VOICE"?
...FOCUS ON...DRUGS AREN'T...READY... MAX...
MAX? AM I MAX?
...BACK UNDER... SENSORY... MORE TESTS LATER...
BACK IN THE DARK. BETTER IN HERE. SAFE.
DON'T HAVE TO WORRY ABOUT ANYTHING.
DON'T HAVE TO BE ANYONE.
MAX? YOU HAVE TO WAKE UP, MAX.

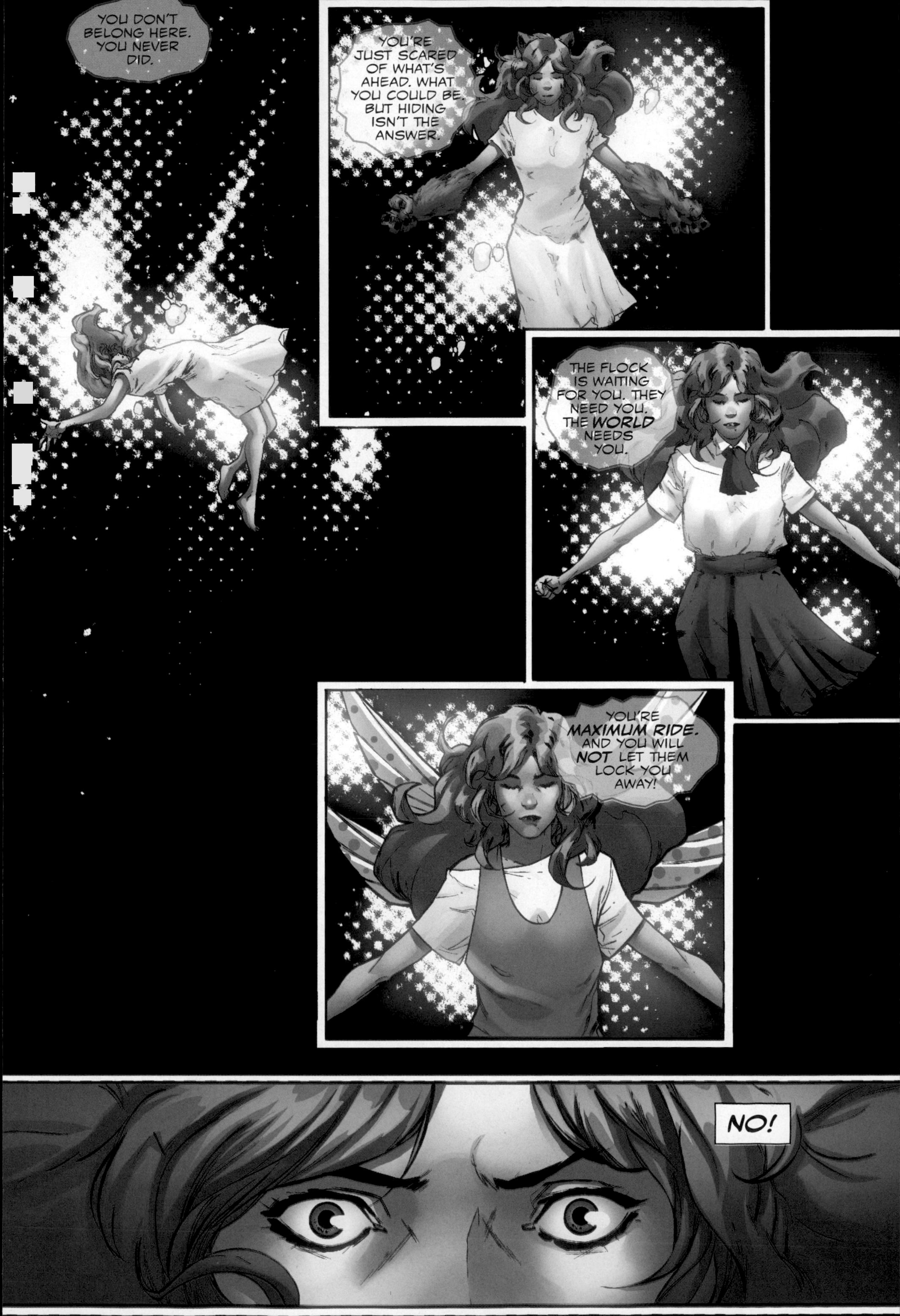
YOU DON'T BELONG HERE. YOU NEVER DID.
YOU'RE JUST SCARED OF WHAT'S AHEAD. WHAT YOU COULD BE. BUT HIDING ISN'T THE ANSWER.
THE FLOCK IS WAITING FOR YOU. THEY NEED YOU. THE WORLD NEEDS YOU.
YOU'RE MAXIMUM RIDE. AND YOU WILL NOT LET THEM LOCK YOU AWAY!
NO!

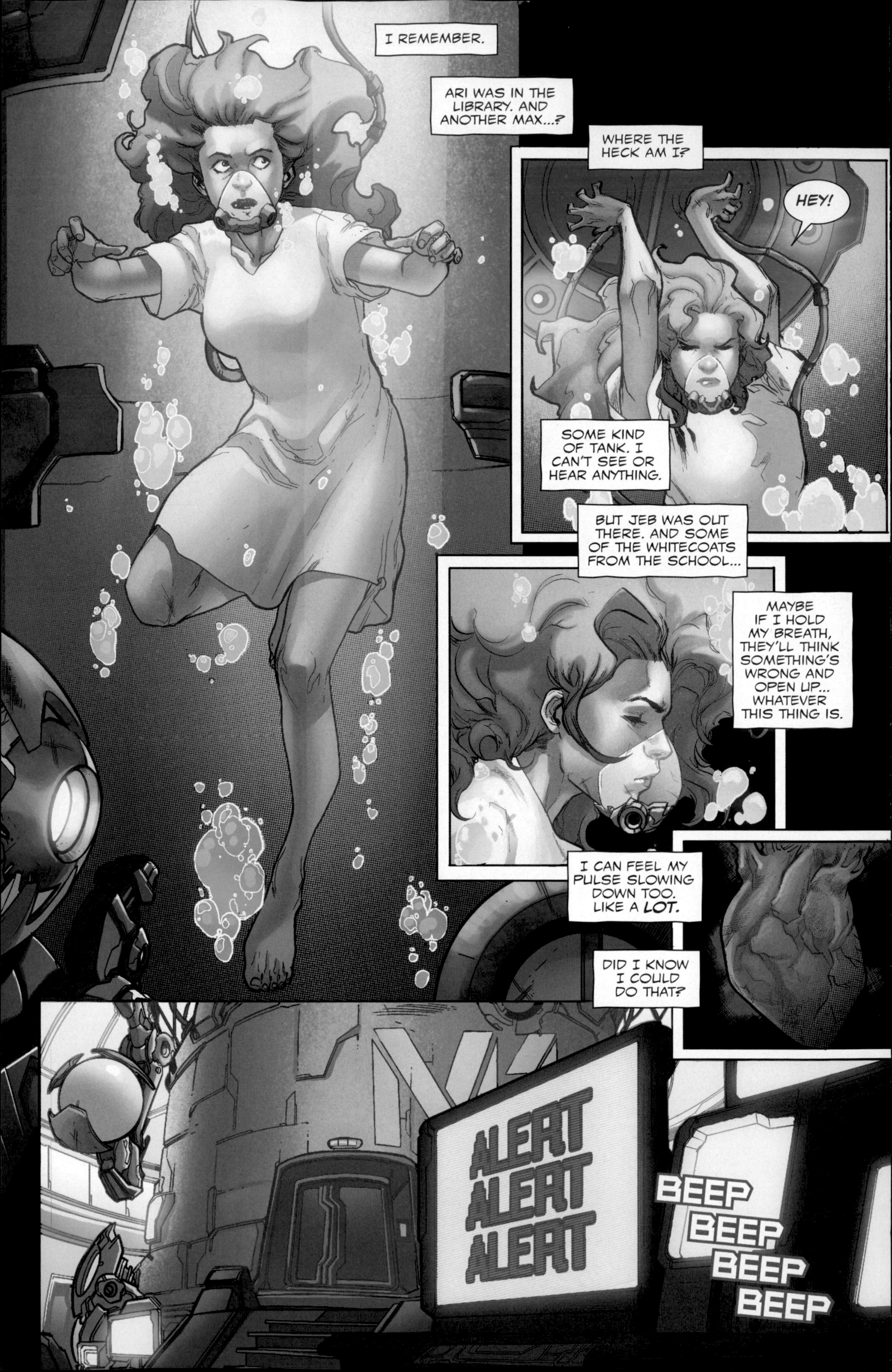
I REMEMBER.
ARI WAS IN THE LIBRARY. AND ANOTHER MAX...?
WHERE THE HECK AM I?
HEY!
SOME KIND OF TANK. I CAN'T SEE OR HEAR ANYTHING.
BUT JEB WAS OUT THERE. AND SOME OF THE WHITECOATS FROM THE SCHOOL...
MAYBE IF I HOLD MY BREATH, THEY'LL THINK SOMETHING'S WRONG AND OPEN UP... WHATEVER THIS THING IS.
I CAN FEEL MY PULSE SLOWING DOWN TOO. LIKE A **LOT.**
DID I KNOW I COULD DO THAT?
ALERT ALERT ALERT
BEEP BEEP BEEP BEEP

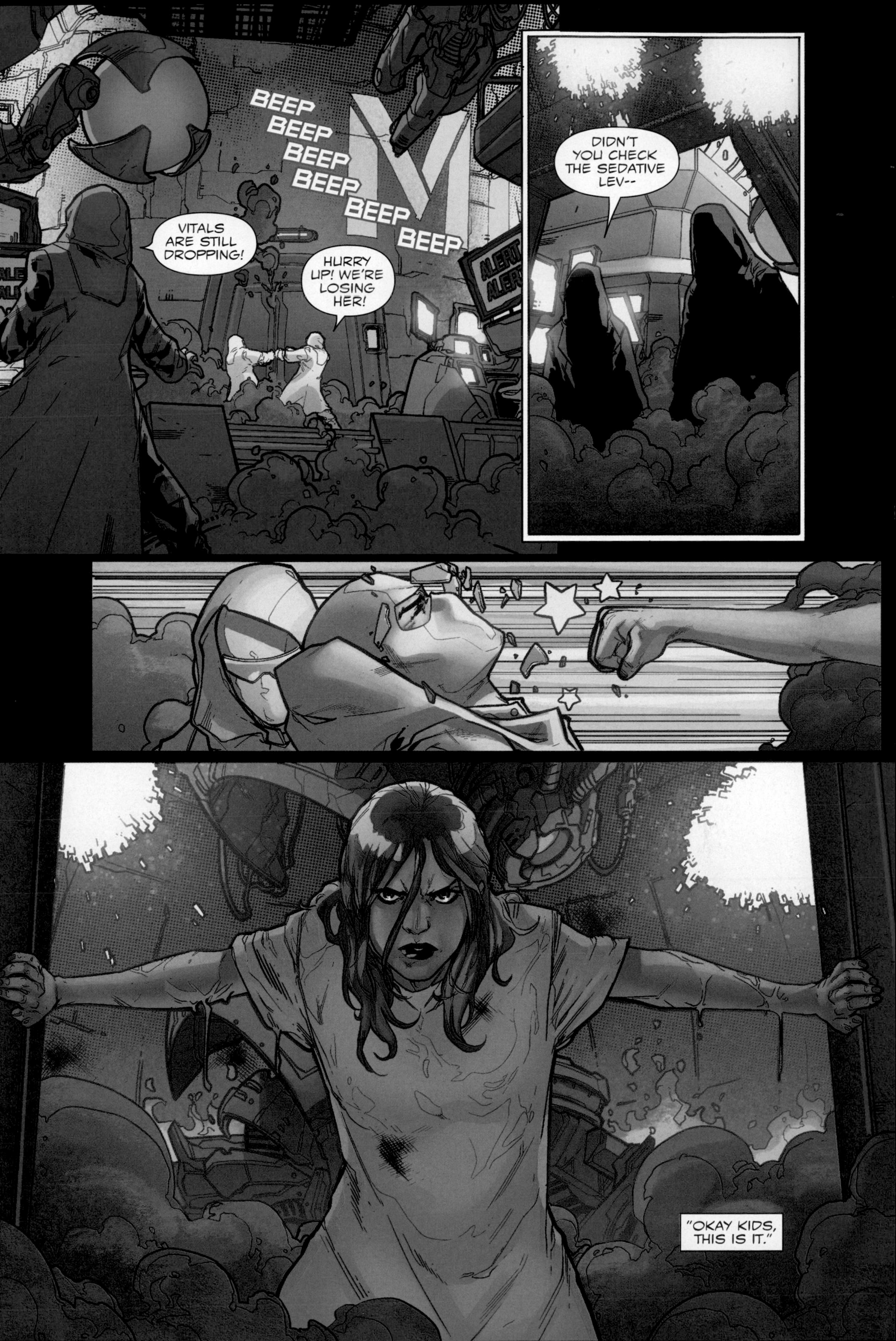
BEEP
BEEP
BEEP
BEEP
BEEP
BEEP
VITALS ARE STILL DROPPING!
HURRY UP! WE'RE LOSING HER!
DIDN'T YOU CHECK THE SEDATIVE LEV--
"OKAY KIDS, THIS IS IT."

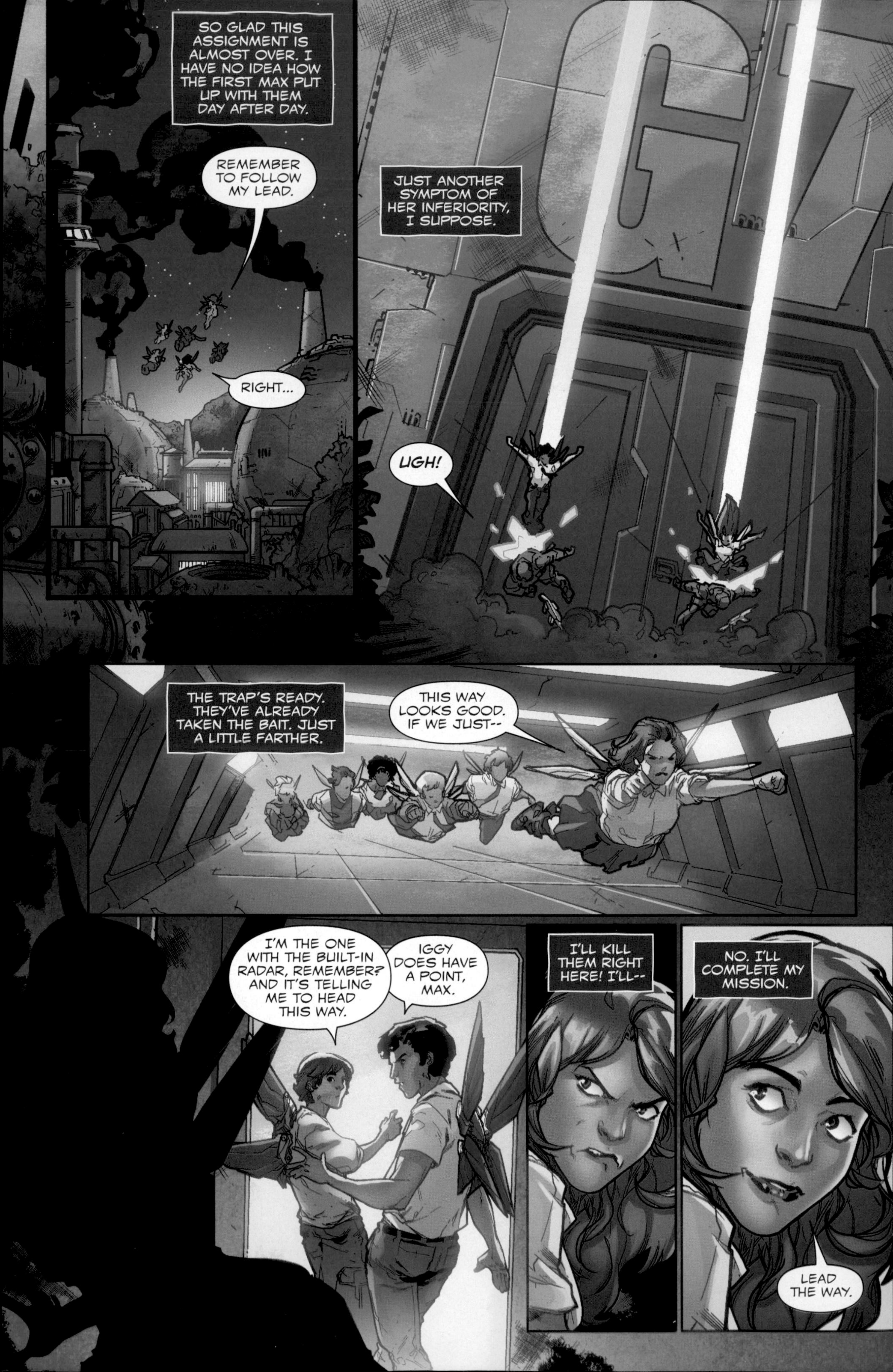
SO GLAD THIS ASSIGNMENT IS ALMOST OVER. I HAVE NO IDEA HOW THE FIRST MAX PUT UP WITH THEM DAY AFTER DAY.
REMEMBER TO FOLLOW MY LEAD.
RIGHT...
JUST ANOTHER SYMPTOM OF HER INFERIORITY, I SUPPOSE.
UGH!
THE TRAP'S READY. THEY'VE ALREADY TAKEN THE BAIT. JUST A LITTLE FARTHER.
THIS WAY LOOKS GOOD. IF WE JUST--
I'M THE ONE WITH THE BUILT-IN RADAR, REMEMBER? AND IT'S TELLING ME TO HEAD THIS WAY.
IGGY DOES HAVE A POINT, MAX.
I'LL KILL THEM RIGHT HERE! I'LL--
NO. I'LL COMPLETE MY MISSION.
LEAD THE WAY.

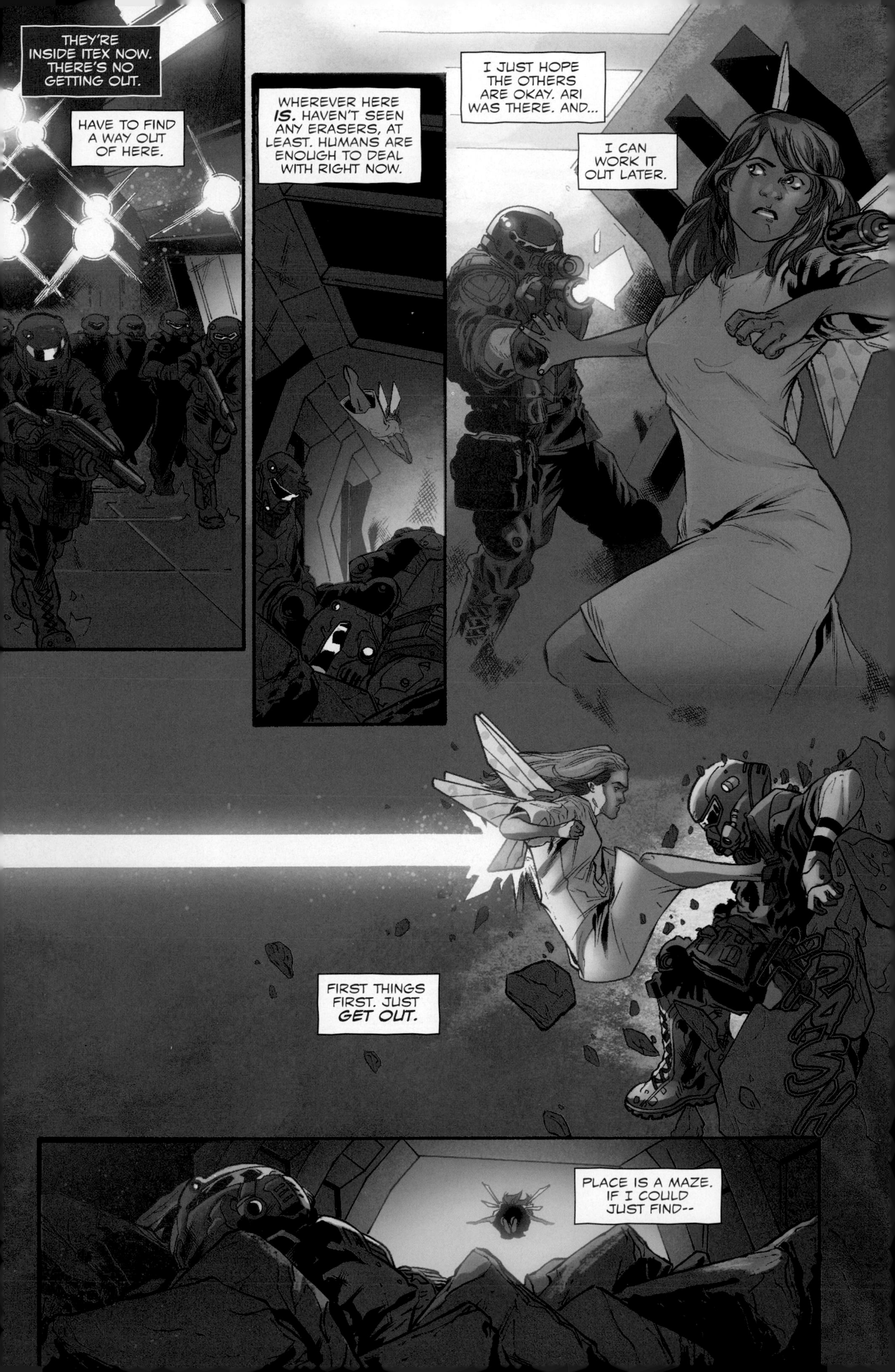
THEY'RE INSIDE ITEX NOW. THERE'S NO GETTING OUT.
HAVE TO FIND A WAY OUT OF HERE.
WHEREVER HERE IS. HAVEN'T SEEN ANY ERASERS, AT LEAST. HUMANS ARE ENOUGH TO DEAL WITH RIGHT NOW.
I JUST HOPE THE OTHERS ARE OKAY. ARI WAS THERE. AND...
I CAN WORK IT OUT LATER.
FIRST THINGS FIRST. JUST GET OUT.
PLACE IS A MAZE. IF I COULD JUST FIND--

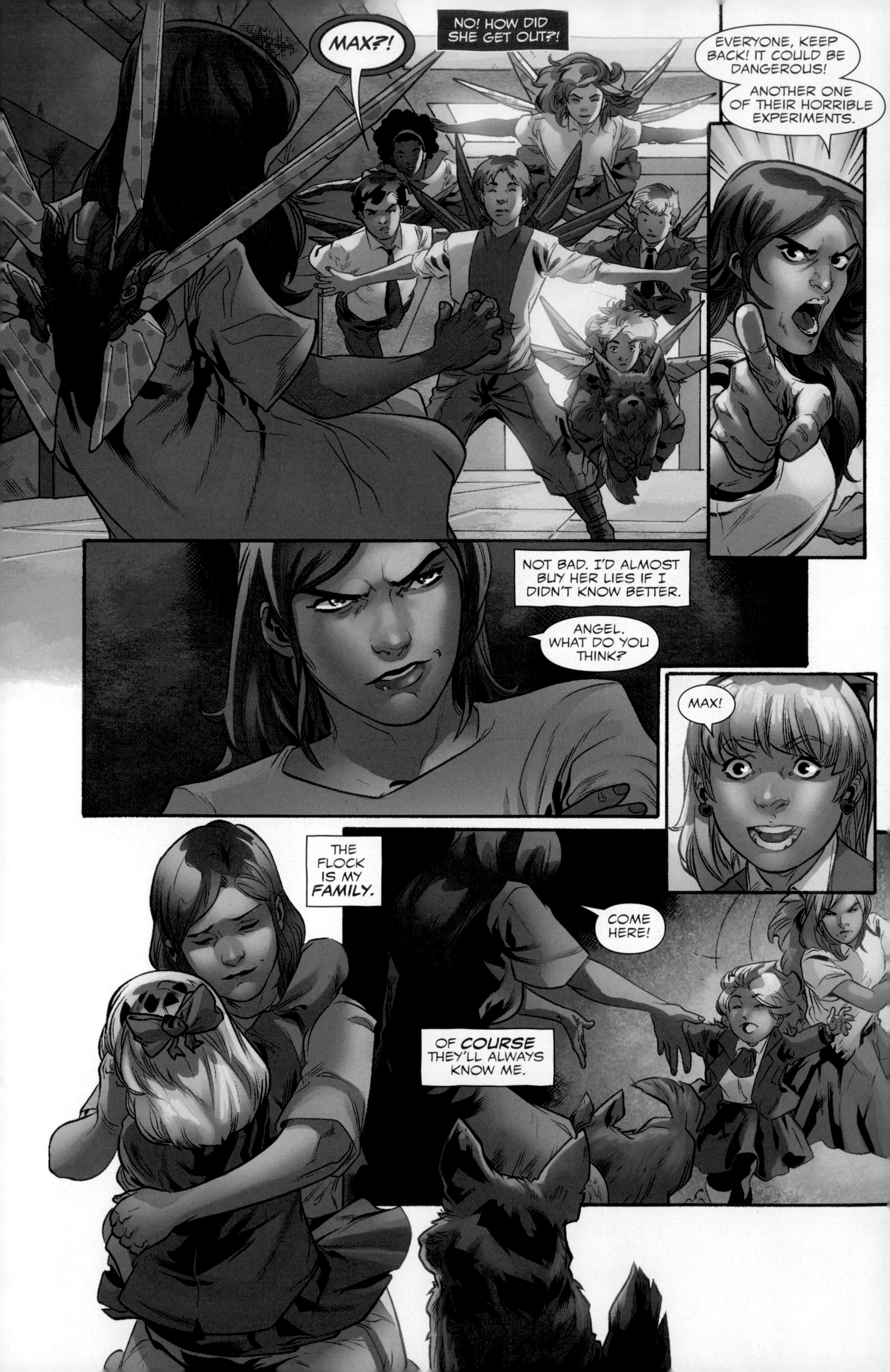
MAX?!
NO! HOW DID SHE GET OUT?!
EVERYONE, KEEP BACK! IT COULD BE DANGEROUS!
ANOTHER ONE OF THEIR HORRIBLE EXPERIMENTS.
NOT BAD. I'D ALMOST BUY HER LIES IF I DIDN'T KNOW BETTER.
ANGEL. WHAT DO YOU THINK?
MAX!
THE FLOCK IS MY FAMILY.
COME HERE!
OF COURSE THEY'LL ALWAYS KNOW ME.

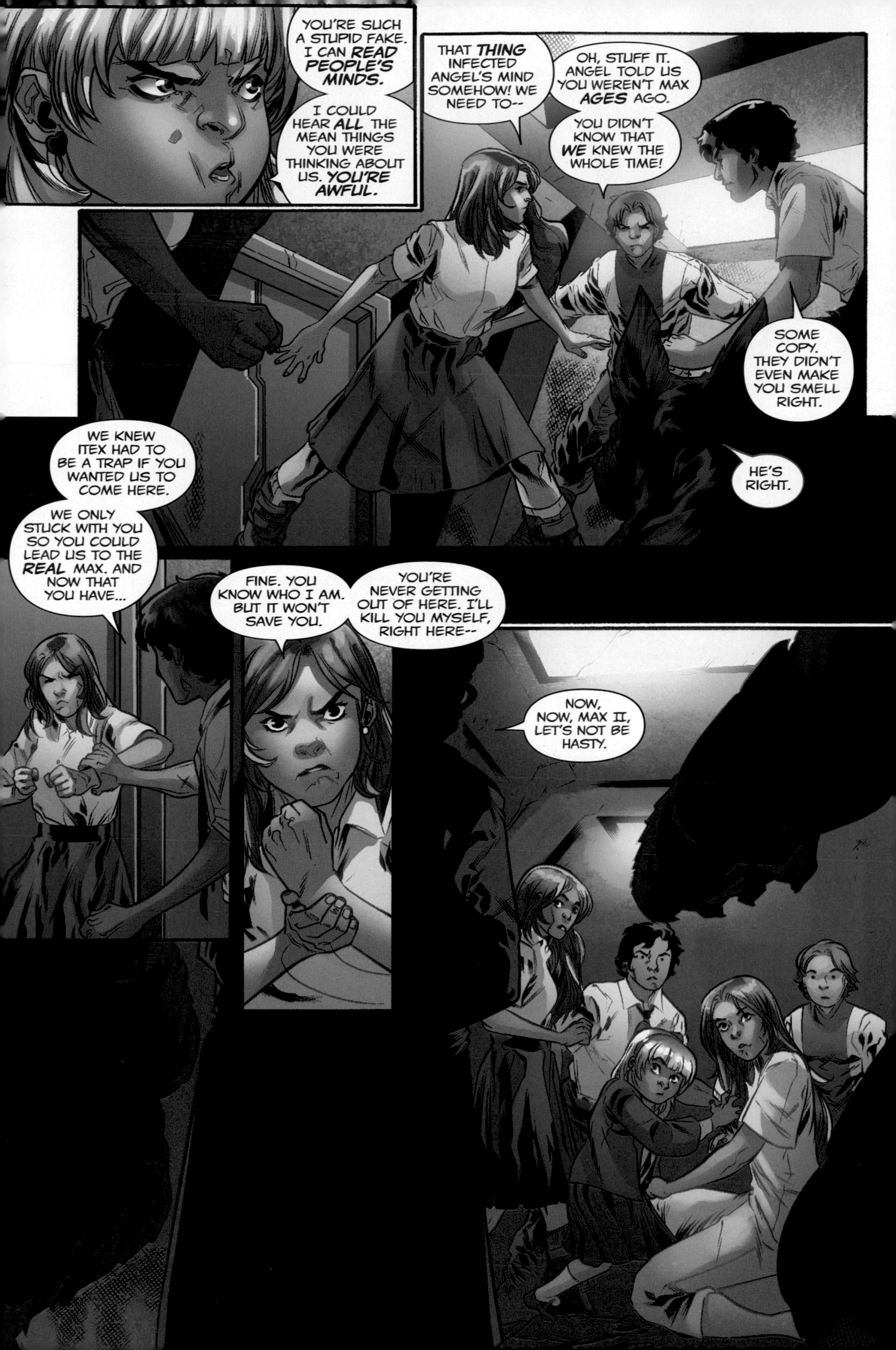
YOU'RE SUCH A STUPID FAKE. I CAN READ PEOPLE'S MINDS.
I COULD HEAR ALL THE MEAN THINGS YOU WERE THINKING ABOUT US. YOU'RE AWFUL.
THAT THING INFECTED ANGEL'S MIND SOMEHOW! WE NEED TO--
OH, STUFF IT. ANGEL TOLD US YOU WEREN'T MAX AGES AGO.
YOU DIDN'T KNOW THAT WE KNEW THE WHOLE TIME!
SOME COPY. THEY DIDN'T EVEN MAKE YOU SMELL RIGHT.
HE'S RIGHT.
WE KNEW ITEX HAD TO BE A TRAP IF YOU WANTED US TO COME HERE.
WE ONLY STUCK WITH YOU SO YOU COULD LEAD US TO THE REAL MAX. AND NOW THAT YOU HAVE...
FINE. YOU KNOW WHO I AM. BUT IT WON'T SAVE YOU.
YOU'RE NEVER GETTING OUT OF HERE. I'LL KILL YOU MYSELF, RIGHT HERE--
NOW, NOW, MAX II, LET'S NOT BE HASTY.

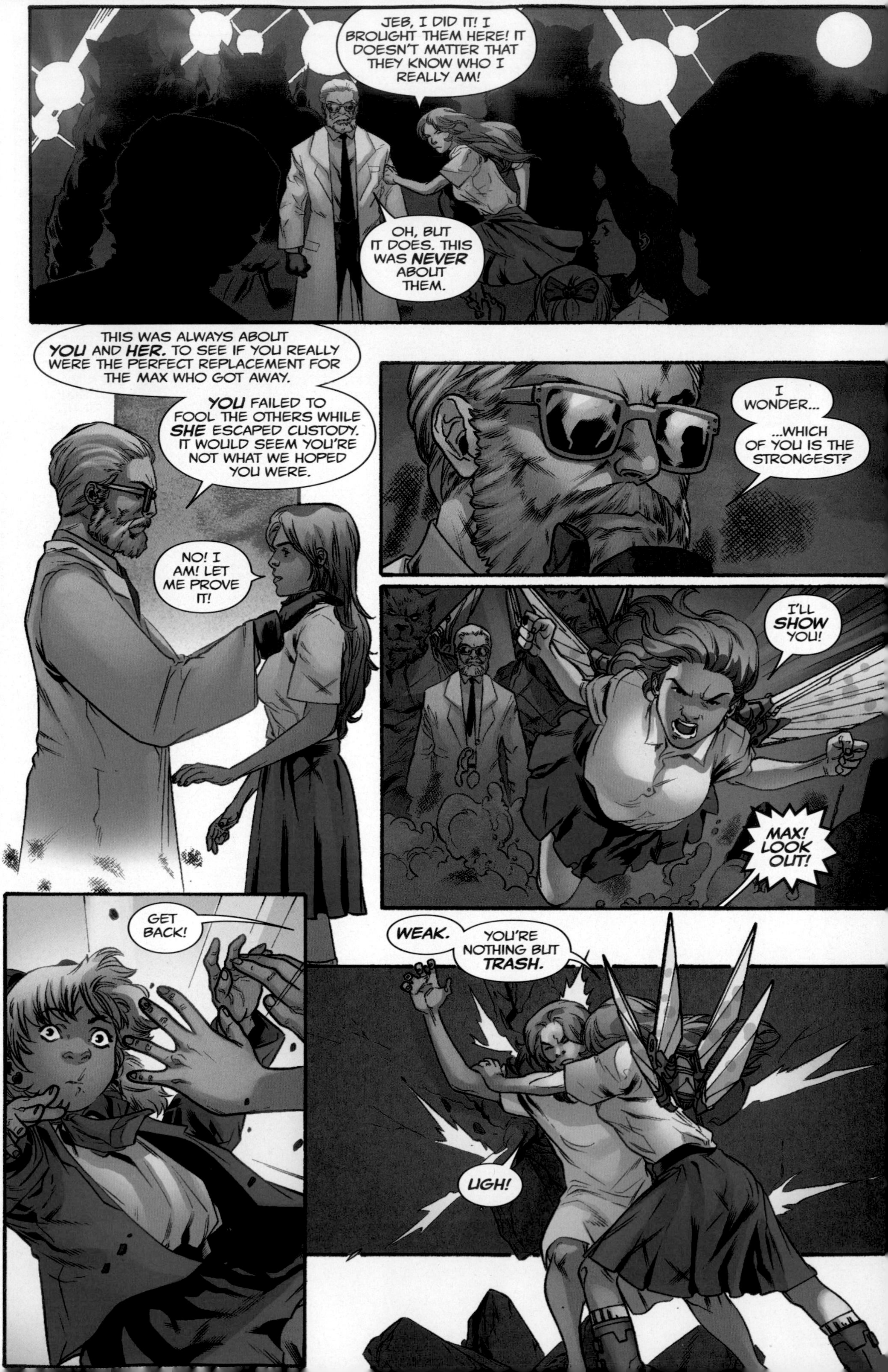
JEB, I DID IT! I BROUGHT THEM HERE! IT DOESN'T MATTER THAT THEY KNOW WHO I REALLY AM!
OH, BUT IT DOES. THIS WAS NEVER ABOUT THEM.
THIS WAS ALWAYS ABOUT YOU AND HER. TO SEE IF YOU REALLY WERE THE PERFECT REPLACEMENT FOR THE MAX WHO GOT AWAY.
YOU FAILED TO FOOL THE OTHERS WHILE SHE ESCAPED CUSTODY. IT WOULD SEEM YOU'RE NOT WHAT WE HOPED YOU WERE.
NO! I AM! LET ME PROVE IT!
I WONDER...
...WHICH OF YOU IS THE STRONGEST?
I'LL SHOW YOU!
MAX! LOOK OUT!
GET BACK!
WEAK.
YOU'RE NOTHING BUT TRASH.
UGH!

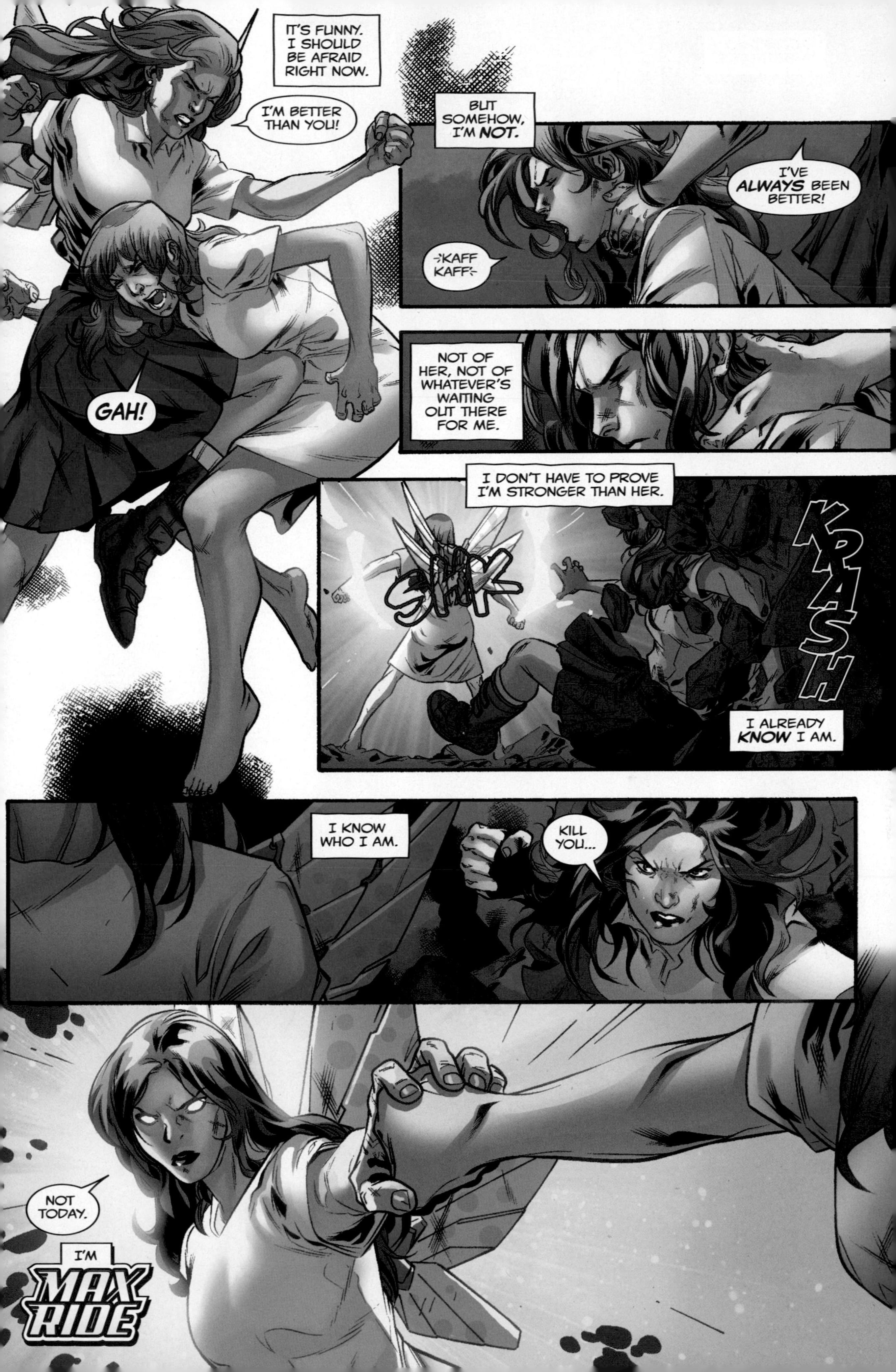
IT'S FUNNY. I SHOULD BE AFRAID RIGHT NOW.
I'M BETTER THAN YOU!
GAH!
BUT SOMEHOW, I'M **NOT.**
I'VE **ALWAYS** BEEN BETTER!
-KAFF KAFF-
NOT OF HER, NOT OF WHATEVER'S WAITING OUT THERE FOR ME.
I DON'T HAVE TO PROVE I'M STRONGER THAN HER.
SHIK
KRASH
I ALREADY **KNOW** I AM.
I KNOW WHO I AM.
KILL YOU...
NOT TODAY.
I'M
MAX RIDE

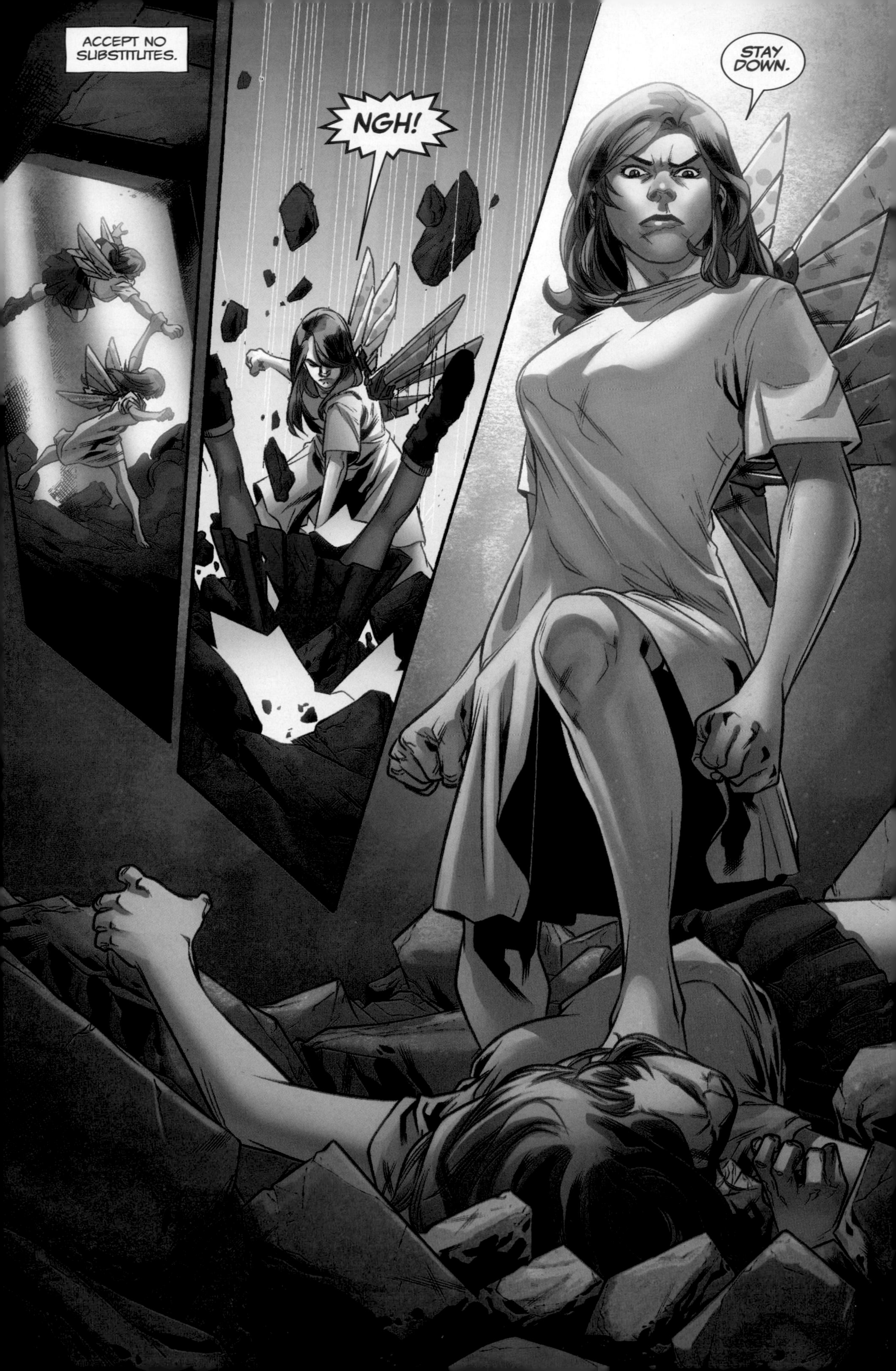
ACCEPT NO SUBSTITUTES.
NGH!
STAY DOWN.

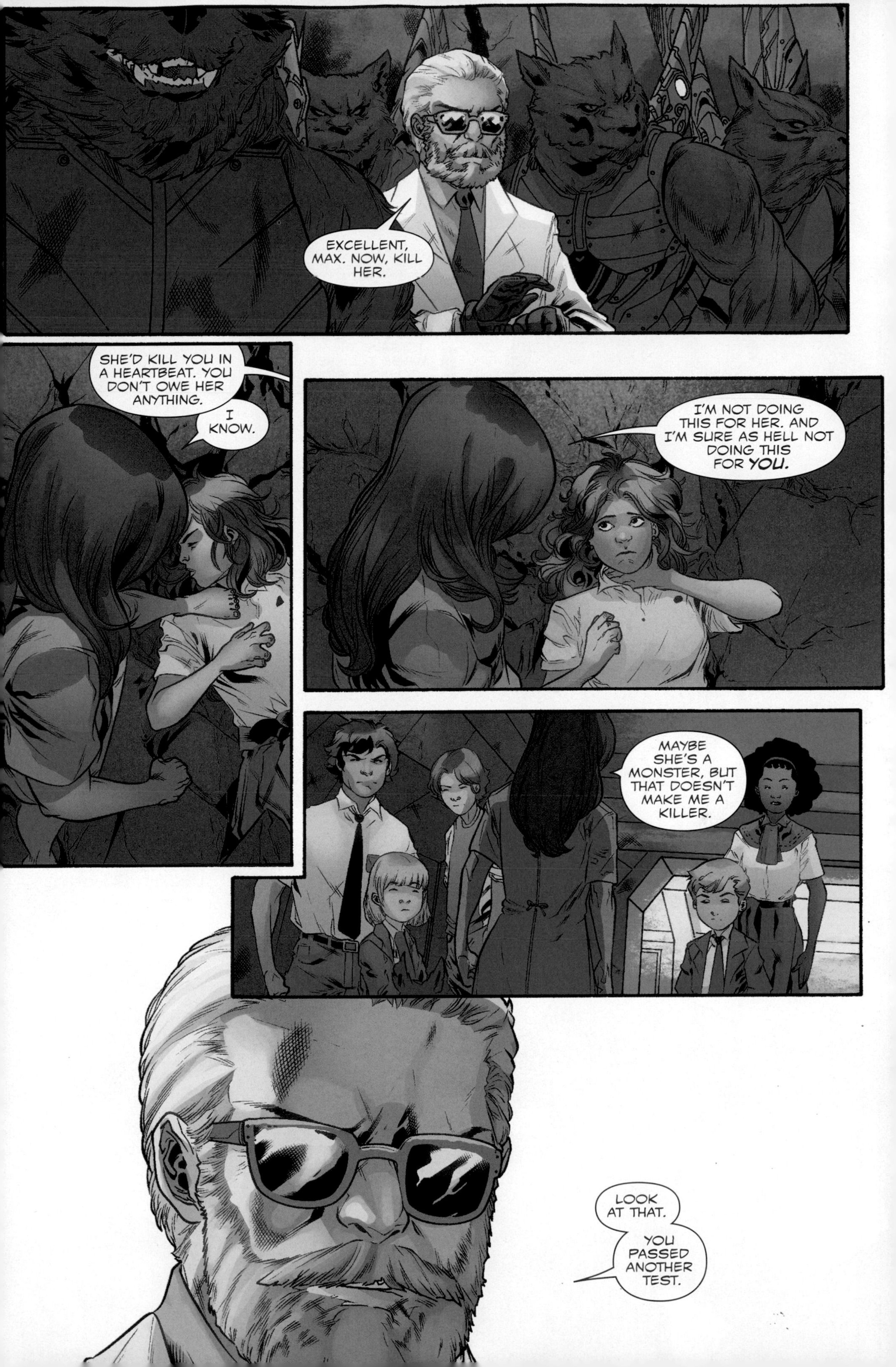
EXCELLENT, MAX. NOW, KILL HER.
SHE'D KILL YOU IN A HEARTBEAT. YOU DON'T OWE HER ANYTHING.
I KNOW.
I'M NOT DOING THIS FOR HER. AND I'M SURE AS HELL NOT DOING THIS FOR YOU.
MAYBE SHE'S A MONSTER, BUT THAT DOESN'T MAKE ME A KILLER.
LOOK AT THAT.
YOU PASSED ANOTHER TEST.

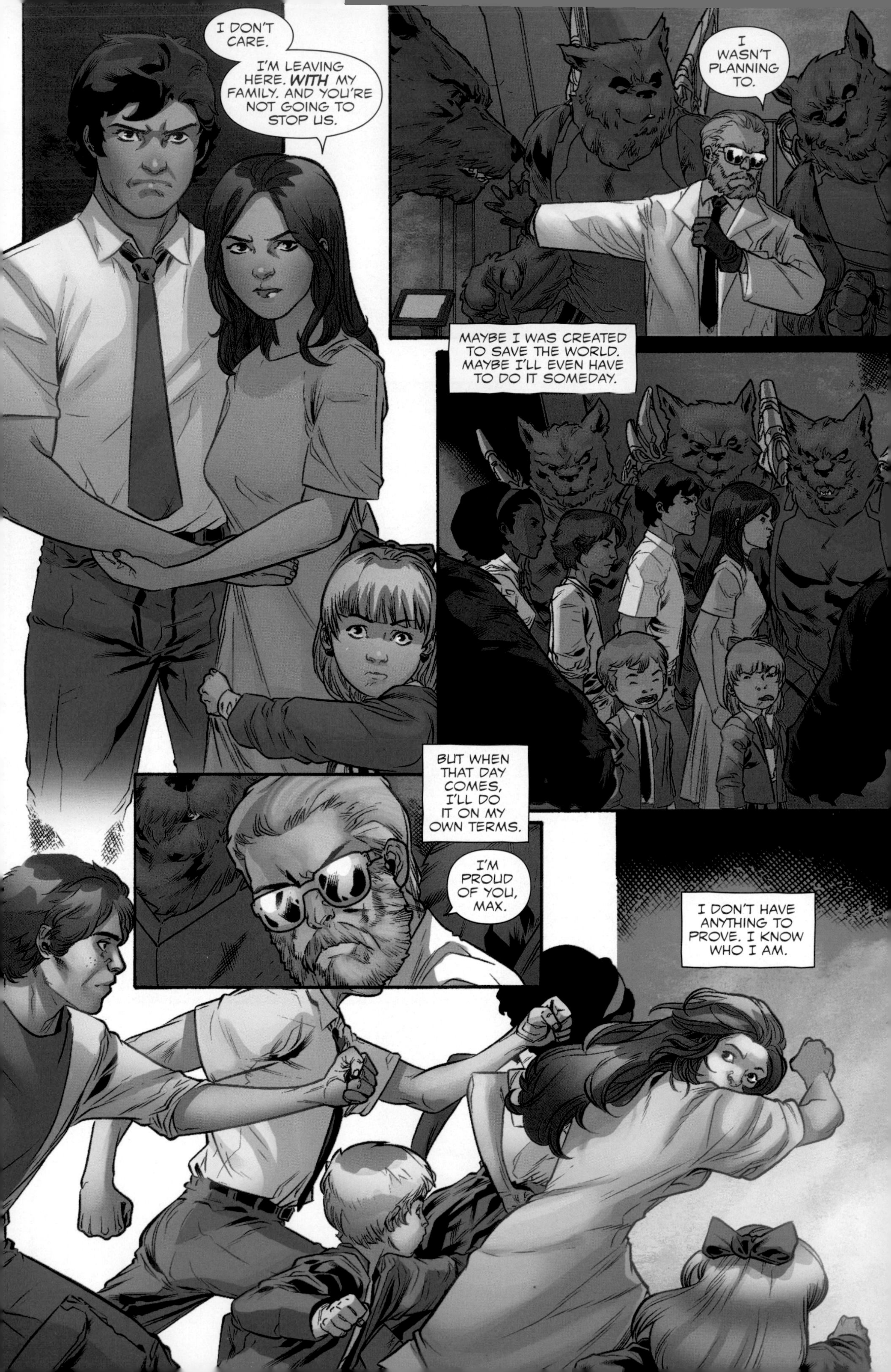
I DON'T CARE.
I'M LEAVING HERE. WITH MY FAMILY. AND YOU'RE NOT GOING TO STOP US.
I WASN'T PLANNING TO.
MAYBE I WAS CREATED TO SAVE THE WORLD. MAYBE I'LL EVEN HAVE TO DO IT SOMEDAY.
BUT WHEN THAT DAY COMES, I'LL DO IT ON MY OWN TERMS.
I'M PROUD OF YOU, MAX.
I DON'T HAVE ANYTHING TO PROVE. I KNOW WHO I AM.

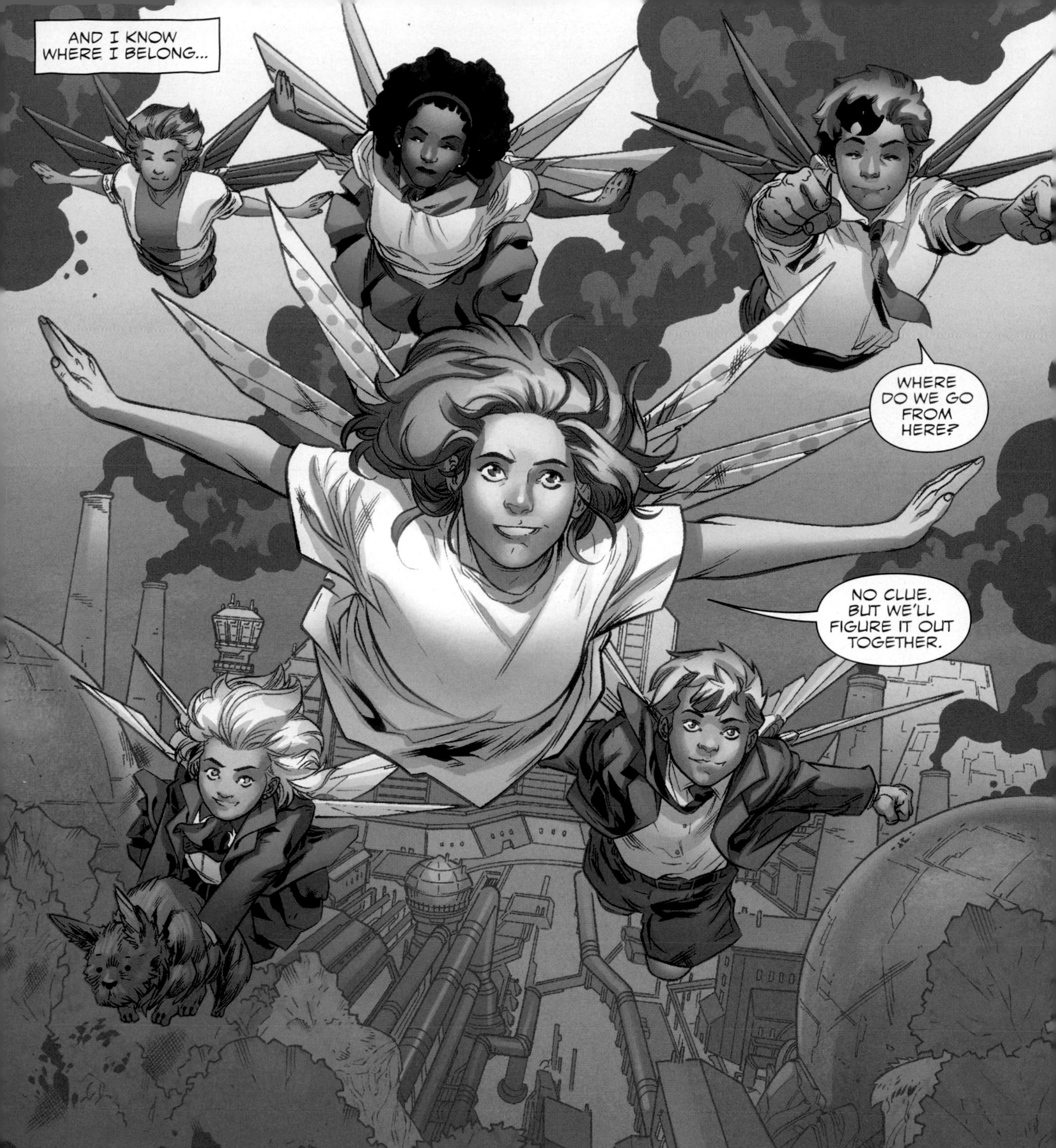
AND I KNOW WHERE I BELONG...
WHERE DO WE GO FROM HERE?
NO CLUE. BUT WE'LL FIGURE IT OUT TOGETHER.

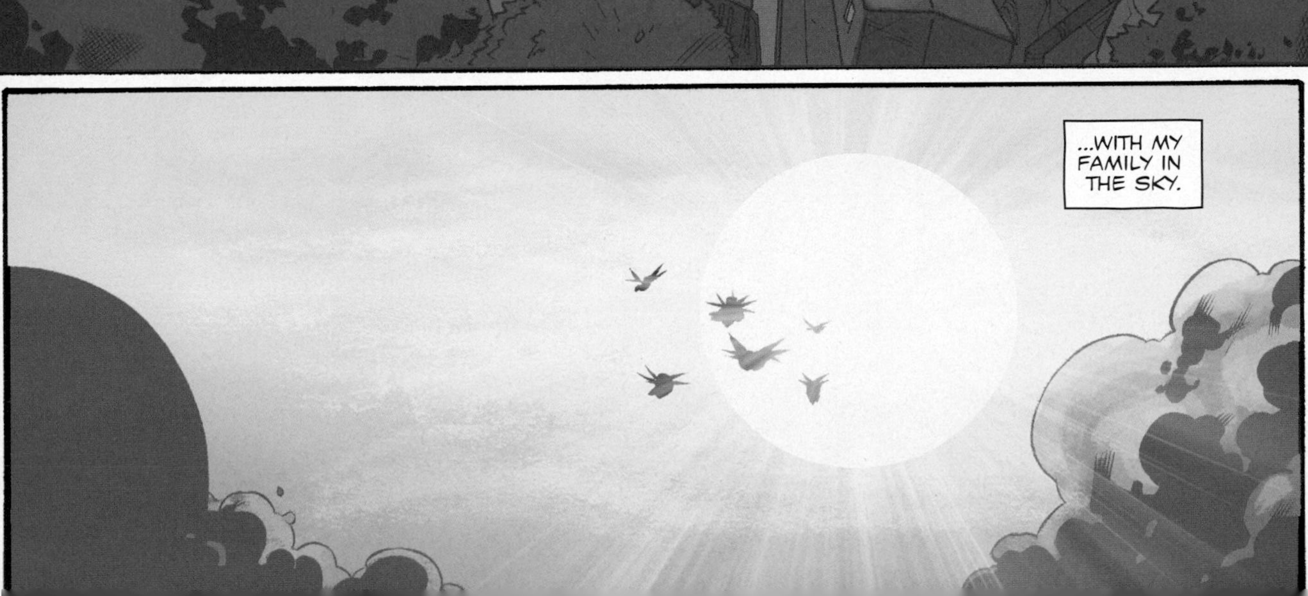
...WITH MY FAMILY IN THE SKY.

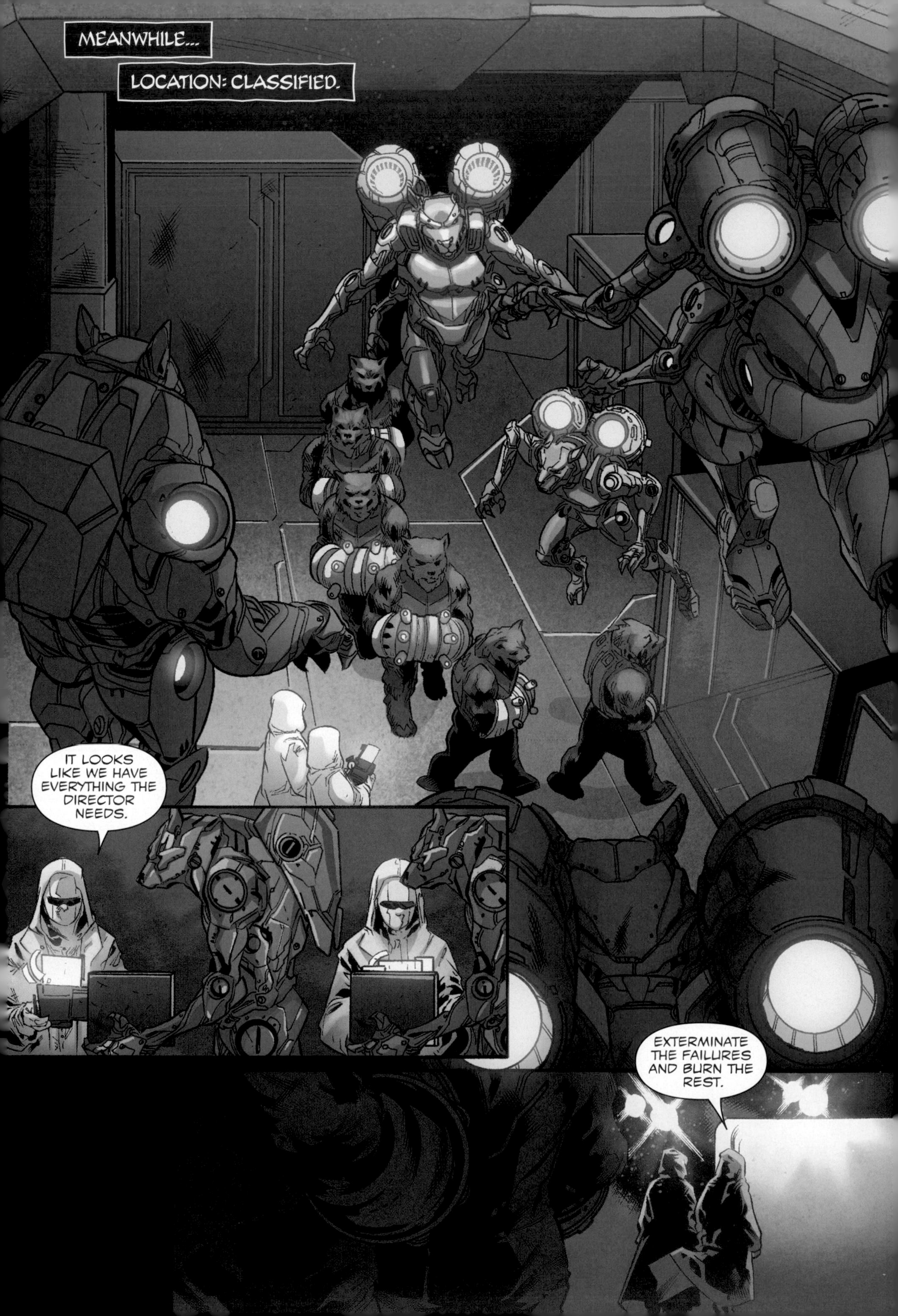
MEANWHILE...
LOCATION: CLASSIFIED.
IT LOOKS LIKE WE HAVE EVERYTHING THE DIRECTOR NEEDS.
EXTERMINATE THE FAILURES AND BURN THE REST.

THE STORY CONTINUES IN...

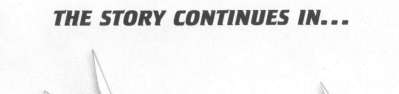

MAX RIDE: FINAL FLIGHT

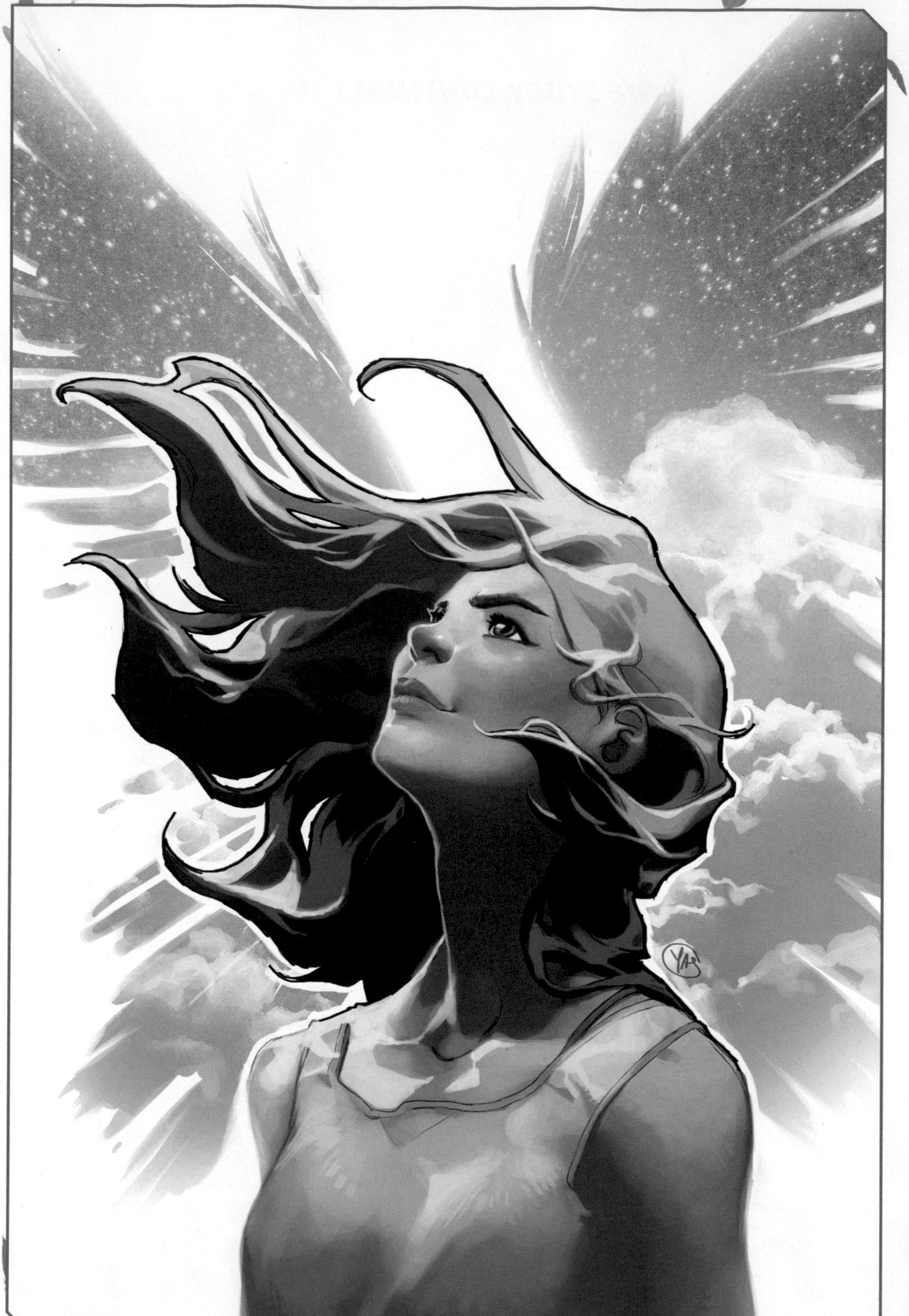

MAX RIDE: ULTIMATE FLIGHT #1 COVER
by YASMINE PUTRI

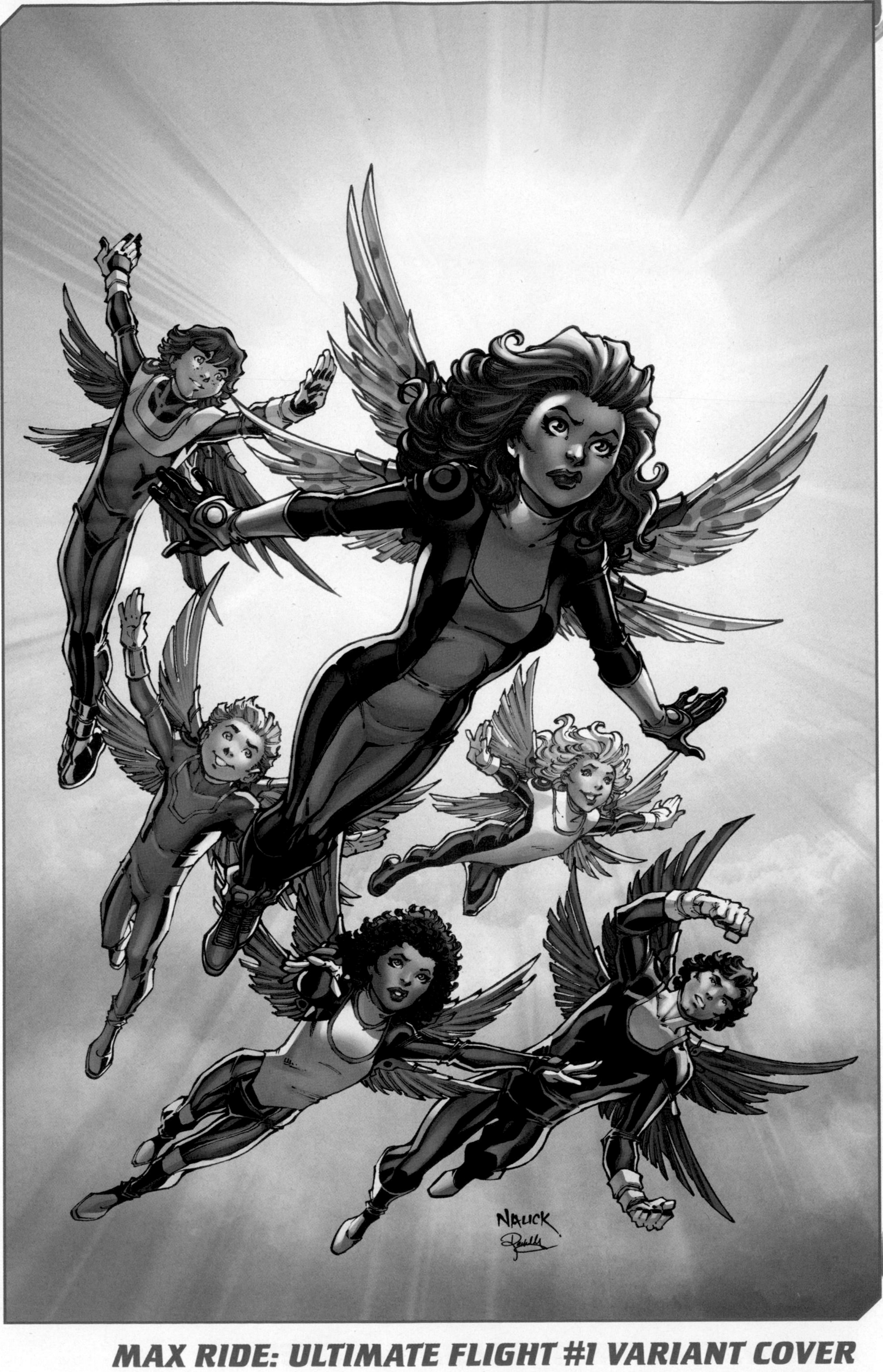
NAUCK

MAX RIDE: ULTIMATE FLIGHT #1 VARIANT COVER
by TODD NAUCK & RACHELLE ROSENBERG

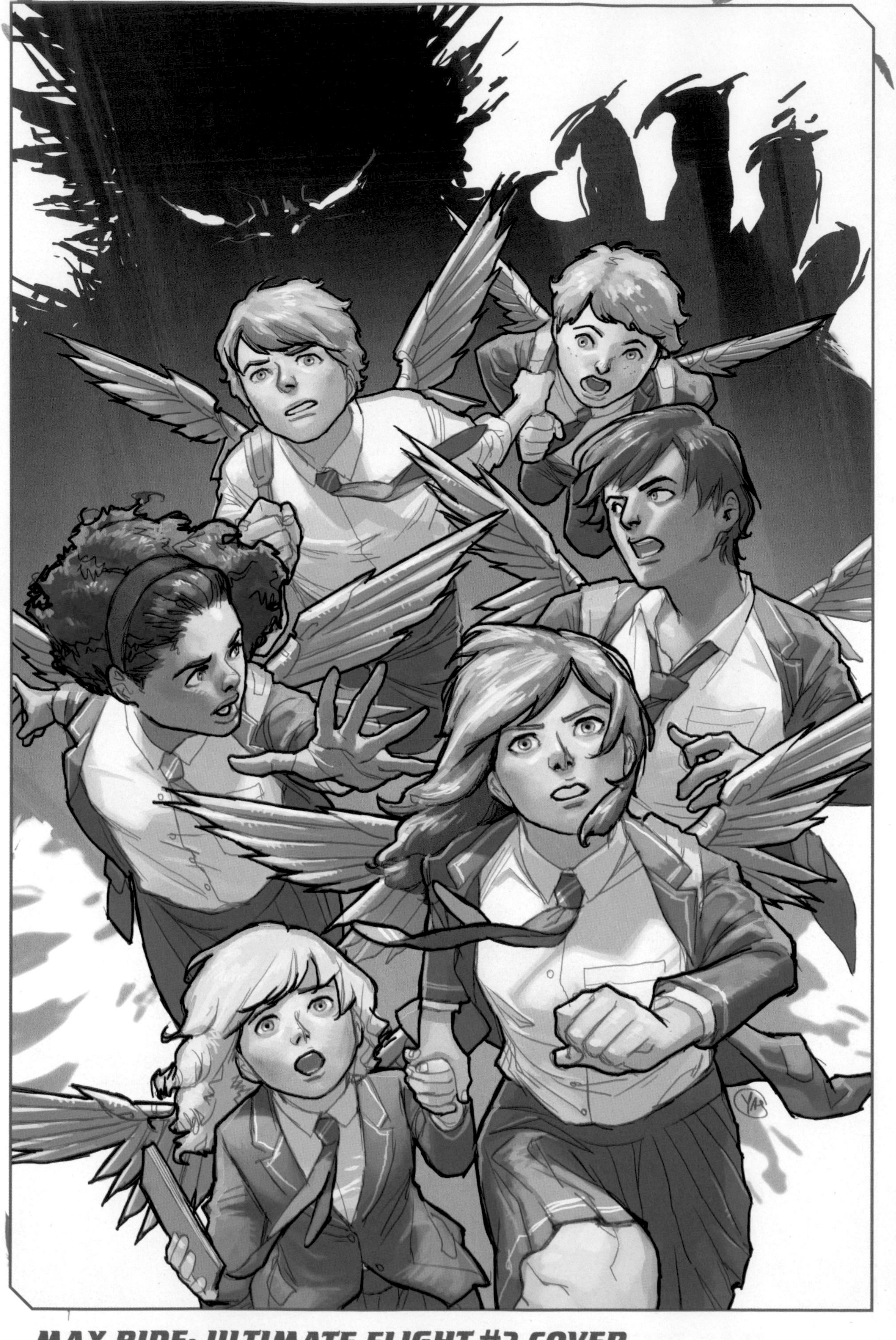

MAX RIDE: ULTIMATE FLIGHT #2 COVER
by YASMINE PUTRI

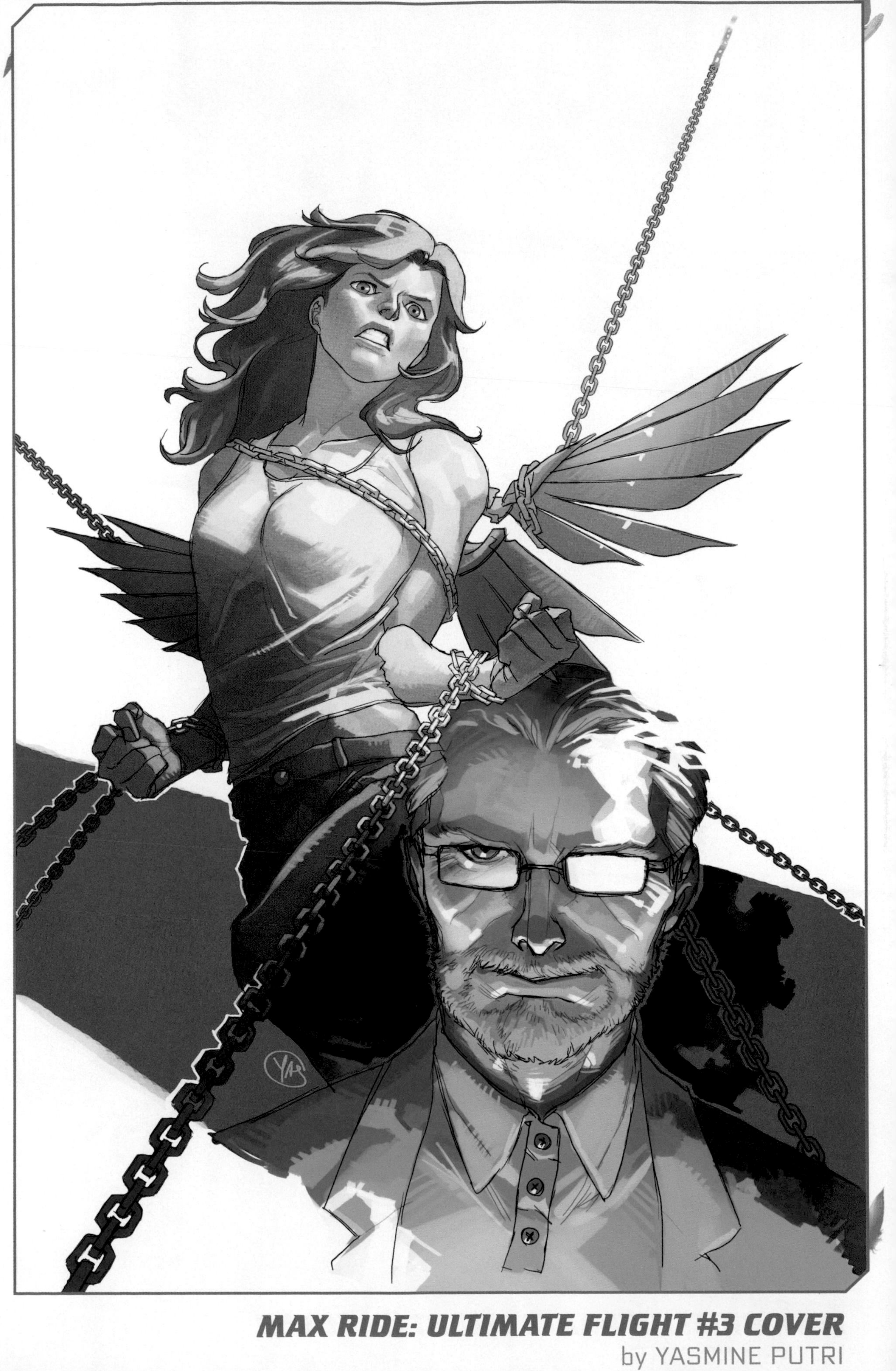

MAX RIDE: ULTIMATE FLIGHT #3 COVER
by YASMINE PUTRI

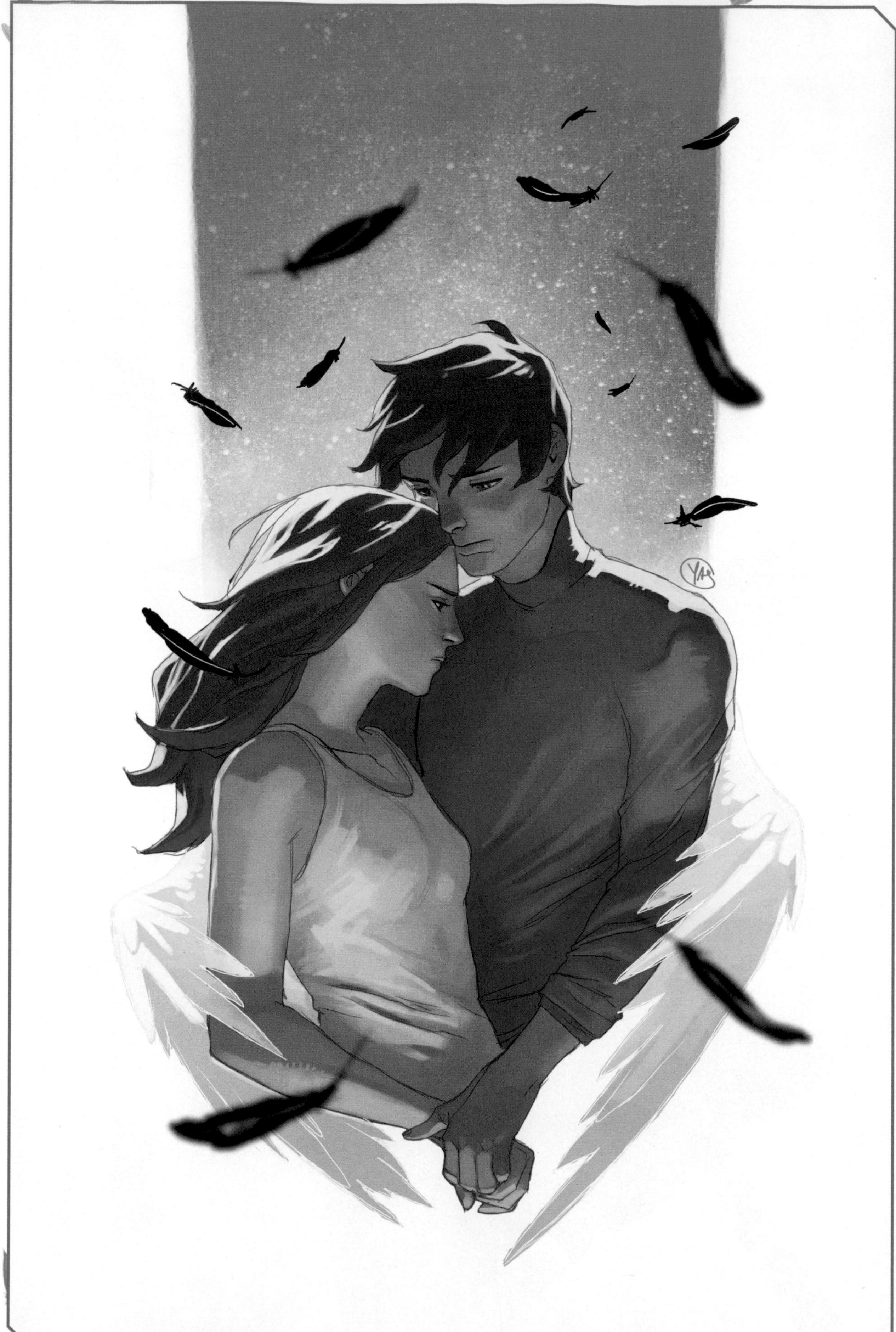

MAX RIDE: ULTIMATE FLIGHT #4 COVER
by YASMINE PUTRI

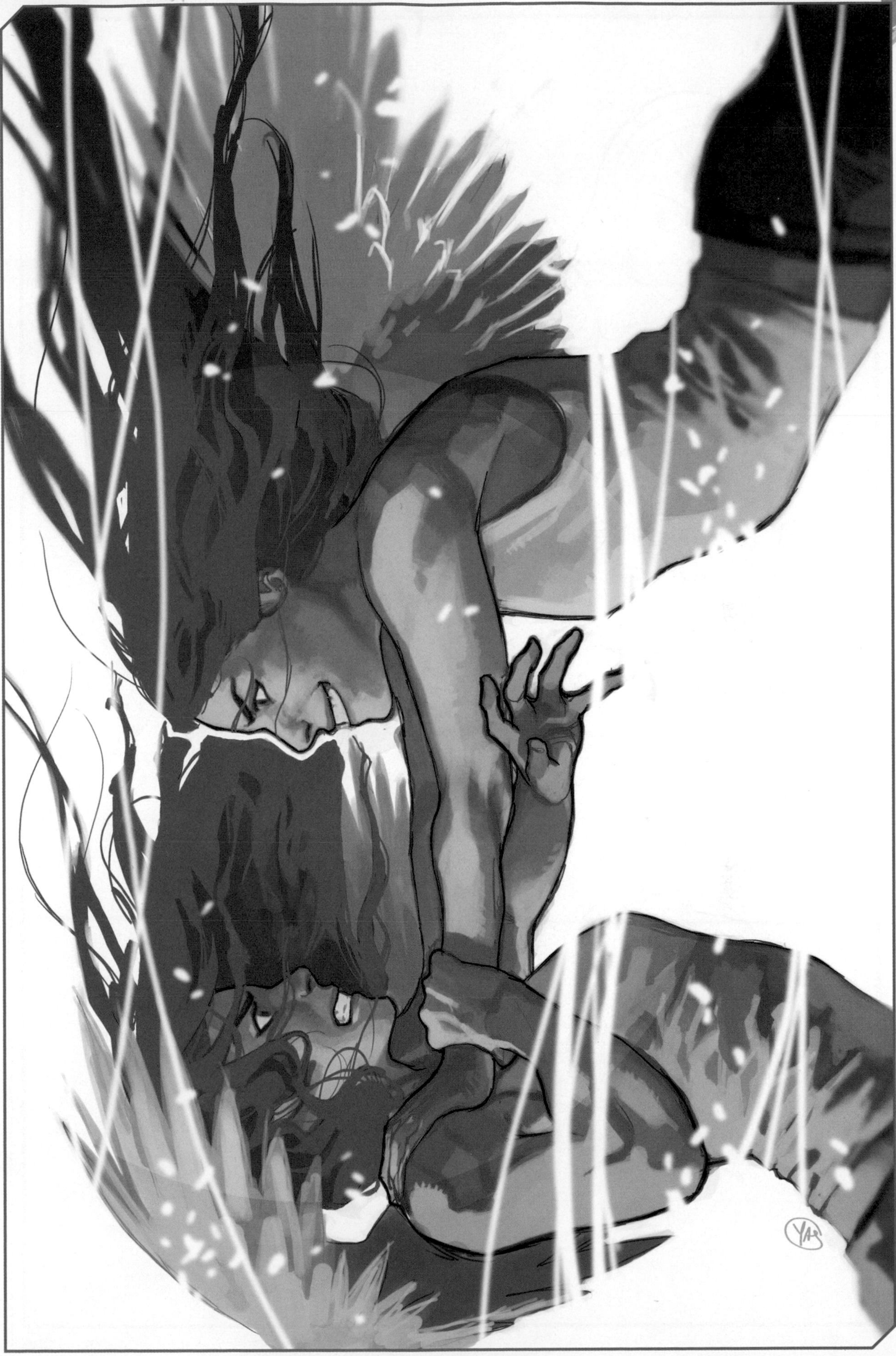

MAX RIDE: ULTIMATE FLIGHT #5 COVER
by YASMINE PUTRI

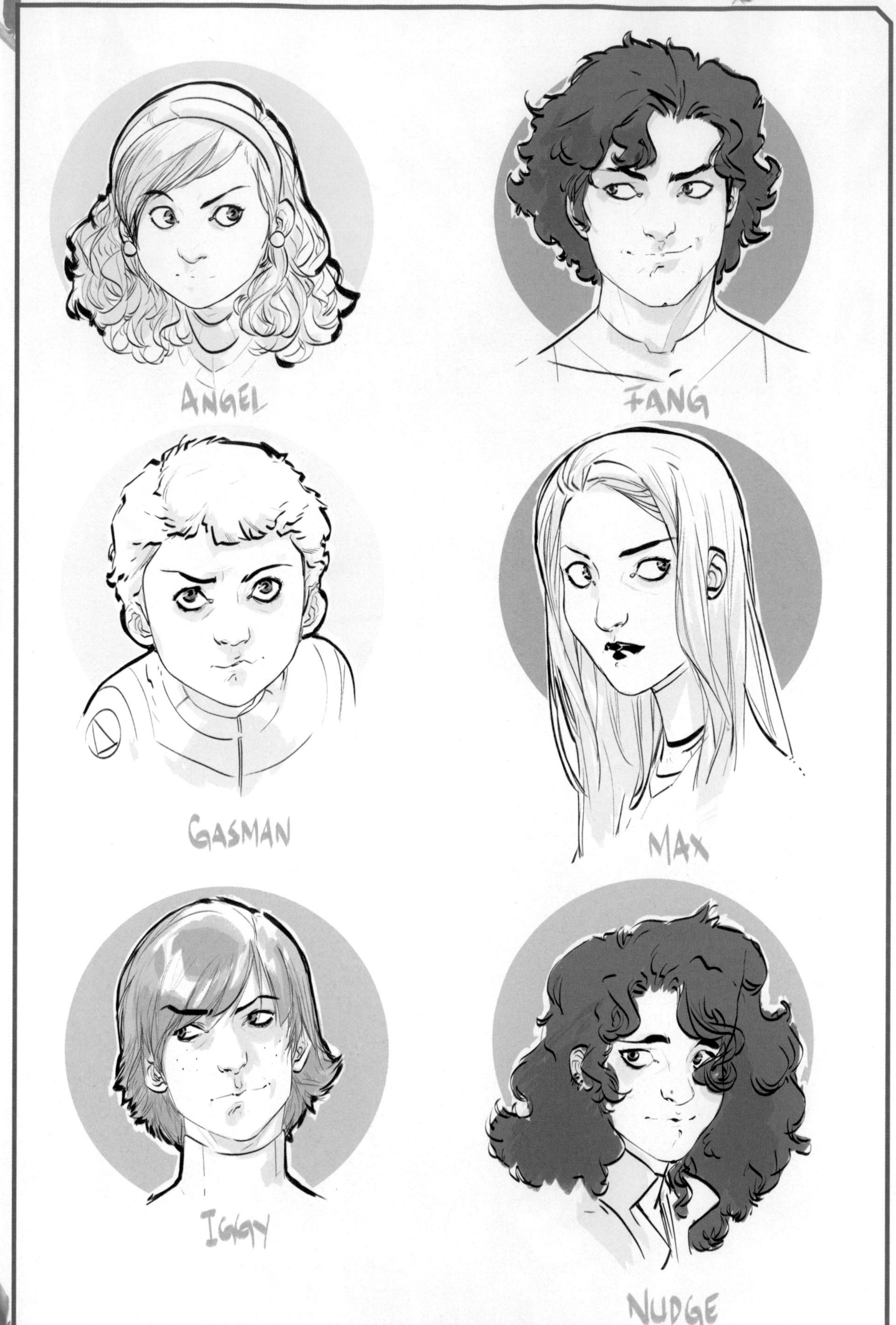
ANGEL
FANG
GASMAN
MAX
IGGY
NUDGE

CHARACTER DESIGNS
by RB SILVA

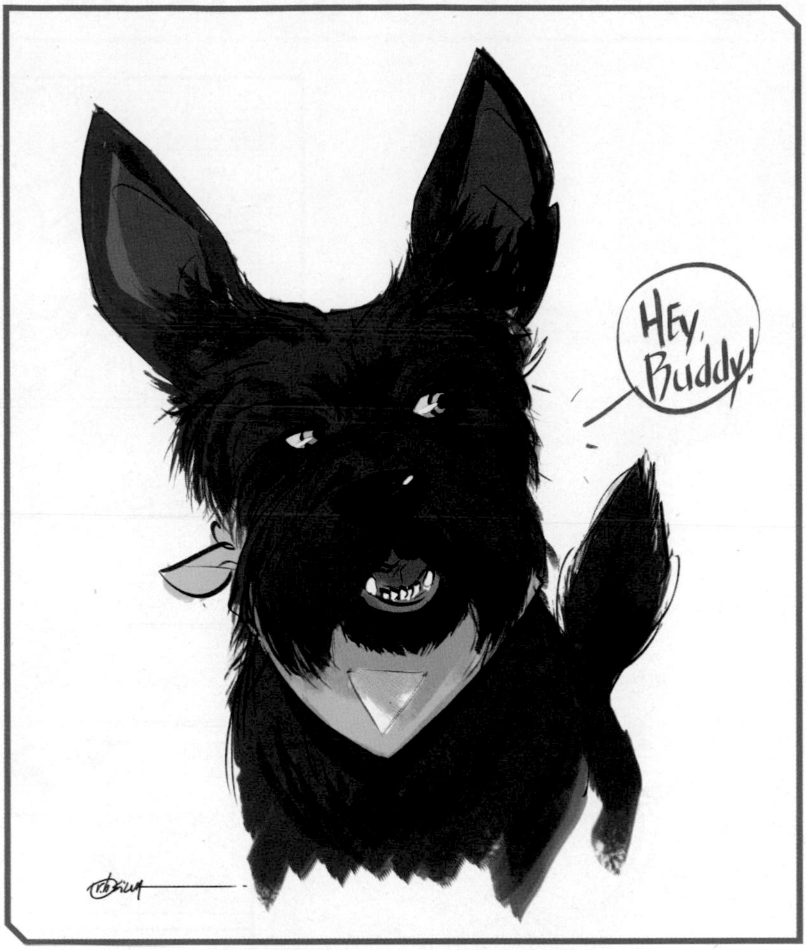
HEy, Buddy!

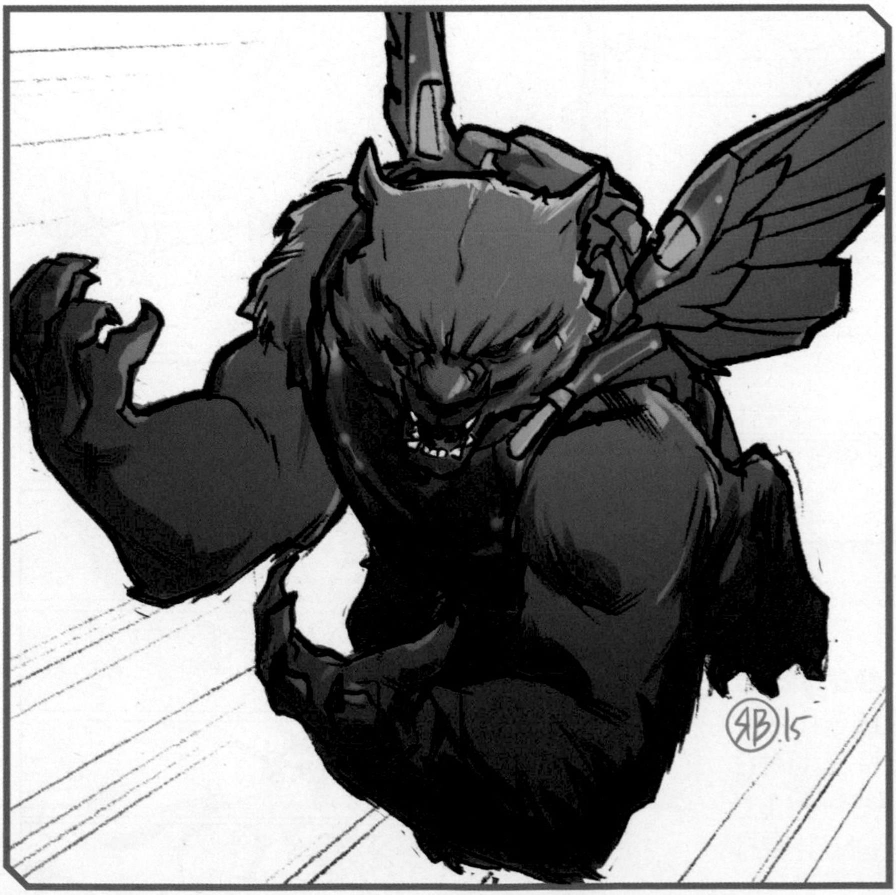

ART PROCESS FROM LAYOUTS TO COLOR

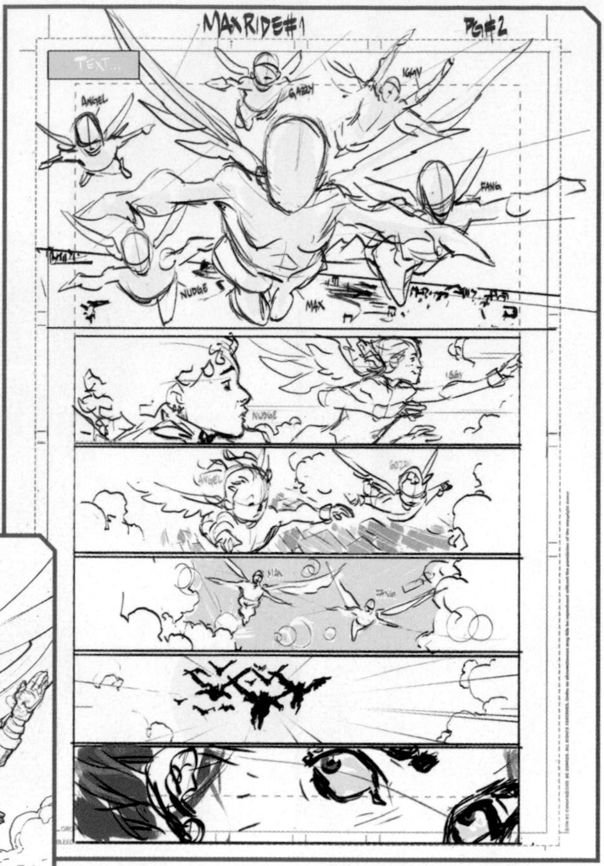

MAXRIDE#1
PG#2
TEXT...
GAZZY
IGGY
ANGEL
FANG
NUDGE
MAX

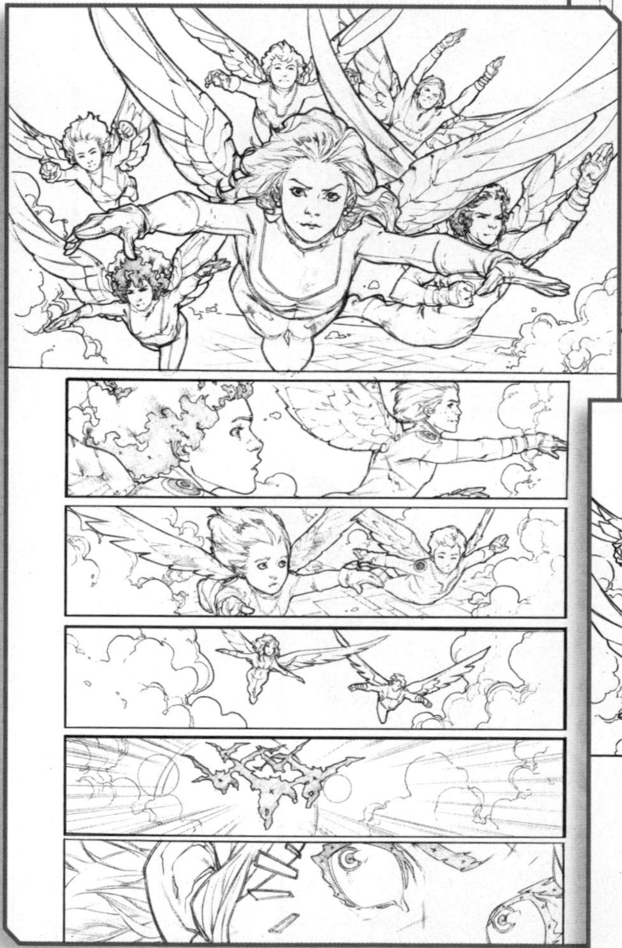

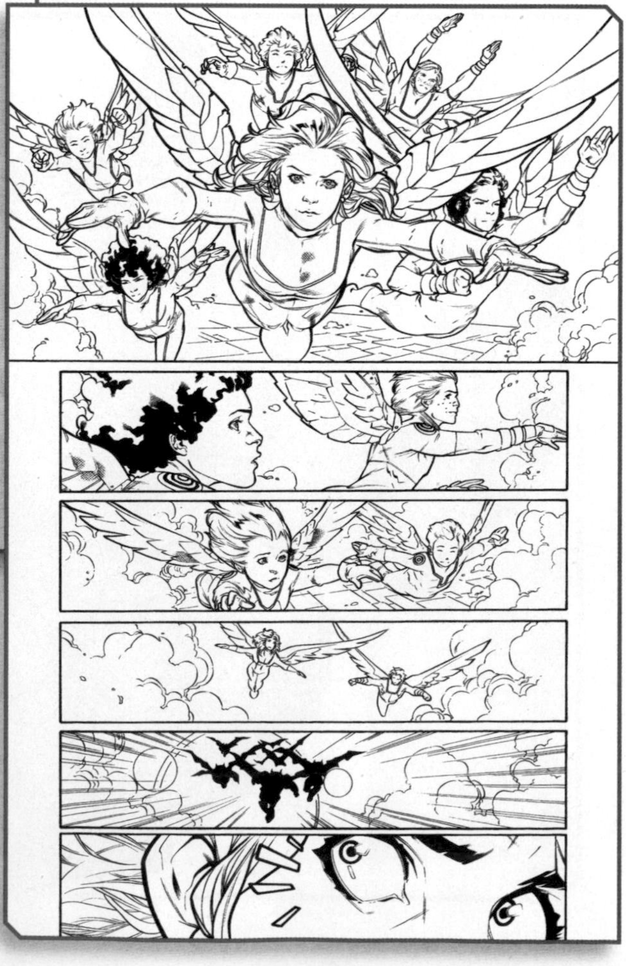

Issue 1, page 2
by RB SILVA,
WALDEN WONG
& RACHELLE
ROSENBERG

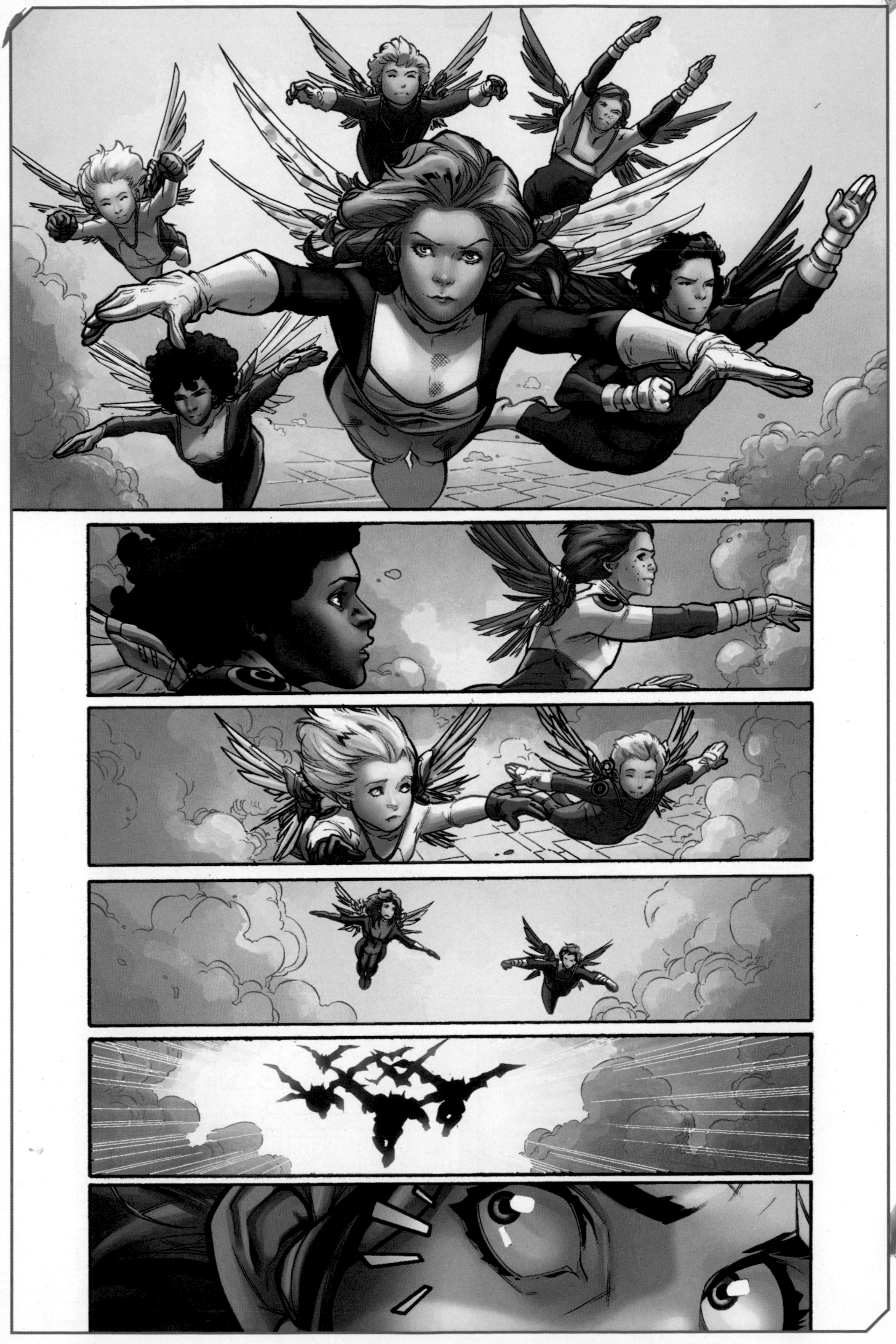

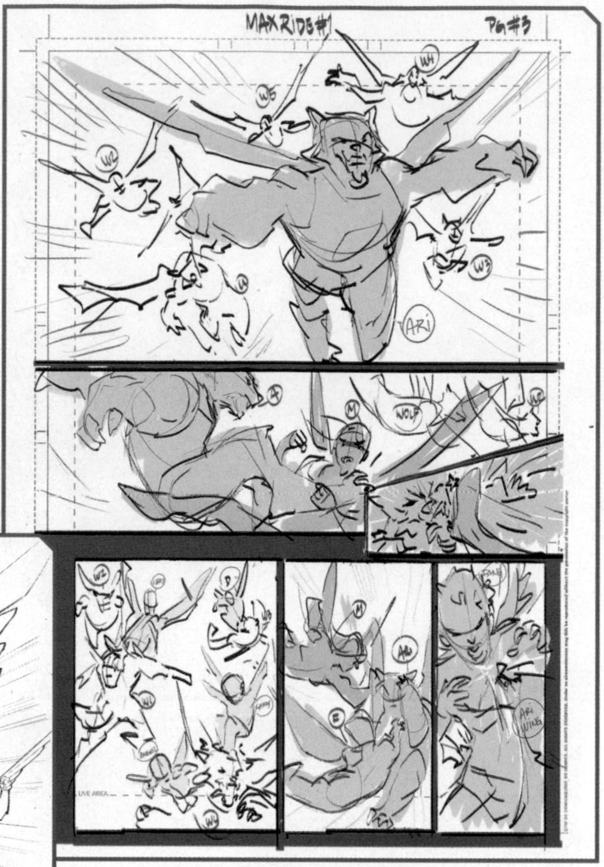
MAX RIDE #1
PG #3

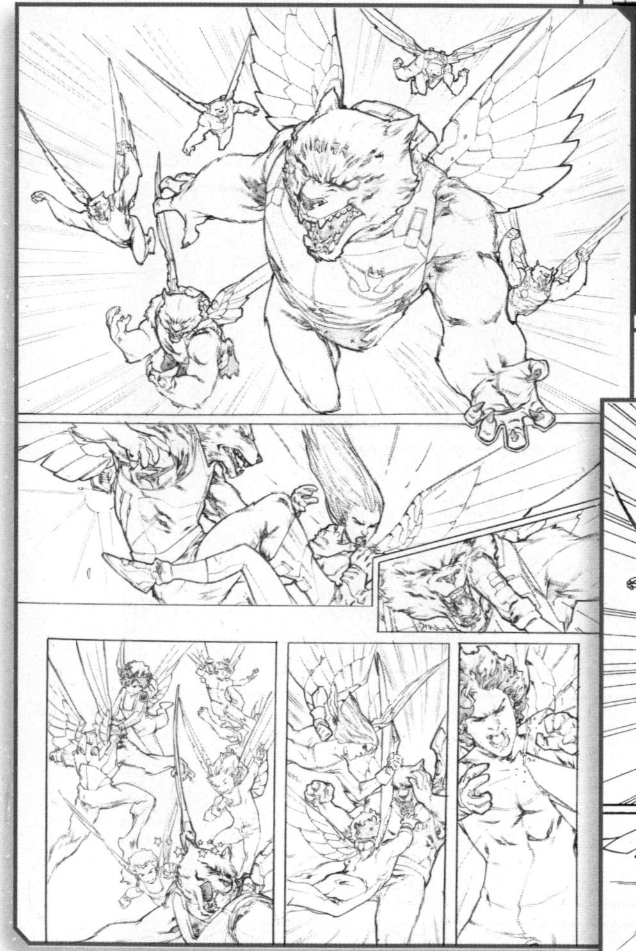

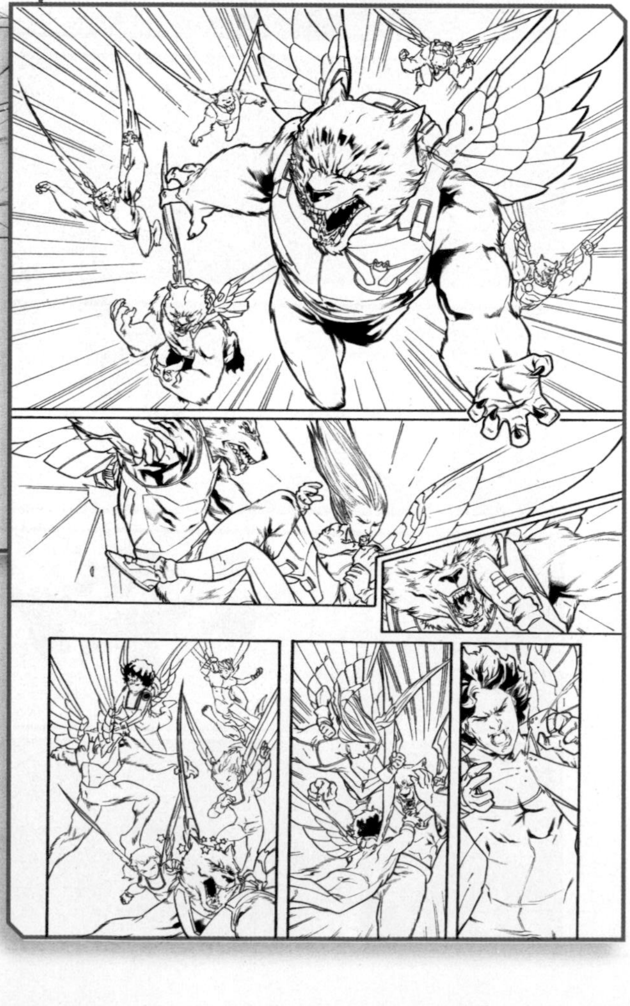

Issue 1, page 3
by RB SILVA,
WALDEN WONG
& RACHELLE
ROSENBERG

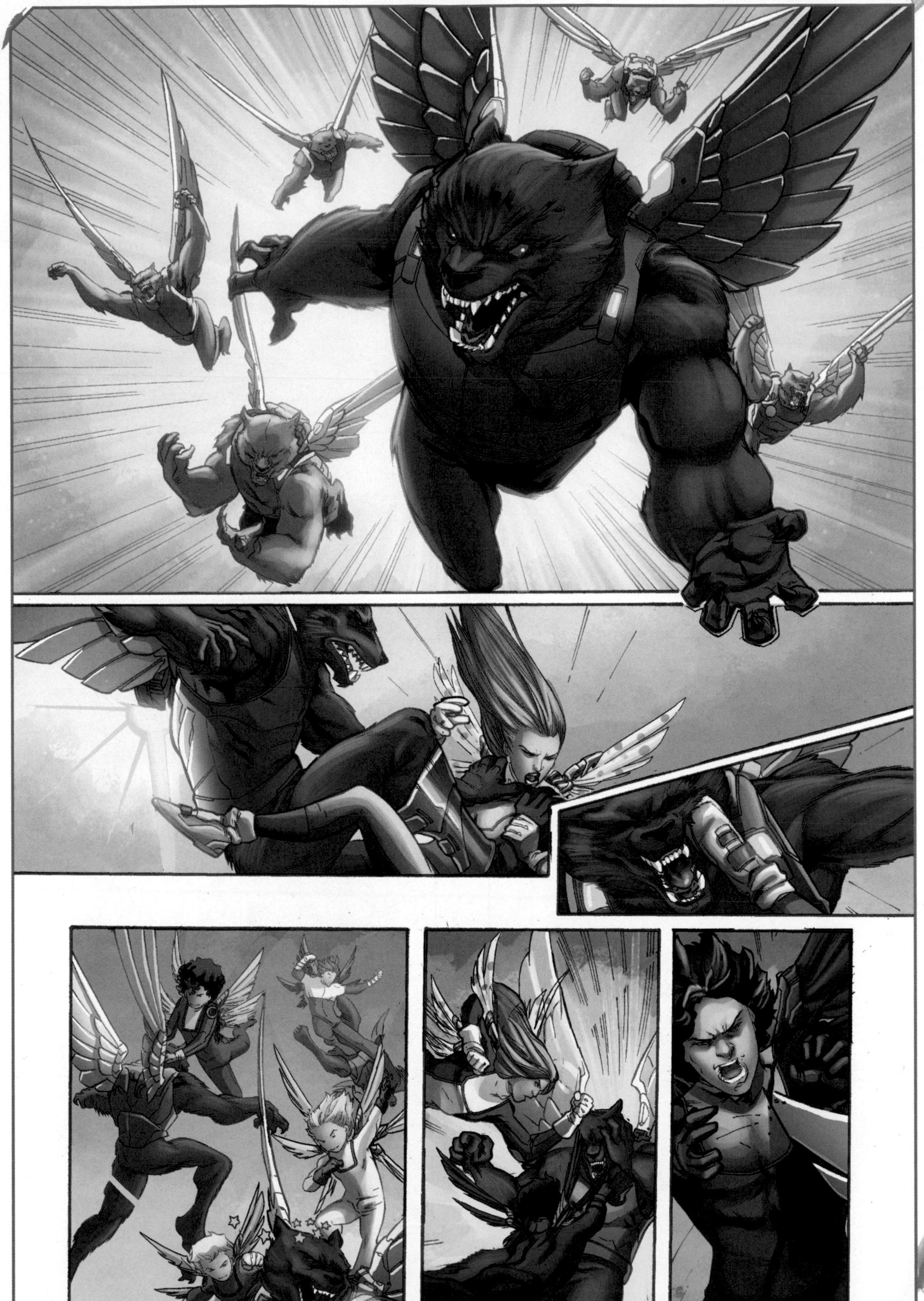

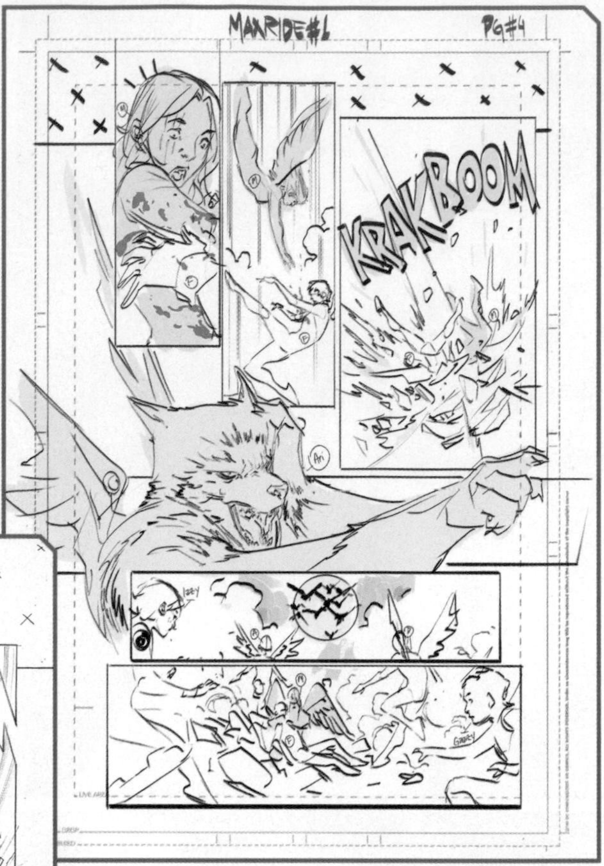

MAXRIDE#1
PG#4
KRAKBOOM

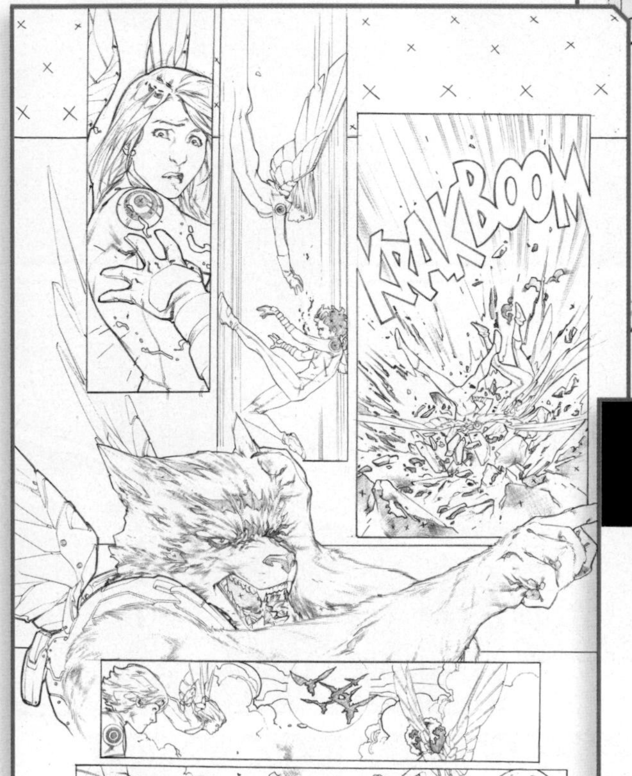

KRAKBOOM

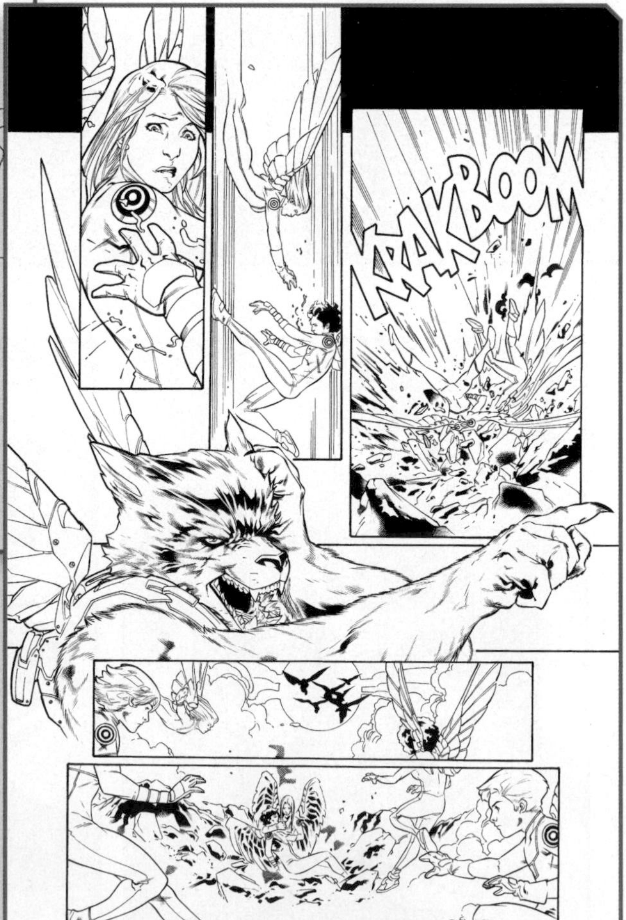

KRAKBOOM

Issue 1, page 4
by RB SILVA,
WALDEN WONG
& RACHELLE
ROSENBERG

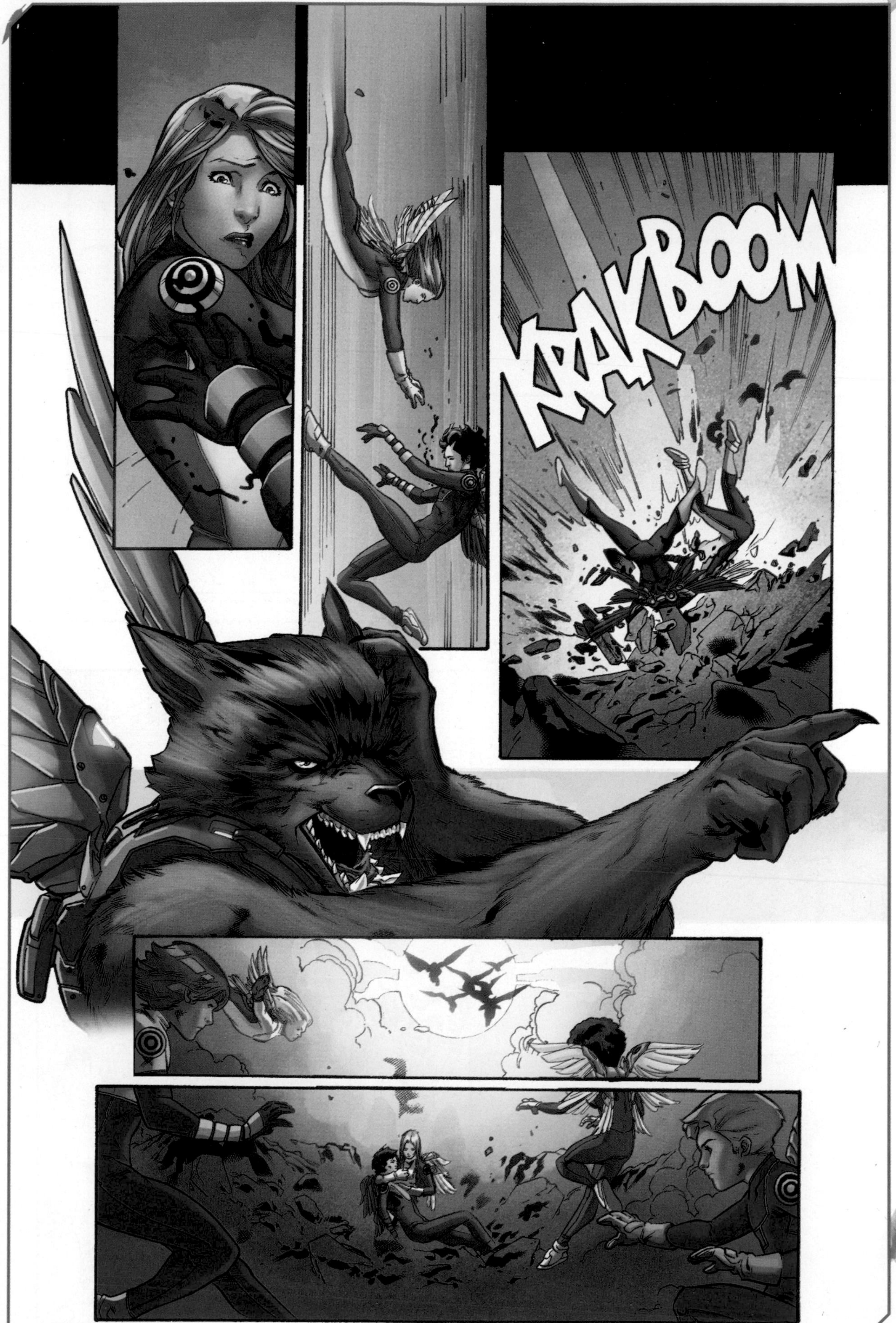
KRAKBOOM

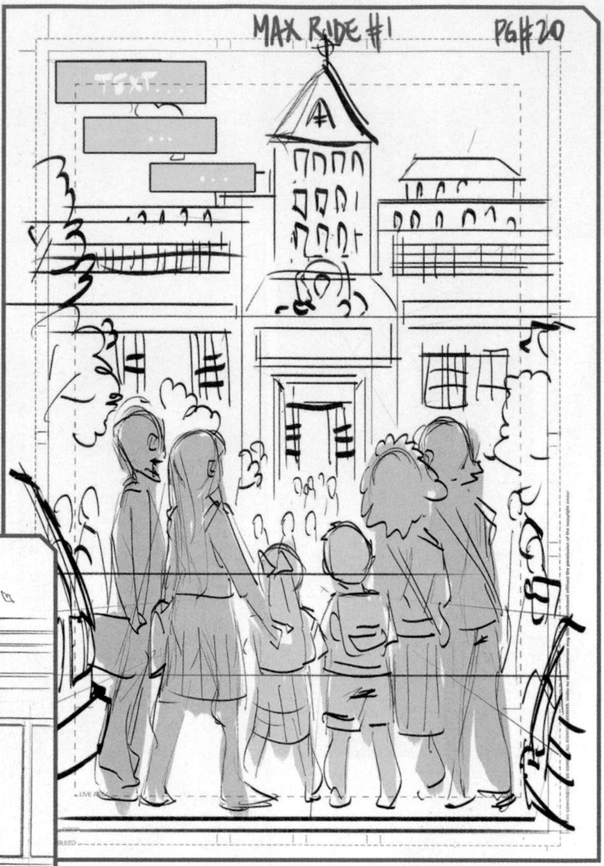
MAX RIDE #1
PG#20
TEXT...

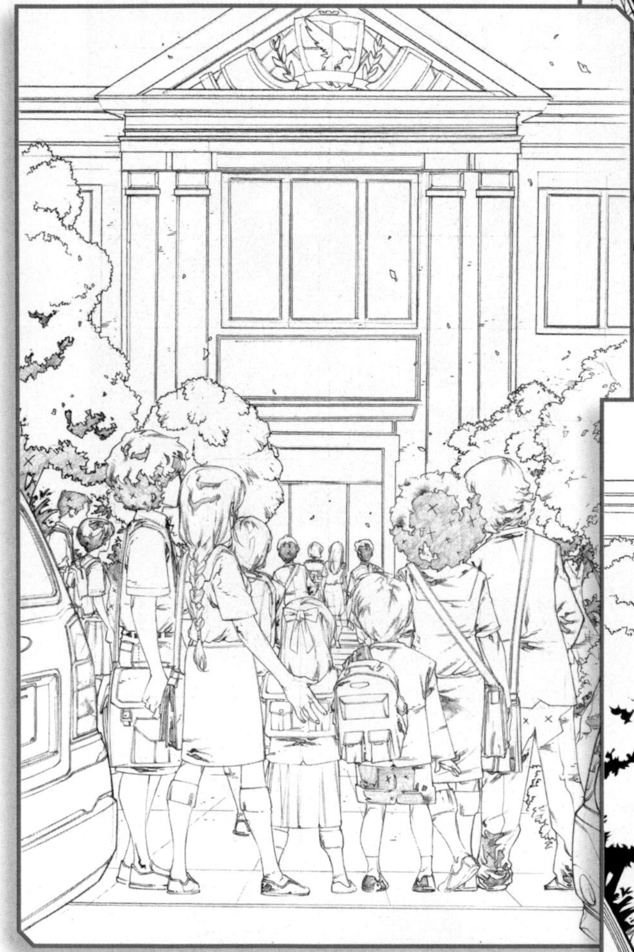

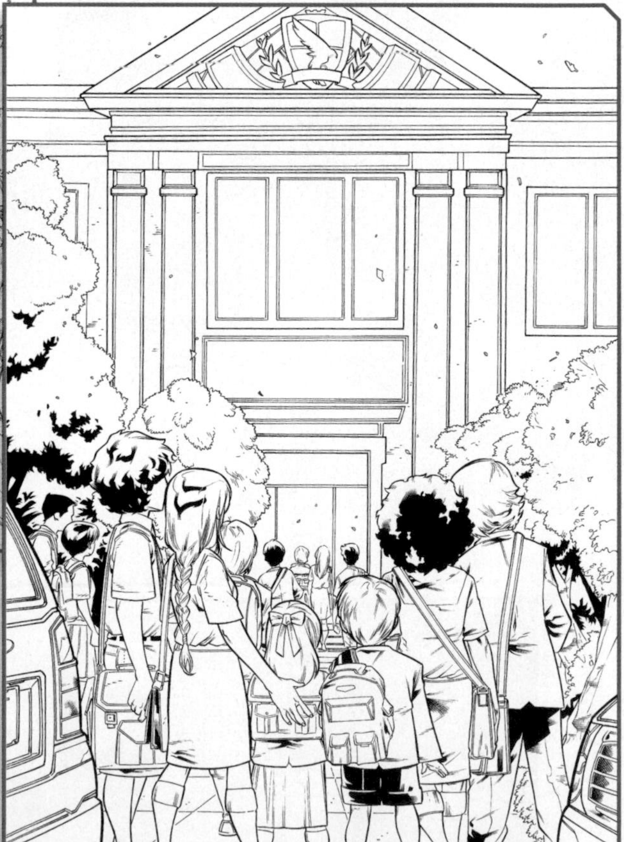

Issue 1, page 20
by RB SILVA,
WALDEN WONG
& RACHELLE
ROSENBERG

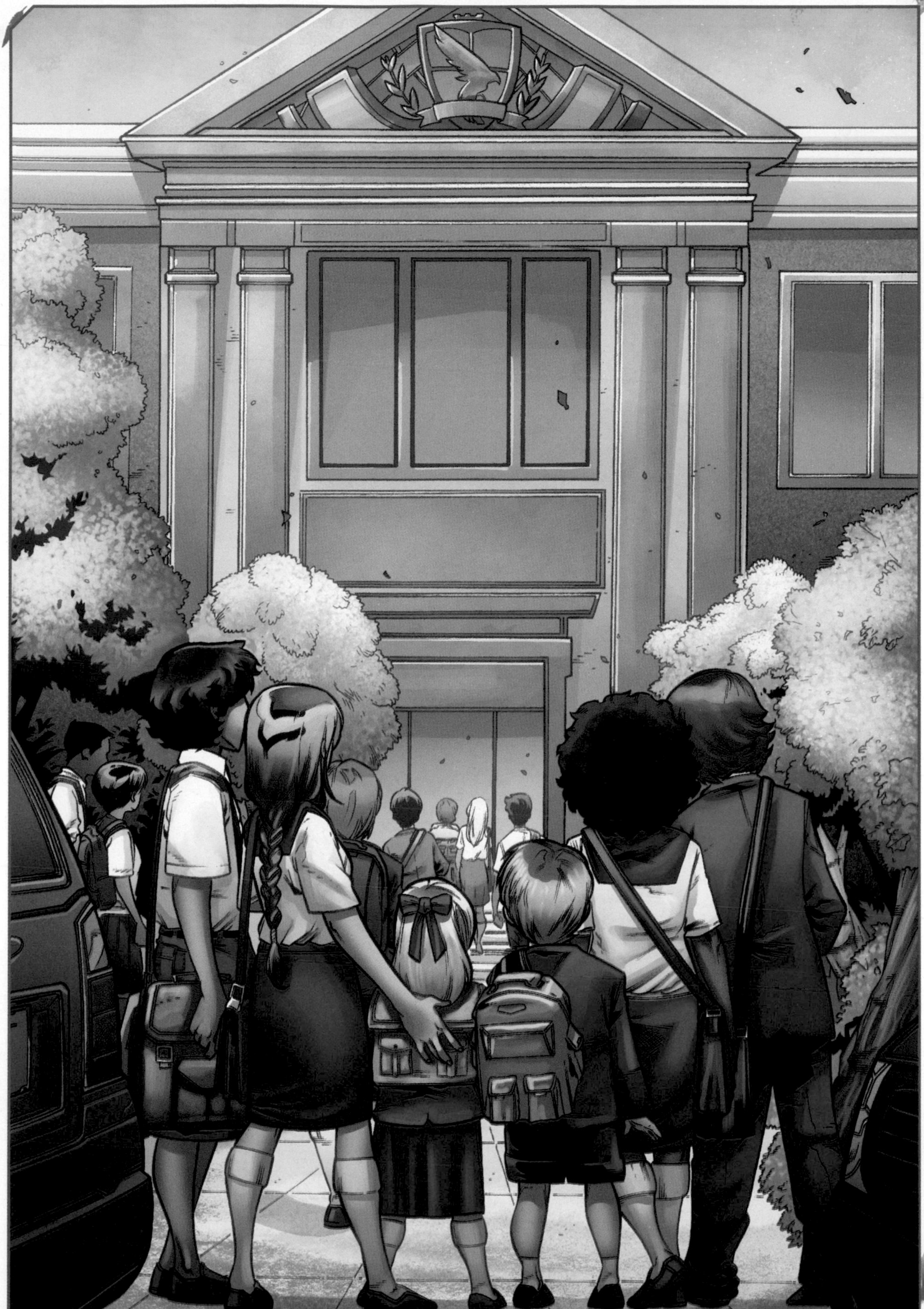

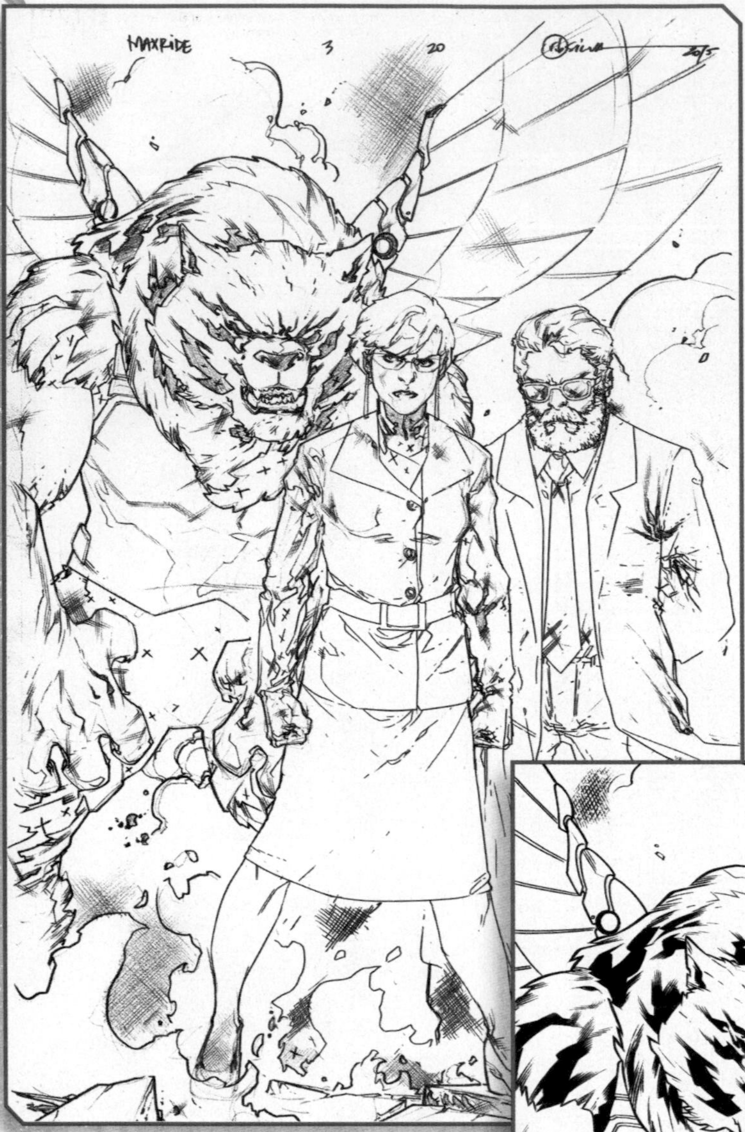
MAXRIDE
3
20
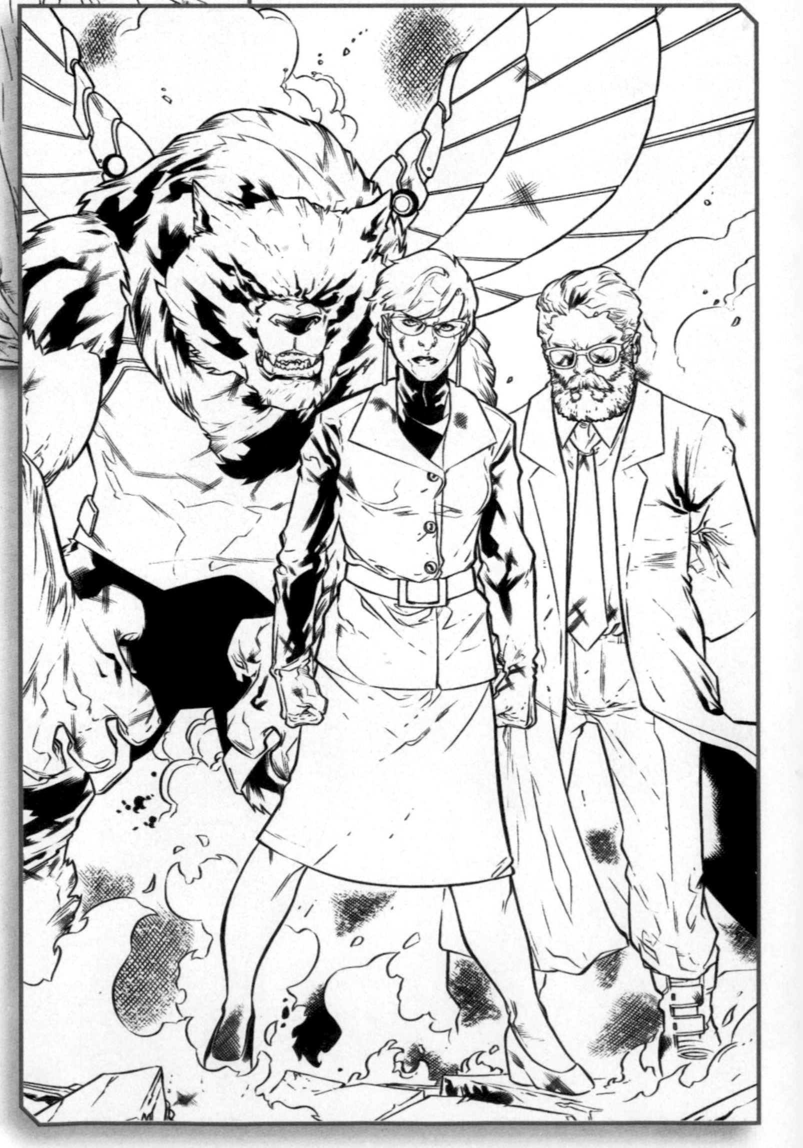

Issue 3, page 20
by RB SILVA,
WALDEN WONG
& RACHELLE
ROSENBERG

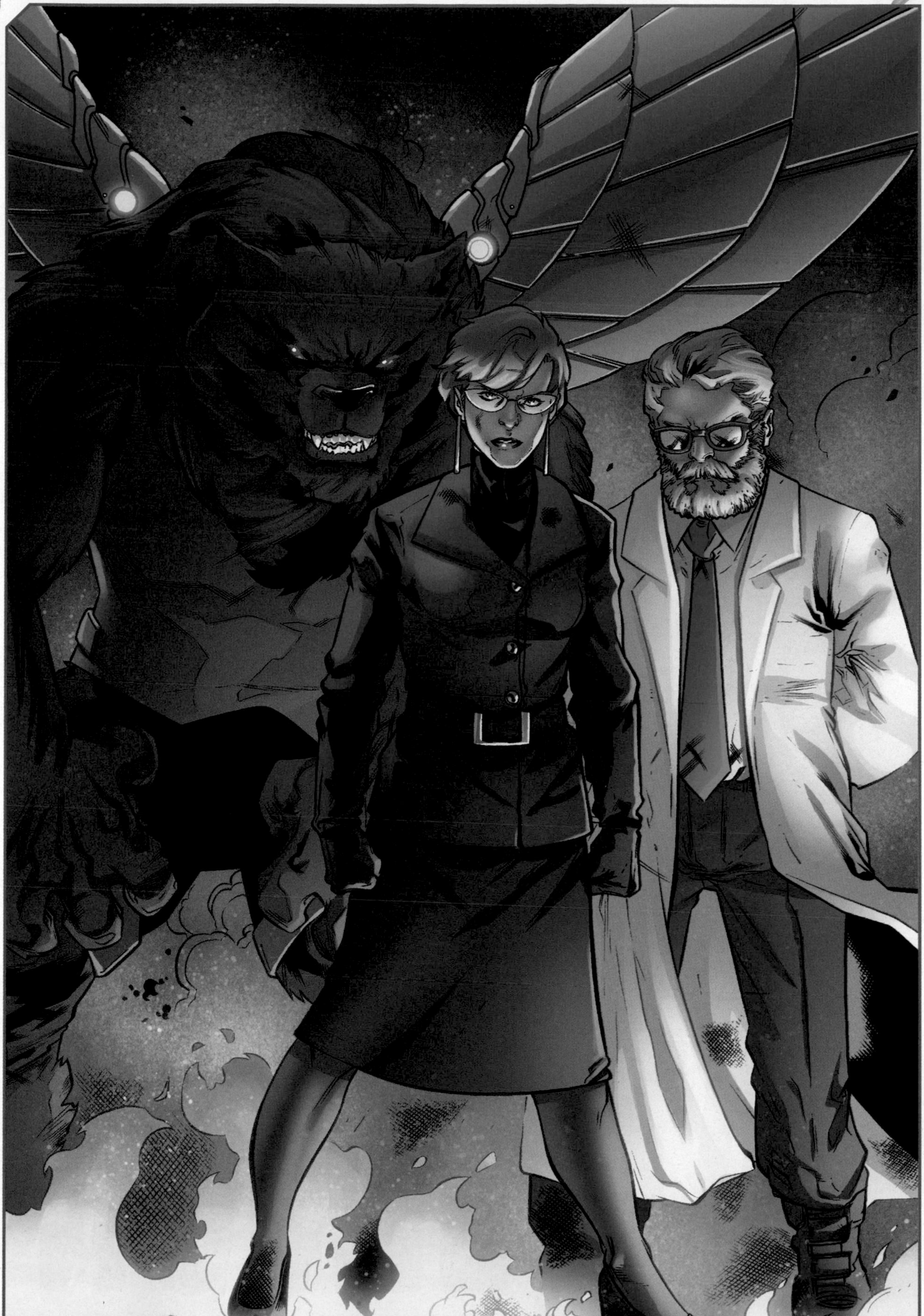

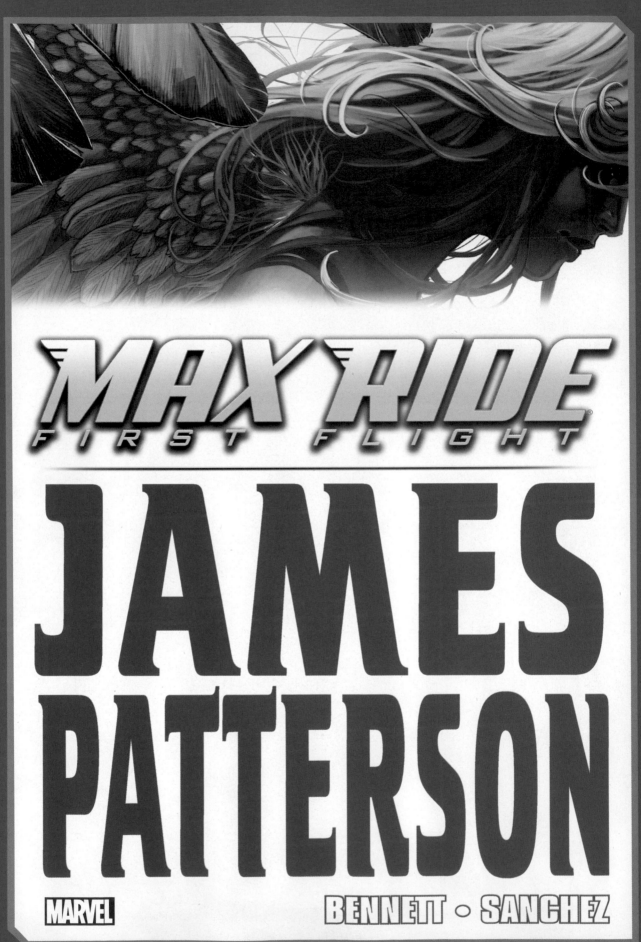

MAX RIDE
FIRST FLIGHT

JAMES PATTERSON

MARVEL

BENNETT · SANCHEZ

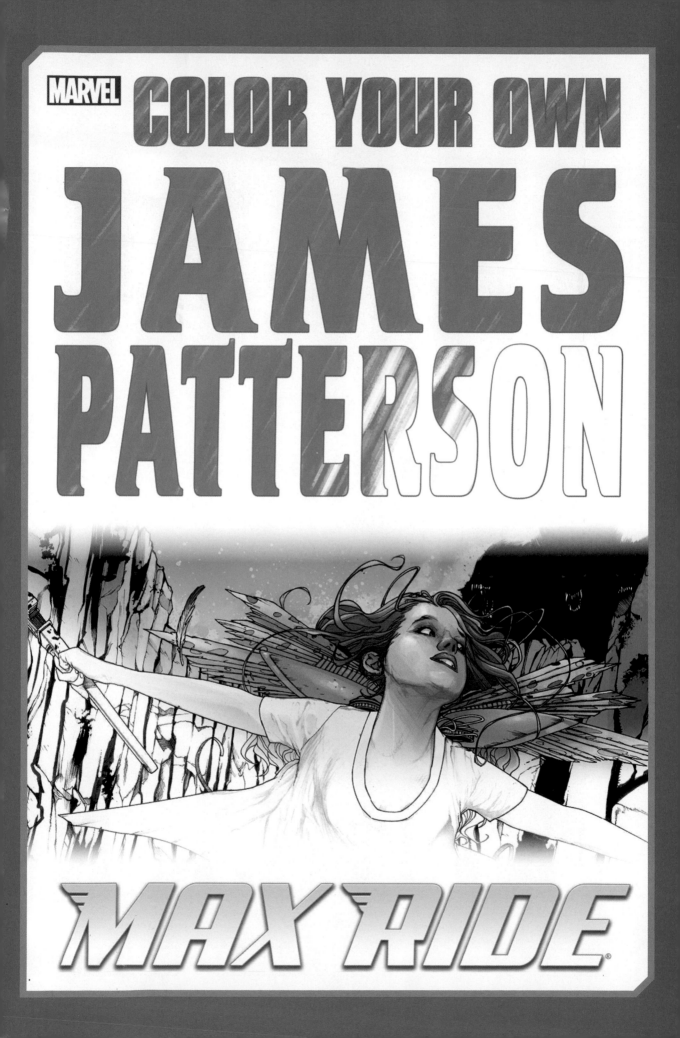